MARY
and
RICHARD

By the same author

Novels

Yes, Farewell

Childhood at Oriol

The Midnight Diary

The Trouble with Jake

Sociology

Mr Lyward's Answer

The Debatable Land

Poetry

Poems to Mary

The Flying Castle

Out on a Limb

Open Day and Night

Play

The Modern Everyman

MARY
and
RICHARD

A True Story of
Love and War

MICHAEL BURN

ARBOR HOUSE
WILLIAM MORROW
New York

For Teddy Hulton

First published in Great Britain by André Deutsch Limited as *Mary and Richard: The
Story of Richard Hillary and Mary Booker*

Library of Congress Cataloging-in-Publication Data

Burn, Michael.
Mary and Richard: a true story of love and war / Michael Burn.
p.   cm.
Bibliography: p.
ISBN 1-55710-042-X
1. Hillary, Richard, 1919–1943.   2. Booker, Mary, 1897–
3. Fighter pilots—Great Britain—Biography.   4. Great Britain,
Royal Air Force—Biography.   5. World War, 1939–1945—Aerial
operations, British.   6. Upper classes—Great Britain—Biography.
I. Title.
D786.H52887   1989
940.54'4941—dc19   88-27335
CIP

Printed in the United States of America

First U.S. Edition

1 2 3 4 5 6 7 8 9 10

Contents

Acknowledgments	7
Illustrations	9
Preface	13
Chapter One	15
Chapter Two	22
Chapter Three: December 1941 – April 1942	52
Chapter Four: April – June 1942	76
Chapter Five: June – July 1942	98
Chapter Six: July – September 1942	116
Chapter Seven: September – October 1942	142
Chapter Eight: October 1942	157
Chapter Nine: October – November 1942	171
Chapter Ten: November – December 1942	189
Chapter Eleven: December 1942 – January 1943	209
Epilogue	227
Bibliography	247

Acknowledgments

I wish to express my thanks to the Richard Hillary Trust, Trinity College, Oxford, for the use of Richard's letters and other documents that form part of the Trust; and to two Trustees especially, John Wright and Dennis Burden, for their help and hospitality during my researches at Trinity College.

I am glad to have met, and am very much in the debt of, Wing-Commander Geoffrey Page, for his recollections of Richard, his advice about matters to do with the RAF, and above all for his account, first verbal and then so courteously written out for me, of the circumstances which in his view caused Richard's final crash.

I am grateful to Mrs Chryss Hillary, second wife of Richard's father, for conversations years ago, when I began to edit these letters; to the late Rache Lovat Dickson, Richard's biographer, for suggesting to me, in 1975, what has now become this book; to the late Rosemary Kerr, whose invaluable recorded memories I have quoted throughout, and particularly for her affectionate account of Mary; to two other dear friends of Mary, Mrs William Inman (Deirdre Hart-Davis) and Mrs Barbara Lindsay, for their encouragement; to Lady (Constance) McIndoe and Mrs Barbara Karmel, for their encouragement and their recollections of Sir Archibald McIndoe and of Richard at East Grinstead Hospital; to the Rev. Geoffrey Fison, for information concerning his father, who was killed with Richard; to Mr J. Frizzel, still living near Duns, for his memories from boyhood of accompanying his father, George Frizzel, to the scene of the crash; to Sir Ronald Swayne, for recollections of Richard at Oxford just before the war; to Air Commodore J. S. Hall, Assistant Surgeon General to the RAF, for inquiries on my behalf; to Gordon Watkins, formerly of the BBC,

7

for his insistence over many years that I should write this story, and to Robert Wales who, with him, arranged and conducted the interview with Rosemary Kerr; and finally to Anthony Thwaite, Howard Davies and Laura Morris, surgeons and midwife to the book, who helped to ease its birth.

Acknowledgements for permission to quote from published works are due to:
Macmillan Publishers Limited, for *The Last Enemy* by Richard Hillary and *The Art of Adventure* by Eric Linklater; A. D. Peters and Co. Ltd, for 'The Birth of a Myth' by Arthur Koestler and *Years of Command* by Lord Douglas of Kirtleside; Weidenfeld and Nicolson Ltd, for *Faces from the Fire* by Leonard Mosley; Corgi Books, for *The Tale of a Guinea Pig* by Geoffrey Page; Putnams, New York, for *Princess Merle: The Romantic Life of Merle Oberon* by Charles Higham and Roy Moseley; Editions France Empire, for Admiral Jubelin's preface to the French edition of *The Last Enemy*; Express Newspapers, for articles concerning Richard Hillary by Robert Pitman and Leonard Mosley; Executors of the Estate of the late Rosemary Kerr, for her recorded memories of Richard Hillary; The National Portrait Gallery, for the portrait by Eric Kennington, reproduced in this book.

Illustrations

1   Richard at Oxford, 1939
2   Mary in her twenties
3a Michael Burn on the morning of capture after the raid on St. Nazaire, March 28, 1942. German newsreel photograph
3b The 16th Annual Reunion of the Guinea Pig Club at East Grinstead (Popperfoto)
4   Richard before the Battle of Britain
5   Richard in uniform after plastic surgery
6a Mary at window, late 1930s
6b The Cottage in Wales
7   Mary, 1941
8   Richard, 1941
9   Alexander Korda and Merle Oberon leaving Buckingham Palace after receiving his Knighthood, September 22, 1942
10 Eric Kennington portrait of Richard (National Portrait Gallery)
11 Richard's last letter to Mary
12 Mary's last letter to Richard

He would speak sometimes of two great sorrows: the
loss of his hands, and the loss of his friends. He
hated war more bitterly than any young man I have met.

Mary on Richard

It is high time that you wrote a book; but
then again, perhaps not, for you might cease
to care about letters.

Richard to Mary

It is not to be rid of history that we study it, but to save from
nothingness the whole past which would be swallowed up without it.
We study history so that even those things which would be lost from
the past may once again come to life in this all-important present,
apart from which nothing really exists. In order that this particular
human story may live anew in all its individual and concrete
complexity, it is enough that we know it. In order that it may enrich
us with its very substance, it is enough that we love it.

Etienne Gilson, *Héloïse and Abelard*

Preface

Re-reading the documents that are the basis of this story, I have grown more detached than I was twelve years ago, when first I came on them. I used to feel that I was taking part in and almost living within an ancient literary cliché: that I was witnessing the unfolding of some tragedy for the stage, of some Greek tragedy in particular. The Fates really seemed to be urging it on, with a chorus to be expected, expounding and lamenting each new step at which the principal character is goaded, by an interplay of circumstance and his own nature, towards a point where they will chant of him that he 'has an appointment with Death', and finally he will go out to keep it.

Now and then I still have this impression, and have allowed it to recur in what follows. But this is not a Greek drama. It is a story of real life. It is all true. Somebody did say that of him, and go out he did.

Scholars and dramatic critics have the task of investigating the machinery a great playwright has employed to move his tragedy towards its inexorable imagined end, and make it seem inexorable. In this story the events and the emotions are before us in great detail as they were in truth; and whereas, in a work of art, under the spell of language and artistic skill, we accept, here we do not. We question: could the end have been avoided? There is no splendour of words nor theatrical acceleration of action to suspend disbelief and sweep aside commonsense. There are no Fates; and we ourselves, the readers, are the commenting chorus.

Chapter One

One night during October 1941, on leave in London from military training, I went to a night-club; and there on the dance-floor was the most beautiful woman I had ever seen. She had come with a party. She did not notice me, and I supposed I should never set eyes on her again.

Next evening I was invited to the flat of Brigadier (later Major-General) Charles Haydon, at that time in charge of the Commandos, in which I was a captain. I rang the bell, and to my amazement this same woman opened the door. She turned out to be his first cousin. She had divorced her husband many years before and never married again. She is the Mary of the ensuing pages.

I talked to her for a short while, awkwardly, not telling her of the impression she had made on me the night before, and feeling that she must be far beyond my reach; everyone must be in love with her. My leave came to an end before I had a chance to see her again. I went back to my billet in Scotland, and on the night of 27/28 March 1942 took part in the Combined Operations raid on St Nazaire, was captured, and spent the next three years in German prison-of-war camps. Very soon after I had been set free and come home, I went in search of her. We were married on 27 March 1947, and were together twenty-seven years. She died in a London hospital on 10 August 1974.

A few days after her funeral I returned to the home in North Wales she had created for us, where we had lived for the past twenty years. I answered the scores of letters, from young and old, from many parts of the world, which had come in praise and gratitude for her life and sadness at her death. This gave me some weeks of respite.

15

But by the beginning of winter it had ended, and I was left in the house alone.

One day during November I felt particularly low. It had rained continuously. I could do no work out-of-doors. I was nowhere near ready to attempt imaginative writing again. I could hardly bear to open the cupboards that held her clothes, all so colourful, each with its memories, left exactly as she had left them on the summer morning five months earlier, when we had set out so unsuspectingly for London. I decided to clear out the boxroom, and there I came on a large neat package.

Inside I found Press cuttings from the war years about the young fighter-pilot and author Richard Hillary, and his book about the Battle of Britain, at one time famous, called *The Last Enemy*; twenty years of minutes of the Trust founded in his memory; correspondence with the painter-sculptor Eric Kennington about his portrait of Hillary, now in the National Portrait Gallery; letters to Mary from Hillary's parents after his death; and the originals of sixty-one letters from him to her, covering nearly the whole of 1942 and ending at 4 January 1943, four days before he was killed. These she had laid lovingly, sheet by sheet, between the parchment-like pages of a beautiful leather-bound gold-tooled album with a brass lock, and prefaced them with Swinburne's lines:

> They gave him light in his eyes,
> And love, and a space for delight,
> And beauty, and length of days,
> And night, and sleep in the night.

Beside the lines she had placed a photograph of him, in an open shirt, taken either on leave before his injuries, or before the war on holiday. She had prefaced his letters with her own account of her first meetings with him.

I also found copies, which she had typed herself to show in confidence to his parents; to Rache Lovat Dickson, his publisher, who wrote his biography in 1950; to the writers Arthur Koestler and Eric Linklater, who published essays about him; and to students, among them a French girl and a young Scandinavian, who compiled theses about him for their universities.

16

She had often told me about Richard. She gave me *The Last Enemy* soon after our second meeting, at the end of the war. I had never known him or, having been a prisoner when the book came out, even heard of him, and felt no conscious jealousy then, or since, or now, of their love for one another. We often spoke of him. We dined with his parents year after year on the anniversary of his death. I dedicated a book I had written in Colditz, my final prison camp, to them; and after the death of his mother Edwyna we remained fast friends with his father Michael. I had always known that the letters were in the house. Mary had told me about them, and suggested I might read them, might perhaps one day write something about Richard. For some reason not entirely clear to me I had not looked at them while she was alive. Maybe I did not want to risk a feeling that I was in someone else's shadow, until I had more substance of my own. Maybe, more simply, I thought that sooner or later there would be time. I had understood that they were in a certain drawer in her desk, and been much troubled when I failed to find them there. When I discovered them in the boxroom, they seemed to have been 'sent': sent to solace me, to give me something to work on, and as a means, for however small an audience of family and friends, of commemorating her as well as him.

I searched on, I read more documents in the package, and within an hour this sense had grown to a compulsion. Papers from Richard, about Richard, were not all I found. I came on an old brown-paper envelope, inscribed with Mary's name, opened it, and discovered thirty-one manuscript letters from her to him, written during the same period as his to her. He had sent them back to her for safe keeping, expecting that he would be killed and that the RAF would destroy them, as they did indeed destroy a few he had no time to send back, his diary, and other private papers.

It was like her to have cherished his letters in their brass-locked leather album, and to leave her own in a faded envelope. Her thoughts had been for him, and what he had written, and might one day go on to write, and not for anything of her own. Of her letters she had made no copies. I imagined, and still think it probable, even certain, that I was the first person to have read them since those months thirty-two, and now forty-five years ago, when, in the RAF

Staff College, in the hospital at East Grinstead for plastic surgery, at Fighter Command HQ at Bentley Priory, and finally in the freezing Border aerodrome, they had been held between Richard's half-mended claw-like hands. She had not told me of them; again, I believe, because she had seen them as no more than part of a story primarily about him. She was without vanity. It would not have entered her head with what admiring wonder I read them; nor that, once detachment had become possible, and I could begin to consider them as literature, I should think more highly of her letters than of his, fine though many of his are; nor that her farewell to him, written to assuage her on the evening of the day she knew he had been killed, would bring such balm to me after her own death. And not to me alone. During the eighties a friend of mine, Goronwy Rees, came to stay frequently with me in Wales. He had recently lost his own wife Margie, and was deeply stricken. I gave him a copy of Mary's farewell to Richard, hoping that it might solace and encourage him as it had me. He took it away with him, and wrote back:

> Reading your wife's letter was both a comfort, and a source of hope, so that I felt that Margie is not altogether lost and I do not have to live entirely without her. And the other night I dreamed about her, and she was exactly as she had been before all her suffering and pain, and I felt that the dream was a kind of blessing on your house . . .

A few others to whom I showed that last letter were much moved, indeed by the whole correspondence, its sadness, its gaiety, and its courage. I spent the following months dovetailing the two sets in chronological order, editing and annotating them, principally for Mary's family, for Richard's parents, and close friends. It was a therapy; besides, were I suddenly to die, no one else, from what she and one or two others had told me, could know the background, the implications, the names, the nuances, so well. Now that so many years have passed, and I have come back to them, I feel that, if they could make such an impression, could give such heart, to a few, then they should be made known to wider circles, and therefore arranged into a book.

18

CHAPTER ONE

Two fresh motives appeared as I researched the story. I discovered with a good deal of amazement how diseased a record much of the printed word to date presents of Richard. Any student setting out to write a thesis about him would be bound at least to consider, and even to conclude, first that he may have committed suicide, and/or secondly that he had had an unhappy love affair.

Both these views are false, and do a shameful injustice to his and to Mary's memory. It became a responsibility to correct them. This I could only do by publishing the true facts as contained in their letters and in other documents belonging to the Richard Hillary Trust, at first in my possession and then delivered by me to Trinity College, Oxford. I have left it until the final chapter to list and discuss these two allegations, or insinuations, since readers will be in a better position to form their own opinions after they have read the correspondence and the narrative which links it.

A second motive was that Richard was becoming forgotten. As the war receded from people's memories, curiosity about him diminished, and, as was inevitable and had happened after World War I, a generation grew up, many of whom wanted little to do with the glamorous or heroic figures of World War II, considering them even as pawns in an Establishment campaign to prepare the climate for a third. Sales of his book fell off; his and Mary's letters lay untouched and unsought in their leather album and brown paper envelope; the dust gathered on his memory. Even those who remembered him had no reason to think of him as a partner in a love-story at least as vivid as his book. Vivid it would be even without its tragic end, even were it to be totally removed from the war, which receives little attention in the correspondence. Stalingrad is besieged, El Alamein is fought, the thousand-bomber raids on Germany begin, the Allies land in North Africa; but we hear nothing of all this. Generals, Marshals of the Royal Air Force, Directors of Naval Intelligence, move fleetingly in and out, but like extras, as aids or impediments to the liaison. Sometimes only the addresses from which Richard writes remind us that there is a war. The war serves to heighten the tensions of a relationship which would compel attention anyhow without it.

* * *

19

A love-affair between a young man and an older woman (Mary was twenty years older than Richard) is a classic relationship, of which the types have often been portrayed in novels, particularly French novels. Here in many respects they diverge from type; he was no stammering boy, hungry for amatory experience or influence; and she even further from the ageing *mondaine* looking for a lover. In pretty well all respects the relationship is so extreme that one forgets how frequently found, in all ages, in all classes, are the basic ingredients. Their difficulties, for example, about finding somewhere to meet in peace, which have exasperated many men and women, married or unmarried, in him produce a chronic frenzy and in her exhaustion. Head versus heart; the determination in both to keep their individual independence; his 'Blimpishness', her romanticism; his preoccupation, after the initial excitement, with the problem of what he is going to do, and her preoccupation with him – all are ubiquitous antagonisms whose familiarity the dazzle of their personalities, their striking awareness of their own emotions, and their articulateness serve often to disguise. 'We are too exaggerated,' she once wrote to him. Perhaps, but from well-known patterns. Exceptional they were, but only in degree, setting forth with clarity, sometimes with wit, sometimes with poetry, always with an underswell of love, the emotional condition if not the milieu of innumerable lovers. To these intensifications of what is usual, crowded into just over a year, add the disaster of his death, and a story emerges which does not deserve to stay hidden in a boxroom.

It lasts the whole of the war-year 1942, overlapping a month one end and a week the other. Although it finishes in midwinter on that bleak aerodrome, most of it is set in spring, summer, and early autumn, at the hub of that lush London enclave, which gossip-writers still call 'Society', and is sequinned here and there with names of men and women once much publicised, and a few of longer fame. Both Mary and Richard were beautiful, charming, intelligent, and extremely privileged. Such circumstances may attract some readers, but not interest, may even repel, seem too exotic, too far out of the common run, to others. It seems as well then to mention at the outset that, though both moved within that world with superficial and successful ease, and had many true friends there, neither of them was in their true element. Both wanted to get out. Richard wrote of 'that appalling London existence', and with irony of 'the Claridge's front'; and, during the time after his book had been published in Britain and he was being lionised, told Mary from the aerodrome, 'my London period sapped my will'. Mary wrote of the same people and surroundings: 'I am in a prison of soft hands, so much more difficult to escape from than the barbed wire variety. I have a strange faith in you . . . that you will get me out.'

It often happens that love between two people strengthens a reaching-out, of which one or even both may scarcely have been conscious, beyond their time and beyond their social boundaries. The fashionable élite among whom their gifts had cast them satisfied neither; it was this latent affinity, and not merely physical attraction, which drew them together. They were spoilt; knew it; and said so, repeatedly. Selfish they were not; by the time their year was up, he had given a life he need not have given, and she her happiness. Nor were they without vision. It is more than a war story, since they were thinking beyond the war; more than a love story, since they were thinking beyond themselves.

Their characters, and what befell them, will emerge from their letters and, I hope, my notes, which I have tried to weave into a consecutive narrative. Although Richard was often likened (wrongly, apart from his looks and gift for words) to Rupert Brooke, and sometimes to Wilfred Owen and Siegfried Sassoon, among author-combatants of World War I, and his book translated into many languages and on the reading list of many schools, I have assumed that few today have even heard of *The Last Enemy*. Certainly no one, her family and friends apart, will have heard of Mary. A preamble is needed to summarise what their lives had been as far as their first meeting.

Chapter Two

RICHARD HOPE HILLARY

was born in Sydney, Australia, on 20 April 1919, of Australian parents; his father of English and Irish, his mother of Scottish and Spanish ancestry. His father had had a distinguished career. He had served throughout World War I with the Australian Expeditionary Forces, being awarded the DSO and OBE and twice mentioned in dispatches in Mesopotamia. From 1921 to 1923 he was Private Secretary to the Right Hon. and rumbustious Billy Hughes, Prime Minister of Australia; was transferred to special duties at Australia House in London, and then to the Sudan Government, in which he became Auditor-General. He and his wife Edwyna lived for many years in Khartoum.

When Richard was three, his parents brought him back to England. He went for a spell to a preparatory school, where he was wretched, and at thirteen to Shrewsbury, where on the whole he enjoyed himself. From that age on, with his parents' reluctant consent, he spent part of his holidays on his own in France and Germany.

At Shrewsbury he became enthusiastic about rowing, and came under the influence of a sympathetic and gifted English teacher, Mr McEachran, whom he informed that he intended to be a writer, and would model himself on John Steinbeck. His housemaster wrote of him that 'he seemed to dislike the conventional view of things, often merely because it was conventional. He would often express views merely because he thought they would be contrary to those of his companions, and would seem disappointed if his ideas were accepted without argument.' He was, and remained, someone who provoked, and liked to be provoked in argument by others.

He went on to Oxford and stroked the champion Trinity College boat two years in succession – 'the best Eight the College had ever seen', wrote the Vice-President after Hillary's death, 'which in making five bumps to go to the head of the river achieved a feat never likely to be eclipsed'. Richard wrote a little and read, in his own word, 'somewhat'. Outwardly an athlete, a hearty, he was very much attracted by women and attractive to them. From childhood he was extremely close to his mother. Women were essential to him. It is hard to think of any writer with so short a life threaded through so many associations with women, whether as son, as lover, or as friend.

At Oxford Richard learned to fly and soon after the beginning of the war, aged twenty, was drafted into 603 (City of Edinburgh) Squadron. Based on the airfield at Hornchurch, twelve miles from London along the Thames estuary, he was in the thick of the Battle of Britain. His Spitfire shot down five German planes and probably three more. Most of his friends were killed early on. On 3 September 1940 his own plane went down in flames into the North Sea. Blinded and terribly burnt about the face and hands, he was rescued by the Margate lifeboat, taken to a clearing station, and thence to the Royal Masonic Hospital at Ravenscourt.

There the great pioneer of plastic surgery, Mr (later Sir) Archibald McIndoe, found him. The old-fashioned treatment of his hands with tannic acid was causing his fingers to curl; his eyes, their lids burnt away, had to be covered quickly with gentian violet. He had the first signs of blood poisoning. McIndoe took him to his own hospital at East Grinstead, removed the tannic acid and gentian violet, and treated the burns with lukewarm brine. There Richard underwent a series of dangerous and experimental operations, surrounded by others in an even worse state and greater pain than he was. More than two hundred of the cases treated there were 'faceless ones', whose burns had stripped away all the skin. Most suffered between ten and fifty operations, and spent up to three years in hospital and convalescence. Richard was one of the more fortunate. The boyish look had gone, his face become a patchwork, his blazing blue eyes been fixed in a framework taken from his arm, which also contributed a straight, pale upper lip, with no middle ridge, in place of his former Cupid's bow; but he was still attractive, and by the end of 1940 had been enabled to see, to read, write a little, and go about in public.

In January 1941 he returned to hospital and got a very bad infection of the ear. Denise, the fiancée of his greatest friend Peter Pease, who had been killed in action, drove his mother down to see him. Together they sat on a table at the end of his bed, where he could see them without having to move. Richard tried to joke, but looked such a ghastly colour they felt they were with him for the last time. The colour was the consequence of a drug. He recovered. He questioned other patients so relentlessly that one slung a rationed egg at him. He wanted their answers for his diary. By March he had managed to finish the first chapter of a book, which brilliantly described his crash. Armed with it, he was introduced by Patricia Hollander to Rache Lovat Dickson of Macmillans, just before closing time and, like a youthful Ancient Mariner, forced him to listen. He read badly; but Lovat Dickson was impressed enough to ask him to come back when the book had been completed.

While recovering at East Grinstead he found a friend, a girl related to a woman, K., connected with the hospital, who will enter briefly and sombrely into the story. He also began a much deeper friendship with a woman slightly older than himself, whose name was Rosemary Kerr. She was the daughter of an Admiral and a close friend of Mary's. I knew her always as Rosie. A few months earlier she had been involved in an appalling car crash; her face had been smashed in and she had sustained seven fractures of the skull. McIndoe managed gradually to rebuild her face; when Mary first went to visit her, she was slung up (like many of the patients) with no nose and a hook in her mouth, and wished to die. As she began to mend, she stayed on as one of the nursing staff, and came to know McIndoe well. Through this triple relationship, with him, with Mary, and with Richard, she had as great an intimacy with the story as anyone. She died in 1986. Fortunately during the early 1980s, when a play about Mary and Richard was in preparation, she made a tape-recording of all that she remembered. Apart from being an extremely brave woman, discreet and loyal, she had a talent for detachment and

24

objectivity, relating tragic and horrifying events in an accurate, clear, and deadpan way of much value to a chronicler; it is to her recording that I owe some of the most important details.

Because of the state of his hands, Richard could not write at long stretches, and then, to start with, only with his left, which he forced himself to use. He felt that he was a failure. He had failed, he wrote to Denise, as a pilot. As for writing, 'it won't come, and I can't help feeling it will always be like this. I've never done anything, and I'm beginning to wonder if I ever shall . . . I'm a sham, gracefully doing nothing and being witty to visitors, and I know it, that's the awful part of it.' But to do nothing was impossible for him. Soon after his meeting with Lovat Dickson, he presented himself to Duff Cooper and Sir Walter Monckton at the Ministry of Information, and persuaded them to send him on a mission to the United States. The United States had not yet entered the war. Richard planned to give talks to American industrial workers and tell them 'something living' about the British pilots they were supplying with planes.

In June, the first of the British war-wounded to confront New York, he got a big reception from the newsmen and a good Press next morning. Things began to go wrong in Washington. Sir Gerald Campbell, Minister at the British Embassy, approved the speeches he had prepared, but was dismayed by his appearance, fearing that the women's clubs he would be obliged to address would take one look at him and say, 'We do not want our boys to die for Britain.' The mid-West especially would be against him; enthusiasm for the war in Europe had fallen off since the days of the Battle of Britain and the Blitz. He proposed that Richard should issue his speeches as a pamphlet and give talks over the networks.

But this did not suit Richard. Mobilising a lobby of powerful sympathisers, including several chiefs of aircraft production, a number of diplomats, and 'all the women with whom I came into contact', he advanced with their backing on the Ambassador himself, Lord Halifax. Unluckily Sir Gerald Campbell had got in already with Sumner Welles, the Secretary of State, who put the case to President Roosevelt 'from the mutilated airman angle'; and the answer had come back from the White House that it would be a 'psychological error' for Richard to appear on public platforms. Lord Halifax had an open mind. He would go to the President and tell him that the case had been unfairly presented, if Richard could win over Sir Gerald. Richard failed; and about the same time an article came out in a Washington newspaper to the effect that 'the presence here of Flight Lieutenant Hillary is not as good propaganda as the British think'.

It was a bitter blow. Always vain of his looks, he had not thought, nor had people at home, that the change in him would so appal. Although he tried to make light of the rebuff, dramatising himself as an international incident ('Shall Hillary Appear?'), he wrote home that 'all this is driving me crazy', and felt cruelly humiliated. Mrs Jeanette Lee, wife of the American Military Attaché in London, met him in Washington and found him extremely nervous and depressed. Once again he seemed to himself to have failed. 'I tried to explain that the shock to American women would be caused not by the sight of him, but by the idea . . . these emotions might just be the beginning of what we in America would have to learn.' It was thought a good scheme that an American surgeon should operate on his hands; but the operation did not succeed, he nearly died under the anaesthetic, and lost all hope of getting normal flexibility back into his fingers.

The Embassy agreed that he should give four broadcasts, which under RAF rules had to be anonymous. They brought him a big fan-mail. His chief comfort became the immense kindness and hospitality of individual Americans, who put him up in their homes for long periods and treated him as one of the family. The banker Edward Warburg lent him an office. There he continued his book, using his broadcasts and the diary he had kept in hospital for the next chapters. He met the French author-pilot Antoine de St-Exupéry, and his translator Lewis Galantière, who admired what he was writing, and found it a publisher, Eugene Reynal, of the firm Reynal and Hitchcock. A contract was signed in early August, before he had even finished; and thus this most English of books was written and first accepted and published in the United States, with the title *Falling Through Space*.

All those who knew him best in America were at one about his gaiety and humour; a youthful charm mingled with an early maturity;

his enjoyment of beauty and music and good living; his delight in excelling, whether in an argument or a game; his kindness; and his carelessness about money. He also had a biting tongue, particularly on the subject of bureaucracies. Mary Warburg, with whom he stayed in New York, thought that his success with women compensated his disappointment about his speaking tour. 'It was not my opinion, nor anyone else's who knew Richard, that the women of America couldn't take it; he would have charmed them all once he began speaking . . . He made one feel perfectly natural, although his scars in those days were quite red and very noticeable. I was only upset when I cut his finger nails. They were thick, and all but two deeply embedded, as the burned skin pulled them down into a clenched position.' Mrs Lee, with whom he stayed in Georgetown, noticed how easily he tired, and how weak his hands were, and had the knobs on all the doors he used adjusted, so that they would move at the least touch.

He made a conquest of Merle Oberon, by now a film star of a magnitude less only than that of Greta Garbo, Marlene Dietrich, and one or two others, already rich, and well on her way to becoming a celebrated hostess and the friend of many of the great. 'She was one of the magic presences of the twentieth century,' say her biographers. 'The rich black hair, the high noble forehead, the smoky opalescent eyes, now hazel, now seeming to be green, the sensual lips, the exquisite neck and shoulders, and the full generous voluptuous body all remain fascinating and desirable in photographs and films. At her best, as in *Wuthering Heights*, the movie for which she is most often remembered, she was an actress of striking gifts. But she was a woman before she was an actress – a woman of rare strength, independence, daring, and style, who was also a true romantic . . . mystical also . . . in spirit walked among the stars . . . could have been a poet; her life was filled with intimations of immortality.'

At the time Richard met her, she had been two years married to Alexander Korda, whom movie-making and other more secret work for Churchill kept busy coming and going across the Atlantic. He had directed her in the first film that made her famous, *The Private Life of Henry VIII*, in which she had played Anne Boleyn. She was now thirty. She and Korda were old friends of Mary's, who had known

27

her first on Korda's pre-war film sets before Merle's marriage. Some considered her hard. She was of Eurasian origin, which she went to lifelong pains to conceal, and had had hard beginnings. Mary loved her, and found her touching. She could no more help breaking hearts than falling in love herself, which happened to her regularly, each time convincing herself that she had found the one who could really make her happy. When Mary once spoke to Richard of the charm of youth consisting in believing oneself wholly in love, she might have been thinking of Merle at almost any age.

She died in 1979. Her biographers give the impression of having spent so much time and energy researching her true background, and her endearing and necessary fantasies about the background she invented, which is the main and fascinating purpose of their book, that they had not enough left to spare for Richard and her relationship with him. They say of him, for example, that 'according to his friend, the distinguished author, Arthur Koestler, he committed suicide', which Koestler does not specifically say, but only hints. Richard, they also say, 'was painfully aware that, whereas he had been rescued from the original crash in the North Sea, others of his crew had died'. They should have known that Richard crashed flying a Spitfire, and Spitfires were single-seaters and did not have 'crews'. And repeating from Lovat Dickson's biography of Richard an abridged clause out of his will, they omit the bequest in the original document of his gold aeroplane clip to Merle, which surely deserved mention in their immensely detailed story of the passions, sorrows, and triumphs of her bejewelled life. More serious divergences will be mentioned later between the account they present of him and what he himself says in his letters to Mary, which they had heard of, since they refer to them, but had evidently not had the time or opportunity to read. The result, if his own account is to be accepted, is rather more prosaic than theirs; but I know of no reason to doubt, in general, their narrative of his first meetings with Merle in New York.

They relate that the daughter of his publisher, Eugene Reynal, introduced her to him at a party, and she 'immediately felt an overpowering sympathy and warmth towards him. She herself had known what it was to see her face destroyed [in a car crash]; she knew in the essence of her being the pain of loss of looks which only

28

a beautiful human being can know. And she had been lucky; she had regained her looks, with only slight scars left behind to mark the torment of her ordeal.' According to Tessa Michaels, of United Artists, her publicity agent, and other friends, Merle was 'overwhelmed by desire for Hillary. He brought out the frustrated maternal element in her nature as well as the healing element she had inherited from her mother, who had worked as a nurse. She wanted to give Hillary back a sense of his lost manhood; that he could still be attractive to a woman of great allure. She knew that by reawakening his dampened and suppressed sexual fires she could give him back his virility and self-confidence.' And, according to Tessa Michaels, so she did.

Lovat Dickson, whom Merle's biographers also quote, puts it more coolly, perhaps because he was a Scot. 'Merle was just what Richard needed at the time . . . Merle helped him to laugh and have fun. She *gave* him laughter – he always said . . . that their affair was not heavy and major, but it was lighthearted, cheerful, and took his mind off' his humiliation by the British Embassy. This corresponds more closely with what Richard also says to Mary, and certainly rings true of Merle, who had a great gift for laughter and for making others laugh. The affair lasted until Richard returned to London, taking with him a letter of introduction from Merle to Mary.

As a writer, his most important encounter was with St-Exupéry, who had gone into temporary exile in New York after the fall of France. *Vol de Nuit* and *Terre des Hommes* had made him worldfamous; critics were already saying, and continue to say, that his books did for aeroplanes and the adventure of the air what Conrad's did for ships and the adventure of the sea. St-Exupéry had had it in mind to write a preface to *Falling Through Space*. His own latest work *Pilote de Guerre* (*Flight to Arras*) came out from the same house on the same day, and had much in common with Richard's. Set in May 1940, just before France surrendered, it commemorates the comradeship against desperate odds of St-Exupéry's deathless squadron 22/3, in a defeat St-Exupéry refused to accept as a defeat, as Richard was commemorating his own squadron in their victory.

St-Exupéry deepened in him a sense of something like guilt that he had been shot down too soon; a disquiet that sooner or later more would be demanded of him, that he owed more to his fallen fellow-pilots than a book. He did not live long enough to learn that St-Exupéry, wounded like himself, would force his way back to the survivors of his squadron in North Africa; persuade the American General under whose command they were operating to grant him, though at least a decade over regulation flying age, permission to make sorties with them over occupied France, and meet his death among them. Did the veteran in exile ever convey something of this intention, this expectation, this fulfilment, to the young Englishman, and so strengthen a determination to return to combat with the RAF? Reflections such as these may explain the occasional aloofness one of his hostesses noticed in him, the craving to withdraw from the fêting and the parties. Miss Levine, who typed his manuscript and would have typed its sequel, which was to have been called *Dispersal Point*, knew all along, she wrote after his death, that the sequel would never be. 'He was too anxious to return to flying, and when he walked out of the office, I told Mr Warburg I had a feeling we would never see him again . . . He always gave me the feeling of someone living on borrowed time, as if he had been granted a short reprieve from the grave . . .'

Richard might have stayed on. He had become enchanted with Americans, and longed to see more of the country than New York and Washington, but the Air Ministry were demanding his return. The straightforwardness of those Americans he met, their inquisitive and restless minds, found an immediate response in his own. He had many talks with the young of draft age, whose sentiments struck him as 'identical with our own just before the war . . . They too thought that the world was their oyster, and the war to be fought so that they could gain experience of life. They, as we before them, have the inestimable advantage of not going forth waving flags, only to come back cynical and disillusioned. We were cynical and disillusioned before it started. Our so-called Lost Generation found itself quickly enough, and I have no doubt that the Americans will have the same experience. The only difference I can see is, that when we held a debate, even on pacifism, we had some difficulty in taking ourselves seriously; the younger Americans, never.'

They all wrote of him to his parents afterwards, that parish of rich and generous and intelligent American women who had looked after him. Mrs Carola Warburg Rothschild, for example: 'No one who ever knew him can forget his luminous quality. The star-dust that was his portion has left a glow, which guides us towards the ideals for which he gave his life.' Mrs Lee recalled how well he got on with her eight-year-old daughter. He loved to take his meals with her, and told her fairy stories. (Strange – another resemblance; about the same time, St-Exupéry was finishing *Le Petit Prince*.) Two years after Richard's death the U.S. air commander Collyer wondered to Mrs. Lee if Richard would have been great had there been no war. 'I cannot answer that question,' she wrote. 'I only know that the influence he had on all of us was great.'

He returned to Britain in October 1941 and gave the completed galley proofs of the American edition of his book to an astounded Lovat Dickson, on whose recommendation Macmillans at once agreed to publish it this side. It was re-named *The Last Enemy*. Richard referred to it as a novel. He took occasional deliberate liberties with the truth. It is of the type of *Bildungsroman*, which relates an author's growth out of youth into what he deems to be maturity. There have been many such, often written by men and women in middle age, able to spread themselves over a wide canvas. Richard's tragedy, wrote Jules Roy, another French pilot, contrasting him with St-Exupéry, was that his entire 'adventure' had been confined to war. Yet his days of active service were few, and in the school edition of the book comprise only fourteen pages of the total 161. What makes it live is his 'born writer's' gift for describing fact with laconic but intense detachment, and the chronicle of his spiritual development that runs through. Composed swiftly under a fierce compulsion, as if in a blaze about a blaze, it remains a remarkable and, for someone so young, quite extraordinary record of a self-confessed, self-fascinated, egocentric transformed by suffering; his own, and, yet more, that of others.

So much for an editorial précis of events, some used in the book, others (including the American) not. Since his fame rests on the

31

book, which is almost entirely autobiographical, let us see, commenting now and then, what he made of those events.

[ii]

THE LAST ENEMY

opens with the chapter describing his crash, which he had forced on Lovat Dickson before going to America. The next chapter is a flashback to his days at the University, and makes rather odd reading now, set alongside what the eighties have come to associate with Oxbridge in the thirties. He was not a spy. He was not a pacifist. He was not homosexual. He was not a born-again member of the Oxford Group. He was not a Communist; nor even, in the terms of that time, Left-wing; nor Tory; but by no means unconcerned with politics. It was his idiosyncrasy to select as prophet not Marx, nor Keynes, but the nineteenth-century American land-and-tax reformer Henry George.

George and his huge book *Poverty and Progress* were no longer much thought of, if at all, but Richard's originality of choice put him in good company from the past. Alfred Russell Wallace, writing to Charles Darwin in 1881, had called George's book 'the most startling, novel, and original of the last twenty years and, if I mistake not, will in the future rank as making an advance in political and social science equal to that made by Adam Smith'. Bernard Shaw wrote: 'when I was swept into the great Socialist revival of 1883, I found that five-sixths of those swept away with me had been converted by Henry George.' Sun Yat-sen declared George's teachings to be 'the basis of our programme of reform' in the new Chinese republic. Tolstoy thought that nobody who had read the book could fail to agree with it. Keir Hardie told Philip Snowden that, though George was not a Socialist, *Poverty and Progress* had given him his own first impetus towards Socialism. Snowden too had been influenced and when, as Chancellor of the Exchequer in 1931, he tried to introduce his land-taxes, he spoke with a fervour that echoed George. How Richard came upon George, who put him in touch with *Poverty and Progress*, I should like to know. The enthusiasm may help to account for his fascination with America, and places him emphatically on the side of radical reform.

Henry George had been the impassioned advocate of free trade and 'the single tax'. Sickened by the poverty and exploitation he had witnessed in the States, particularly in California and along the courses of the new railroads, he came to believe that, as economic development advanced, so land became ever scarcer and scarcer, and rents higher, with the consequence that idle landowners made ever larger and larger profits at the expense of productive capital and labour. This unearned economic rent, he argued, should be taxed away by the State, and all other taxes abolished; the income from this one tax would become so huge, that it would provide a surplus for public works. He was far from anti-capitalist; apart from the nationalisation of all land and some public services, he favoured a mixed economy. The theory was finally propounded in 1877 in *Poverty and Progress*, which had enormous sales and was translated into many languages. For years most of the Roman Catholic hierarchy condemned it, since they deemed it, wrongly, to be hostile to private property. Marx despised it: 'the whole thing is simply an attempt, decked out with socialism, to save capitalist domination and indeed to establish it afresh on an even wider basis than the present one . . . on the other hand, George's book is significant because it is the first if unsuccessful attempt at emancipation from the orthodox political economy . . . He is a talented writer (with a talent for Yankee advertisement too) . . . he also has a repulsive presumption and arrogance which is displayed by all panacea-mongers without exception.' George did not come up with the all-too-obvious retort, but merely called Marx 'a superficial thinker, entangled in an inexact and vicious terminology . . .' and 'the prince of muddleheads'.

Any teaching repudiated by both Roman Catholicism and Marxism was likely to appeal to Richard. The political causes of the time seem to have left him fairly unmoved. His attention was not engaged by the civil war in Spain. From Cambridge, a short while before, his near-contemporary John Cornford had been killed there. From Oxford, Auden and Isherwood were turning their backs on the ideologies and settling down in the United States. Evelyn Waugh had long since been received into the Roman Catholic Church, and was about to be accepted into the Royal Marines. Stephen Spender would soon be volunteering for the London Fire Brigade. Richard

33

plumped for the University Air Squadron, though the river took up most of his time. He worked for his degree just hard enough to expect a decent Second and, in his own epigram, row his way after his father into the Sudan, that country of blacks ruled by Blues.

His rebelliousness, such as it was, was satisfied by a comfortable and fairly conventional iconoclasm, unattached to any movement; a do-your-own-thing individualism, conducted well within the limits of his upbringing and his class. His friends were well-to-do, athletic, radiating 'an atmosphere of alert Philistinism . . . of necessity that part of the University with which I came in contact, but I venture to think little differing in essentials from the majority of young men with a similar education. We were disillusioned and spoiled. The Press referred to us as the Lost Generation, and we were not displeased . . . without any Holy Grail in which to lose ourselves. The war provided it, and in a delightfully palatable form.' No heroics here; rather 'an opportunity to demonstrate in action our dislike of organised emotion and patriotism, the opportunity to prove to ourselves and the world that our effete veneer was not as deep as our dislike of interference, the opportunity to prove that, undisciplined though we might be, we were a match for Hitler's dogma-fed youth.

'For myself I was glad for purely selfish reasons. The war solved all problems of a career, and promised a chance of self-realisation that would normally take years to achieve. As a fighter-pilot, I hoped for a concentration of amusement, fear, and exaltation, which it would be impossible to experience in any other form of existence.'

There follows an account of training in England and Scotland; landscapes, airscapes, characterisations of his fellow airmen, all done with a quick accomplished brush; and then, in chapter five, the entry of the major theme and of the hero, if there can be said to be a hero in a book crowded with young men who do not like the title.

He is Richard's blood brother, also six foot two, also handsome. He is called Peter Pease, heir to an estate in Yorkshire. He refers to Richard as 'our Mr Hillary', and thinks him rather eccentric, the sort of person who crash-lands, as Richard once did, in the grounds of a house where a cocktail party is going on. Richard uses Peter's Christian and patrician idealism as a foil for his own outsider creed. 'You', he informs Peter, 'are going to concern yourself after the war

34

with politics and mankind; I am going to concern myself with Richard Hillary. I may or may not be a man of my time, I don't know. But I know that you are an anachronism. In an age when to love one's country is vulgar, to love God archaic, and to love mankind sentimental, you do all three. Me the mass of mankind leaves cold. My only concern outside myself is my immediate circle of friends, to whom I behave well, basically, I suppose, because I hope they'll behave well towards me.'

Peter retorts that one day Richard will change his tune. 'It won't be long either. Something bigger than you or me is coming out of this, and as it grows you'll grow with it. You are not entirely unfeeling . . . it needs only some psychological shock, some affront to your sensibility, to arouse your pity or your anger sufficiently to make you forget yourself.' Richard answers that he doubts it, and there, with the Luftwaffe offensive getting into full swing, they leave it, on Peter's part for ever, to take up their stations on the aerodrome at Hornchurch. The next pages describe their squadron's part in the Battle of Britain, with its recurrent litany, 'From this flight So and So did not return', as far as Richard's own crash.

The second part of the book begins with a no less gripping account of Richard's hospitals. In the first, the clearing station, he spends four days 'floating in a great sea of pain'. Arrived at the Royal Masonic, he faints and the house surgeon 'took the opportunity to give me an anaesthetic and removed all the tannic acid from my left hand'. Under the anaesthetic he has a vision of Peter Pease, a smile on his face, chasing a German Messerschmidt, with another Messerschmidt unseen on his tail. 'For two seconds nothing happened. I had a terrible feeling of futility. Then at the top of my voice I shouted, "Peter, for God's sake look behind!" I saw the Messerschmidt open up and a burst of fire hit Peter's machine. His expression did not change, and for a moment the machine hung motionless. Then it turned slowly on its back and dived to the ground. I came to, screaming his name, with two nurses and the doctor holding me down on the bed.' Two days later a letter from Colin Pinckney, another of his squadron, with whom Peter and Richard had formed 'a triangle of friendship', tells him that Peter has been killed.

35

For the first few weeks only his parents were allowed to visit him, 'and they came every day. My mother would sit and read to me by the hour. Quite how much she suffered, I could only guess, for she gave no sign. One remark of hers I shall never forget. She said, "You should be glad this has to happen to you. Too many people told you how attractive you were, and you believed them. You were well on the way to becoming something of a cad. Now you'll find out who your true friends are."'

After a while there arrives Denise, the 'heroine' of the book, to whom Richard dedicated it. She comes many times. He loves women to wear bright clothes, and if she arrived in mourning or in khaki would say in mock exasperation, 'Not yet, not yet. You've mistaken the place again.' They talk, about Peter, about all kinds of things. He has time and has recovered enough to think. His thoughts are not, like those of St-Exupéry, poetical or mystical. He is young, and they are practical thoughts, like those of thousands, tens of thousands of other young Englishmen, in ships, in the desert, in prisoner-of-war camps, about the England after the war they believed themselves to have taken up arms for. Who would rule? Some wanted to go back to the old order. Not Richard. Some looked to the working class. Not Richard. Some dreamed of a religious revival. Certainly not Richard, one thinks, though bearing in mind the powerful Christian impulse that drove Henry George, one might be wrong. He remembers from his squadron Brian Carbury, formerly a shoe salesman in New Zealand, now a Flying Officer with the DFC; and Pilot Officer Berry, 'commonly called Raspberry, who came from Hull . . . short and stocky, with a ruddy complexion and a mouth that was always grinning or coming out with some broad Yorkshire witticism impossible to answer', now also with the DFC; and many others. And he thinks:

It was to the Carburys and the Berrys of this war that Britain must look, to the tough practical men who had come up the hard way, who were not fighting this war for any philosophical principles or economic ideals; who, unlike the average Oxford undergraduate, were not flying for aesthetic reasons, but because of an instinctive knowledge that this was the job for

36

which they were most suited . . . while their more intellectual comrades would, alas, in the main be killed. They might answer, if asked why they fought, 'To smash Hitler!' But instinctively, inarticulately, they too were fighting for the things Peter Pease had died to preserve.

Was there perhaps a new race of Englishmen arising out of this war, a race of men bred by the war, a harmonious synthesis of the governing class and the great rest of England; that synthesis of disparate backgrounds and upbringings to be seen at its best in RAF squadrons? While they were now possessed of no other thought than to win the war, yet having won it, would they this time refuse to step aside and remain indifferent to the peace-time fate of the country, once again leave government to the old governing class? . . . Would they see to it that there arose from their fusion representatives, not of the old gang, deciding at Lady Cufuffle's that Henry should have the Foreign Office and George the Ministry of Food, nor figureheads for an angry but ineffectual Labour Party, but true representatives of the new England that should emerge from this struggle? . . . Could they unite on a policy of humanity and sense to arrive at the settlement of problems which six thousand years of civilisation had failed to solve?

And even though they failed, was there an obligation for the more thinking of them to try to contribute 'their little drop', however small, to the betterment of mankind? Was there that obligation, was that the goal towards which all should strive who were left, strengthened and confirmed by those who had died?

Or was it still possible for men to lead the egocentric life, to work out their own salvation without concern for the rest; could they simply look to themselves – or, more important, could I?

I still thought so.

He starts to go out with Denise. They wander through an evacuated zoo, and discuss the Darwinian theory. They go to the première of the movie about the Battle of Britain, and he insists that she must not come in uniform. In the streets one or two people look at him with pity, 'and for a moment I was angry'. He smiles at one girl, 'and she smiled at me. I did not speak to her for fear of breaking the spell, but walked back to lunch on air.' Most evenings, from tea-time until eight o'clock, when he is supposed to start back for the Royal Masonic, he spends with Denise at her home in the centre of London. The Blitz is still on, they have to go down to the shelter. Sometimes he tells her stories. Sometimes he is so tired that all he can do is sleep; and in his sleep he fights Germans all night long.

Closed in on herself, she wishes only to see him and Colin Pinckney, the other member of that 'triangle of friendship'. Colin is likely to be drafted to the Far East, and Richard, months before the surrender of Singapore, tries to persuade him not to go, it will be suicide. He goes on talking with Denise. 'So warm and sincere was her nature, that I might have thought myself her only interest. Try as I would, I could not make her think of herself; it was as if she considered herself a person that was dead . . . There seemed nothing I could do to rouse her to consciousness of herself, thaw out that terrible numbness, breathe life into that beautiful ghost . . . Concern with self was wholly gone out of her. I tried pity, I tried understand-ing, and finally I tried brutality.' Her heart, he says to her, 'tells you that Peter will be with you always, but your senses know that absence blots out people. Colin will go away. I shall go back to hospital. What are you going to do then? Live alone? You'll try, but you won't be able.'

Intelligent, aware of what he is up to, she replies that she supposes him to be trying to hurt her in order to give her strength . . . 'but you're only hurting yourself. I have the strength. Peter and I are eternally bound up together.' And so is he, Richard, she goes on, 'in spite of all your intellectual subterfuges and attempts to hide behind the cry of self-realisation. You lay in hospital, and saw Peter die as clearly as if you had been with him. You told me so yourself.' So he had, though her confirmation of his vision is not in the book. Denise had paid several visits to Kent, trying to ascertain how Peter had been killed, and found a policeman who had watched the battle in the sky and been first on the scene after the crash. When she had asked Richard if he would like to hear, he struggled with his bandages to sit up, and said, his eyes alight with excitement, 'Before you tell me, I will tell you.' What he told her was what he had seen under the anaesthetic, corresponding exactly with what she had learnt from the policeman.

The book goes on with this age-old argument between her, the believer, and him, the hard-core cynic, about the influence of the beloved dead on those they leave behind. She quotes Donne's *Devotions* to him, which she had just been reading, and which he had made use of in his book: the famous passage in Meditation XVII:

> No man is an island, entire of itself. Every man is a piece of the continent, a part of the main: if a clod be washed away by the sea, Europe is the less, as well as if a promontory were, as well as if a manor of thy friend's, or thine own were. Any man's death diminishes me, because I am involved in mankind . . .

'You too are involved, Richard,' she tells him. 'Do you really believe you can go through life to the end, always taking and never giving . . .? You have given to me in a way that would have been impossible for you before Peter's death. And what have you got out of it? Nothing! . . . certainly you are going to realise yourself, but it won't be by leading the egocentric life. The effect you will have on everybody you meet will come not only from your own personality, but from what has been added to you by all the others who are now dead – what you so ungratefully absorbed from them.'

Again he is moved; again, not very deeply. He leaves her, thinking to himself that although Peter 'was in fact the touchstone of my sensibility at that moment . . . the mystical experience of his death something outside my experience, which had still to be assimilated . . . and yet . . . and yet . . . this sense of closeness, of affinity, must fade, its very intensity was in part false, occasioned by being ill, and by meeting Denise so shortly afterwards . . . I could not feel that their experience was mine, that it could do more than touch me in passing.'

The following two penultimate chapters, with their taut reportage of pain and endurance of pain, are called 'The Beauty Shop' and (after his Oxford friends) 'The Last of the Long-Haired Boys', and became famous. They describe the hospital for plastic surgery at East Grinstead, implicitly Richard's admiration for McIndoe, explicitly the burns, injuries and treatment of the patients, among them not only pilots, but a little girl of fifteen, terribly burned by boiling sugar her first day in a factory. They make no bones about Richard's far from muted fury at anything that goes wrong, his rows and reconciliations with one or two of the nurses, and include an account of his mastoid infection. He had to be given regular shots of morphine, and for long periods became delirious. 'After the plastic operations I had felt no discomfort, but now, with this continuous throbbing agony in my head, I thought I must go mad. I would listen with dread to the footsteps of the doctors, knowing that the time was come for my dressings, for the piercing of the hole behind my ear with a thin steel probe to keep it open for draining, a sensation that made me contract within myself at the mere touch of the probe on my skin.'

A 2500-lb bomb lands a hundred yards away, but does not explode. He wishes in his agony that it would. 'For a moment I thought it had . . . but as I realised slowly that it had not, I found that the tears were pouring down my face. I was sobbing with mingled pain, rage, and frustration. Sister immediately gave me another morphia injection.' Conscious again, and told that he must be moved to the improvised huts outside the hospital, he explodes himself. 'That night McIndoe came to see me. He was still wearing his operating robes, and sat down at the end of the bed. He talked to me for some time – of the difficulties of running a unit such as this, of the inevitable trials and setbacks which must somehow be met . . . I had had a tough break, but I must try not to let it get me down. I noticed that he was tired, dead tired, and remembered that he had been operating all day. I felt a little ashamed.'

McIndoe tells him that he will not operate again for three months. His mother comes, and tells him that one of those to whom he had been closest in the University Air Squadron, Noel Agazarian, has been killed. 'That left only me . . . the last of the long-haired boys.' And still he is not touched. 'I was horrified to find that I felt no emotion at all.'

The moment of truth arrives in the last chapter, which also became famous and much quoted, and, because of the 'happening' round which it pivots, is called 'I see they got you too'. He starts by telling his readers that, despite his own injuries, despite the Beauty Shop,

40

despite the deaths and the little girl, despite Peter Pease and Denise, 'I was self-centred enough to have survived any attack on my position as an egocentric'. He gets a letter from a friend from Oxford days, a pacifist called David Rutter, a man he had respected 'for an integrity as great, in a different way, as Peter's, an instinctive deep-rooted hatred for killing which no argument could touch . . . Now he was a broken man. In the last year he had stood by and watched his ideals shattered one by one. As country after country had fallen to Hitler, his carefully reasoned arguments had been split wide open . . . Never in the course of history had there been a struggle in which the issues were so clearly defined. Although our peculiar form of education would never allow him to admit it, he knew well enough that it had become a crusade . . .' 'After much heart-searching,' Rutter tells Richard, 'I finally decided that with the outbreak of war I had failed in my own particular struggle. I had not now the right to refuse to fight: it was no longer a question for personal conscience, but for the conscience of civilisation . . . Now I suppose I shall join up. Do you think I should?' Richard answers that he does not know. 'That's a question which only you can decide.'

Returning to the centre of London through the East End, he gets caught in a particularly concentrated air-raid. After the all-clear has sounded, the wardens ask him to help clear the ruins and get out the bodies. Under the wreckage of a house they come upon a working-class woman, still alive, clutching the body of a child who has been killed. Descriptively he is at his best, a master already of the sordid, the horrifying, the epic. He has a flask of brandy and holds it to her lips. Most of it runs down her chin. She reaches for the child and starts to cry. '"Thank you, sir," she said, and took my hand in hers. And then, looking at me again, she said after a pause, "I see they got you too."'

He walks away, totally out of control of his so guarded self, and curses her. 'Could she not have died without speaking, without raising those cow eyes to mine?' He grows calmer. It comes to him that 'all humanity had been in those few words . . . that that woman should die was an enormity . . . not just the German bombs, or the German Air Force, or even the German mentality, but a feeling of the very essence of anti-life that no words could convey. This was what I had been cursing . . . Evil itself, which Peter and the others had instantly recognised, and to be destroyed utterly . . . And it was in the end, at bottom, myself I had cursed . . .' He perceives with clarity, it may be only temporary clarity, the futility of his own self-centred arrogance, which experience after experience has been accumulating to reveal to him. He has done nothing for his dead friends, not even for the tormented pacifist who had paid him the tribute of consulting him. 'Do you think I should join up?' Rutter had asked. 'I had been disturbed a little, but when he had finished I had said nothing, given no sign, offered no assurance that he was now right . . . shying away.' Rutter's creed, like his own, had joined the flames and rubble of the houses. What flower could be plucked from them?

'I could write . . . To write I needed two things, a subject and a public. Now I knew well enough my subject. I would write of these men, of Peter and the others . . . And to whom would I address this book? That too I knew. To Humanity . . . yes, that despised Humanity which I had so scorned and ridiculed in Peter.

'If I could tell a little of the lives of these men, I would have justified, at least in some measure, my right to fellowship with my dead, and to the friendship of those with courage and steadfastness who were still living and who would go on fighting until the ideals for which their comrades had died were stamped for ever on the future of civilisation.'

Arthur Koestler called these final passages 'helpless stammering'. Others have found them rhetorical. They are, a little; and a little long. Rhetoric is often a substitute for emotion, a masquerade of an impermanent conversion. St Paul on the road to Damascus is done better, and more briefly, in the Acts. So is the prophet Isaiah's 'Here am I, O Lord. Send me.' Richard did not yet have the technique to convey belief through action or the interplay of character. At the moment he was writing 'for Humanity', and, though Humanity includes critics, it was not primarily their approval he was looking for. Nor did he greatly need the stimulus of their doubts (Koestler, V. S. Pritchett, Middleton Murry, for example) of his sincerity, since a large part of his brief existence was to become an interrogation of it. Soon, in a letter to Mary, he will be found questioning that very

42

peroration. Meanwhile, to most of the audiences he was reaching out to, in the States and here, that episode of the dying woman and her dead child being hauled out of the ruins became the harrowing climax, indisputably true, of a harrowing book. It is a measure of Richard's urgent need to brand on to the printed page what so far had been taking place within him, as well as no little literary skill, that he was to tell Mary that he had imagined it.

The book was done. It would be out in America in February, and in Britain as soon as war conditions permitted. What next?

On the day America declared war (8 December 1941), he wrote to Mrs Lee thanking her for all the help she had given him:

When I came to you I was practically at the end of my tether . . . I regret so much that I left before the war finally broke out in the Pacific. The American reaction is something I would have given a great deal to see. The let-down feeling after coming from America to this London, now suffering all the inconvenience of war without any of the excitement, is very depressing, and I cannot face going into hospital again . . . I have applied to do some reporting for the RAF in the Middle East . . .

On medical grounds, the application was refused, as was an application to train American pilots. There was nothing for it but to return to East Grinstead for a spell.

Rosie happened to be with his old girl-friend and her relative K. when he telephoned. As soon as the girl was out of the room, K. treated Rosie to a picture of an impossibly conceited youth, using the glamour of his injuries and the Battle of Britain to augment his attractions and get on; a picture of someone so scheming and unpleasant that Rosie expected a Mephistopheles. 'Instead, this rather jolly creature came in.' His sojourn in the States had matured him. The courtship of the girl ended amicably. At the end of the year, equipped with his letter of introduction from Merle Oberon, he went to London to call on Mary.

He was twenty-two.

MARY

was forty-four. She was born at Petropolis, near Rio de Janeiro, on 10 March 1897, the second of four children of Charles Hamilton Walter, a well-to-do merchant trading between Britain and Brazil, and also a connoisseur and collector, from whom she derived an instinct for beautiful things and a considerable knowledge of them. Her mother was Ada Yeats, a first cousin to the poet W.B. and the painter Jack, the only brothers I can think of who possessed pre-eminent genius in two different arts. She came to England as a child, and went to school there. Her father died in 1912. Her mother married again during World War I. Mary married Henry Booker, a London insurance broker, on 23 January 1918 at Brompton Oratory, when she was not yet twenty-one. She had two daughters by him, both of whom were grown up at the time this story begins. She obtained a civil divorce from her husband in the early thirties.

It is easier to speak of her, or leave the letters to speak, than to write. Those who did not know her are likely to be put off and rendered sceptical by an account of someone over and over again described as 'unique', that vacuous epithet. All human beings are unique. What then did she have, that caused so many to find her so different?

Of her beauty there was no doubt. A few are left who still remember their first sight of her, and thought then the same that I had thought. 'Once seen, never forgotten,' remarked a man who had not set eyes on her for forty years. A girl, meeting her about the time she first met Richard, said, 'Oh, how I wish I could look like that! and be like that!'; and another, aged eighteen, after Mary's death: 'I grew up always knowing that she was there . . . the perfect example for a girl of womanhood. She always questioned me and listened to my answers, ever interested in my childish problems and I think fascinated to watch me growing up . . .' Deirdre Hart-Davis, of all those friends dear to her perhaps the dearest, wrote after her death: 'No other friend has been to me what she was. Through all the years she never failed me for even a minute. Her warmth and generosity, her spontaneous response to humour and delight as well as to other people's joys and sorrows was like a limitless well. She never counted the cost to herself, and she had also a wonderful innocence . . .

Beauty, illumined by gaiety, tenderness, and compassion – photographs convey something. Those who tried to paint her conveyed something: Yakovleff her positive challenging look in youth, Csato her stillness later. Siegfried Charoux the Austrian sculpted her, but made her too marmoreal, achieving mainly the perfection of bone-structure. People always mentioned the high cheekbones. McIndoe met her and told a friend that in all his experience he had never seen a more beautifully constructed face. A poet wrote of her 'mainsail brow' (one sees it too in W. B. Yeats); someone else of 'Renaissance eye-sockets', settings for 'tawny eyes' (they were deep hazel, it seemed with flecks of gold, and the whites pale blue). Richard told her that her mouth was so perfect, she might have had something done to it (she had not), but her eyes could not lie. To two schoolboys she always remained 'the magnolia', because of her white – Richard called it ivory – complexion. She never sunbathed and used little make-up, and to the end of her days her face stayed almost without lines; with, in her own phrase once, a 'challenging rampage of hair'. As sometimes happens to those who begin very Latin, very dark, it went white in her twenties, a gleaming electric silver-white rising from her forehead in two curves that reminded me of rams' horns. She was of middle height, her body as well-formed as her features; walked lightly, springily, much as she talked. Sometimes when she smiled, she wrinkled her upper lip and nostril, putting me in mind of a rabbit nibbling a lettuce.

What enhanced her beauty was her apparent unawareness. At one time she had been a 'Society beauty', much fêted, much photographed, at pageants, charity balls, apparelled as a Venetian, as Marie Antoinette, and so on. She thought these photographs a bit ridiculous, and stowed them away. She disliked being shown off, and it was alien to her to show herself off. (She does not appear in Cecil Beaton's *Book of* (so-called) *Beauty*.) But now and then, dressed-up, perhaps coming down the traditional stair, she would seem suddenly to know that she was beautiful and take joy in it, like an athlete, or a dancer, and take one's breath away. Perhaps such people are best left undelineated, for the reader to imagine. Helen of Troy is the precedent. All Homer gives us of her is that, when she appeared upon the city walls, the old men ceased their chattering. Mary coming into a room had much the same effect.

Inwardly she knew all about the power of beauty, as in those lines of Auden's:

> That power to do harm, that power to excess
> The beautiful quite naturally possess.

When she was a girl, at her first dance, a man fell in love with her and would not leave her. 'This is power,' she told herself. 'I must be careful of it.'

Claud Cockburn, nimble-minded erstwhile Communist, saw her once and labelled her 'that obviously Tory woman'. I took him to mean it as derogatory. If he meant 'conventional', it was true that she observed conventions. She shopped at Harrods. She was Catholic; had tried, until her husband put it beyond her, to make a success of marriage; cared deeply and practically for her daughters; was someone to whom personal kindness came more naturally than social theories, which scarcely came at all. Yet after the war Ernst Fischer, the Austrian Communist leader and later doyen of the then version of the New Left, on his first visit to London, wanted nothing so much as to call on her; and declared that, given the right man and the right cause, she would have gone to more courageous lengths than the most ardent intellectual. She had read a good deal, but was not cerebral, and told Richard, 'You are more intellectual than I am, but I'm far more intelligent.' Rebecca West, not a conventional woman, meeting Mary for the first time, found it 'extraordinary' that such an apparently 'Society woman' should be so intelligent. So much for labels.

Strange, I think now, that a book Mary always hoped to see filmed was *A Woman on Horseback*, that amazing chronicle from the mid-nineteenth century of another Irish woman, Eliza Lynch, who became the mistress of the Paraguayan dictator, Francisco Lopez, wished to make him the Napoleon of South America, accompanied him throughout a war which decimated the country, and after his defeat and death ended as a refugee in South Kensington. Perhaps it was the boldness, the adventure, the initial dream of liberty in that

46

wild liaison, which appealed to Mary; of Madame Lynch's ambition, deceitfulness, and cruelty, she had not a trace.

Things people often find difficult and fuss about seemed to come naturally to her. Of the more profound, her religion was innate, straightforward, simple. A priest said of her kind of Christianity that her problems were more practical – how to help people – than theological; she did not study Encyclicals, and could hardly believe what Pope Paul VI had laid down in Humanae Vitae about birth control and the 'safe period'. 'All those thermometers and charts! Surely not!' Another priest, who knew her less well, called her after her death 'a holy woman'. What a face she would have made! One knew what he meant. His comment recognised her spirituality; but seemed to sever her from the flawed world she lived in unjudgingly, loved, and tried to understand, and placed her behind a cordon of formidable and ascetic saints, where she did not belong at all. She was against guilt; if you are going to do something you know is wrong, she once said, at least be sure that you enjoy it. Richard said that she saved one the trouble of defining the word 'good'. Rosie said the same: 'She was very very good . . . so selfless, loving, so terribly good to me . . . so very understanding and wise . . . made no lethal remarks, would never have blamed anybody, never boasted . . .' It begins to read like St Paul's Letter to the Corinthians, and all of it is true.

Of less important things, the same naturalness. Clothes, for example: a gossip-writer in the thirties wrote that she could have put the contents of a salad-bowl on her head or round her neck and make it look part of a *grande toilette*. She spent little on clothes. At one time a famous couturier dressed her free, but mostly she did not bother, and did not need to. She had few jewels; those she had were one-off, exquisite, and not particularly valuable. With household things, with cooking, the same, when her devoted housekeeper Vera retired and, later, the money began to give out, and she did everything herself: the same swift touch, the same absence of fuss. Rooms she created for herself or for others expressed the flair and the experience she had from her father. Things did not 'match', any more than her friends 'matched', nor did they deliberately clash. Each had its individuality; all together they got on, had style, had colour. At one time no demolition sale seemed to be complete without her; she discovered pieces of carved wood, and made of them a door, a fireplace. It seemed so easy.

What did she do, what was her occupation? After her divorce she set out to support herself and her children by her own work. Through Alexander Korda she tried films, but was no good. She was too reticent. (Her reticence, the shelteredness of her life, were of course what Richard was at once to pick on.) With two friends, Peter Lindsay and Edward Hulton, she went into the business of interior architecture (not merely decoration), and did well. After Richard's death she became London manager of Miles Aircraft. I have tried and tried to discover what she was doing during that war year with Richard, but had no success. At the beginning of the war she was a nurse, but that did not last. Her letters speak of being 'cluttered', of work that demanded great concentration, but give no details. At one point she talks of 'turning down a job in the Ministry of Supply, in spite of the salary, and going to the Americans'. Early on she had been friends with some of the top American journalists who came over to report the Blitz. She had friends too among the French, and those parachuted into France, and in the Foreign Office. Admiral John Godfrey, Director of Naval Intelligence (and said to have been a model for M in Ian Fleming's James Bond books) admired her greatly. I thought she might have had to do with something secret; but Rosie considered this 'most unlikely', though Mary was 'extremely discreet'. It must be left at that. To Rosie she was just someone who was 'always there'. During the Blitz she was lucky to remain 'there'. The house she shared then with lodgers got a direct hit, and many of her possessions were destroyed; but no one was hurt, and she was not in.

Her diary shows that she had one or two people with her, or was out with someone, almost every evening. She had too many friends for peace, and gave them too much of herself, especially anyone in trouble, to switch suddenly to someone who wanted everything. Her husband's possessiveness had developed in her, and raised almost to an article of faith, a passion for independence, perhaps Irish. After her divorce she did not become as, much courted, she might easily have become, a *grande amoureuse*. It was not in her nature. She

48

could have married wealth, but it was not what she wanted. For a number of years before the war she had one great friend, to whom, and to his wife after he married, she remained devoted. Something unusual about her among women of great beauty was that many of her closest friends were women; they trusted her, and put her outside the fields of jealousy.

In one letter to Richard she writes of 'three pagan interludes'. If I am thinking of the right men, two were foreigners, gifted, by nature artists, not indigenous to the world surrounding her. Richard too was a kind of foreigner; born in Australia, with Irish and Spanish blood. And Mary herself: half Irish, born in Rio. Perhaps it helps to elucidate the attraction. Physically, when he came into her life, she was alone; spiritually, had been so a long time. Twice in the correspondence she uses the phrase, 'alone, as I was before you came'. Family, friendships, work (whatever it was), concern for others, enjoyment of life, made up for solitariness only in part. She could cope with it from her richness of inner resources, but it did not come naturally to her.

People often spoke of her reticence, of her serenity. Serenity was probably always there in her expression. But what readers will surely, and very soon, remark, is that passage after passage in her letters appears to contradict it, and much else of what I have so far written. Over and over again she is, as Richard is also, insisting on anything but reticence between the two of them when alone; far from serene; far from being a woman to whom things came easily. One finds her torn by anxiety when he is in hospital; trying not to telephone; exasperated by his arrogance and badgering; passionate in his company; hardly able to bear his absences; jealous of others and of the air; frightened by the strength of their love; furious with the futility of her as well as his social life and their lack of privacy; insecure; sometimes exhausted; and near despair at her inability, as their crisis approached, to give him peace and to be ordinary, to transfer herself into (using RAF slang) the easy-going, 'Wizard', 'jolly good show' class.

One answer of course is that the impression given so far is the impression she gave quite naturally, to friends, to company, to people she loved, but was not in love with, and in the letters that follow she is in love. The lightning had struck, out of the blue, before she had had time to instal, as she was well able to, a lightning conductor. She becomes, as he is, someone to whom it is all or nothing.

But that is not the only answer. The serenity is still there, deep down, and springing not only from her religious faith. It springs also from brief but unshaken visions of a shared and perfect understanding between them ('There is nothing you could do I would not understand'); and also, whenever those visions failed, from a self-discipline which over many years had weaned her from caprice, and given her a truly extraordinary power of detachment, so that she could view their few rows as (twice in capital letters) 'IDIOTIC'; could steel herself, though hating it, to go away for weeks; could treat jealousy lightly; and could consider both herself and him sometimes with amusement and wit ('God help us if we ever lose our sense of the ridiculous!'), sometimes merely (and coldly) 'with great interest'. It enables her to stand aside and look on them as some god might, who 'had chosen us as the two people most spoilt and in need of character-building, and . . . thrown us together to show us undreamed-of possibilities of happiness and then put in the way just the sort of obstacles most frustrating to our particular natures. Just to see if we could take it, or destroy the gift'; or, elsewhere, 'as though some humorously-minded chemist had thought fit to take two cool still fluids and gently pour them into the same cauldron to watch the result . . .'

From experience she knows the potency of this detachment to destroy; and in their most crucial exchange of all, when she asks him to revert to friendship, to their initial relationship, 'so critical, so intolerant, so hard-headed', is amazed and reconciled to find from his reply that he is not only aware of this potency, but possesses it, and is equally scared of it himself. Thus, though she lived from the heart, she had a strongly controlling mind and will, was both romantic and classical; one of those whose light is confined to a small space only among people, an unrecorded place in time, but which is nonetheless both true sunlight and true moonlight, capable in other circumstances of warming and illumining a great landscape.

I should like readers to imagine her, not only in the letters, but in the intervals between them, exercising one of the rarest of her rare

50

endowments: listening. Let them picture her, denting her cheek with her forefinger, listening to him, so different, so male, outwardly so buccaneer, so young, even at times so childish, yet found at root to have grown wise and adult; Mary with her disillusion about the goodness of human beings way back in the past, long since mastered, and grown tolerant; Richard with his very recent disillusion about their unimportance to him conveniently exploded into a book, but not yet by any means conquered in himself.

Chapter Three
December 1941-April 1942

On a December evening in 1941 Mary was walking across Hyde Park to her flat. A damp mist was rising. Dead leaves rustled about her feet. 'Everything', she wrote of herself later, 'had gone wrong with her personal life during the past two years of war.' She came to the conclusion that all thoughts of individual happiness must be put aside, and directed instead not just to winning the war, but towards a peace which would atone for the 'blind selfishness' of the years before.

Her flat was on the third floor of a block across the Bayswater Road, a few hundred yards from Marble Arch. She noticed that the black-out was not fully drawn in her living room, letting a chink of light through, and wondered who could be there. Vera met her in the hall and told her that a young man had been waiting for some time.

She went in. 'He lay sprawled out and fast asleep in the largest armchair. From the table behind him the light shone on his fair hair.' She sat down and contemplated him. 'In RAF uniform, the top button carelessly undone, his legs straddled out before him, he looked oddly alert in spite of his deep sleep. His closed eyes, widely spaced, were without eyelashes. Sparse irregular eyebrows and discoloured skin on a broad intellectual forehead told of terrible burns. Above the wide humorous mouth a small nose tilted with similar humour. His hands, hanging limply over the arms of the chair, bore traces of beauty, despite the fact that the fingers of both were drawn up like the claws of a bird.

'His eyes opened slowly and met hers. He was up in an instant, standing slim and tall in front of her, and looking as shame-faced as a small boy. She laughed at his discomfiture, and he gave her a smile which transformed the tragedy of his face into a look of impish charm.'

They talked for an hour or so. He gave her messages from Merle Oberon, and told her about the fiasco of his mission to the United States, the failure of the operation on his hands, the kindness and hospitality of individual Americans, the impending publication there of his book, and its acceptance in the United Kingdom; of his crash, and his time in hospital. He spoke with what struck her as 'a pose of nonchalance, and a slightly aggressive attitude to life'; concealed beneath she was aware of 'a sensitivity which must have caused him a degree of mental suffering far beyond the physical torment of those months after his rescue from the sea'. Before he left, he asked her to have dinner with him some night, adding, 'I suppose one can dine in public in London?' She saw a dreadful uncertainty in his eyes about her answer, and replied at once that she badly needed to be cheered up. 'He cocked his hat at an incredibly rakish angle', and went away.

'Three evenings later the telephone rang, and a young voice drawled, "I feel incredibly low and confused. May I come round?"' He came, to her amusement 'installed himself in the same armchair, and plunged straight into the subject on his mind. What was he to do next? He had to have one or two more operations on his eyes and hands. He had an offer to go on a course at the RAF Staff College. Should he have his operations straight away, or wait till he had done the course? Should he accept the Staff College offer at all? Would it not mean that he might have to do a Staff job, or, worse, have to sit in an office for the rest of the war?

'He was moody and depressed, and filled with a deep sense of frustration, switching from one subject to another, and always returning to his place in relation to the war. Life had been so simple, before he was brought down; just shooting Germans out of the skies. Now he had to re-adjust himself and make decisions. Writing was his passion. All his belief in himself lay in this one gift which, but for the war, would have brought fulfilment of all that he most desired. She had never come across anyone with such a passion for living. It expressed itself in every mood, and every gesture of his hands: in those sudden flashes of gaiety, with which he pulled himself out of his self-absorption in order to regain his balance by ridiculing himself, and in the violence underlying his attack against everything that stood in the way of freedom to experience all that life could offer him, and use it for his writing.'

He remained on leave until the New Year. She found herself looking forward to returning home from work and discovering him there, as she often did. According to his mood, 'they would either play a lazy pingpong with ideas, or start sparring with a ruthlessness which at times reached a white heat of antagonism'. There was no end to his curiosity, on all subjects. He fired questions at her about what had happened to her, what she had done, what she had felt and thought, asked with a straightforwardness and lack of self-conscious-ness that disarmed her completely. 'By nature very reticent', she found to her own surprise that she was answering with equal candour. The way he went about it made her smile: he flattered her with his intense interest in her, and he stimulated her with an attitude which was not just humorous but, enlivened by his talent for words, interpreted all he spoke of in ways that were new to her.

Roused, they were 'well-matched, with swift, pointed minds . . . He loved to goad her out of what he termed the still detachment of her mind, accusing her of not daring to face unpalatable truths, of viewing human beings through pink veils of illusion. He would not rest until he had provoked her out of her calm into furious indigna-tion, as he always succeeded in doing. He would then laugh gleefully, and proceed to take endless pains to charm her back to harmony by being absurdly funny and insisting on taking her out to dance . . . She was old enough to impart an experience of life he considered of value to him, and not too old for him to enjoy taking her out . . .'

During this time they grew to know one another so well that the 'ideal conditions for companionship existed between them . . . having everything in common mentally, and expecting nothing emotionally . . . Since he took a healthy interest in sex, they discussed sex with the same detachment as, it might have been, the problems of post-war housing . . . When he was a small boy at school, he told her, he always took special care crossing streets, because he lived in constant fear of being run over before he had had his first experience of sex. With great delicacy and charm, and above all with that lightness of touch which was so characteristic of him, he informed her about all his love affairs, starting at the age of sixteen, and announced that he had never been really in love the whole of his life. "No one has ever captured my mind, and I've never wanted them to. I want to be free to do the things I have in mind to do. Even during my first affair, with a girl of twenty-two, I wasn't blinded by the romance. I saw things straight. I shall always see things straight." He laughed when she retorted that the charm of youth, as she had always understood it, was that the young always believed themselves to be totally in love, and she considered what he was saying to be not only sad but hideously cold-blooded . . .' This attitude was altogether too romantic for him.

He spoke of Merle, 'in the warmest terms and with equal detachment'. Mary remarked that he did not speak like a young man in love, to which he answered, '"Oh, I love her. No one could help it," but repeated that he was not in love, and never had been.

'"Has it occurred to you," she asked, "that maybe you are incapable of falling in love at all?"'

'This left him quite unmoved. He was glad that it had never happened to him, and he would fight against it if it ever threatened him before he was ready to cope with it . . . He was nervous that Merle might want to marry him . . . He talked of his determination not to marry, until he had gained the maximum amount of experience to carry out his work for the future, by which he meant his writing. He spoke of the possibility of going abroad as a journalist. "I've got to travel," he said. "I've got to learn, and make a career. I've got to learn to take care of myself before I can take on the responsibility of someone else."'

She continued to make fun of him, to parry, to counter-attack, and warned him that 'these things didn't wait on time, and he'd better be careful lest, by remaining so coolly detached, he lost the capacity he was so sure that he possessed'. And did possess. 'He knew', she wrote, 'what it meant to be wholly in love, and knew that he had the capacity. It would come naturally, he said, when he had found something stronger than himself. This assurance, and inner belief in himself, could not be shaken by outside influences, and contrasted strangely with that sudden collapse of confidence, which would sweep over him when relatively superficial buffetings of the world put obstacles in his way.'

During this time 'he was more single-minded and ambitious than at any other in my knowledge of him'. *The Last Enemy* recounts how, on McIndoe's first visit to Richard, at the Royal Masonic Hospital, Richard had asked him how long it would be before he could go back to flying and, on getting the reply, six months, had been terribly depressed for days. On his second visit Richard had asked again. This time, when McIndoe replied, 'Next war for you. These hands are going to be something of a problem,' Richard had had quite a different reaction. 'I wasn't even surprised. I suppose I had known it for some time.' As at the news of the death of Noel Agazarian, 'I felt no emotion at all'. That had been in 1940. Now, with Mary more than a year later, he 'did not speak of flying at all, and I do not think the possibility of being allowed to go back ever occurred to him. He spoke only of his writing', and revelled in his fencing and exploratory conversations with her, trying to screen her life, as she put it, 'like a kind of *Gone With the Wind*', cramming long stretches of time into a few hours.

'He flung himself whole-heartedly into the game, and there was no subject we did not discuss with a frankness that would not have been possible but for that complete lack of emotional involvement.' In the year that followed, this extraordinary understanding of one another, derived from those initial, precious, and all-important weeks, 'formed the basis of a spiritual strength against which nothing could avail'.

At the beginning of the New Year he left London for a two months course at the RAF Staff College at Gerrards Cross. Although Mary did not remember him speaking of returning to flying, it had never left his mind. On 11 January he wrote to his old friend and patron in New York, Edward Warburg:

After this Staff course I may come out on the Staff in Washington if Bill Thornton [the Air Attaché] will have me. If not, I'm going back to hospital to get medically fit again. I shall fly again. This I think will be possible. I have no intention of taking an office job at the Air Ministry. What do you think of the future of

56

Anglo-American relations now? My view is that above all 'the people are a myth' – that to worry about the Lancashire miner and the Middle Western farmer getting together is a complete waste of time. Why not have two dozen experts who know both countries travelling backwards and forwards to get a united war effort, and half a dozen economists to arrange a post-war system whereby your boys don't grab all the European markets and in your capacity of creditor nation expect us to give you all our trade when we can't afford it? I think we should have a set currency price level and exchange control etc etc etc . . .

His private diary shows continuing lack of confidence. The Staff College left him 'completely exhausted . . . 8 a.m. to 10 p.m. without a break, Monday to Saturday.' He was fearful that his past reputation for plain speaking, unconventional views, and facetiousness had done him harm, and was desperate for Macmillans to bring his book out before the course ended, to prevent his companions 'thinking me entirely imbecile'.

Mary and he wrote to one another and met when they could at weekends. None of Mary's letters from that still uncommitted time have survived, and only three of his from January; in which he seems deliberately and joyfully to be submitting, simultaneously with the Staff College course, to another one in life from her. What the RAF had to say was of much less interest and importance than what she had. He did not mind, he wrote, being made to 'feel low' by her, because 'I know only too well that you are right'. He pleaded 'the arrogance of youth, and a certain shyness'. He asked forgiveness for treating her like *Gone With the Wind*. Now it is going to be Proust, with the certainty that he will gain more from her 'than by the study of that illustrious gentleman'. No, he took that back. In 'general appeal' Proust was too exclusive. Mary was 'more akin to Shakespeare'. He had gone back to Shakespeare, and after her next letter agreed that he 'might perhaps have read *Hamlet* before *The Taming of the Shrew*'.

He thought little of organised religion. His particular butt was Dr Buchman's Oxford Group, whose name had been changed in 1938 to Moral Rearmament. He had once attended one of their revivalist

57

meetings and confessed that his principal weaknesses were 'matrons and Portuguese nuns', which one member had taken earnestly enough to attempt his conversion. Now at Gerrards Cross he found himself sharing billets with another member, a Squadron Leader. Fairly new copy, and therefore to be investigated. 'The Squadron Leader', he wrote, 'gets up at 5.30 and meditates, from time to time putting down the odd gin. The Ten Commandments apparently are a good basis, but do not go far enough. I protested that they went too far, that Moses was an amiable old gentleman putting up a memo to the Almighty with a view to getting a spot of order, when that withered old sourpuss Aaron had to go and put his oar in. Looking around at the high jinks among the youth and beauty, and completely forgetting that he had been young himself once, he was filled with terrific self-righteousness and kept pestering Moses to put in a clause or two against natural inclinations. Finally, as one always does when one is pestered too long, the old man agreed, and the result thousands of years later is people like friend [the Squadron Leader] meditating at crack of dawn on a misconception. He was not convinced and retired to bed, saying that "Sometimes there were times for plain talking and sometimes there were not," – a portentous statement, the exact application of which still eludes me. Work continues to pile up, but not enough to make me forget how much I miss you, and look forward to seeing you at the weekend . . . You are very elusive, but I am cantering determinedly behind . . .'

They had their weekend, and in his third letter (Wednesday 26 January) Richard looked forward to the next, when they will be staying in the country with mutual friends, 'more than anything I can remember for years'. He will exploit his disfigurement 'to pull all manner of hideous faces, so that we may have a compartment to ourselves'. The Squadron Leader had ceased to interest him. After last Saturday and Sunday with Mary he had come to the conclusion that 'the first essential of the complete man is the ability to recognise his own limitations', one of his being an inability to put into words what he thinks about her. Poetry would have to do, a version of Samuel Butler:

> All her perfections are so rare,
> The wit of man cannot declare

Which single virtue, or which grace,
Above the rest has any place.

He had been thinking of her so hard that he had walked into 'the business end of a sentry's rifle, and was compelled for a moment to focus my mind on worldly things. Do not, darling, I beseech you, pucker your lovely brows at this levity, for it is not what it seems but cloaking lightly the agitated palpitations of a bewildered heart! . . . Were I Mr Beverly Nichols, and I had any suede shoes, and were there any daffodils, I would now trip lightly outside and dance among them for sheer joy of living. Thwarted by all three factors, I will now content myself with a stoup of port in the Mess, a slightly smug expression being the only visible sign that inwardly I am hugging myself with joyful anticipation. All my love to you . . .'

It was still a game: fun for him, obviously, with a woman quite unlike the girls he was accustomed to have falling for him, and not like Denise, stricken and in mourning; and fun for Mary too, to be at the receiving end. She on her side had been flattered by many men with or without the gift of the gab. Richard was somebody totally different. The inrush of Richard's young life had swept a challenge into hers that seemed almost unrelated, almost outside the war, and given it a creative impetus she had lately lacked. A pity, then, that we are without her letters at this moment; but a safe guess, from his references, that what he had roused in her in conversation continued on the page, and that they contained a fair measure of criticism, raillery, and counter-provocation, none of it with any other aim.

The weekend put paid to this Platonic idyll. A number of other guests were staying in the house, and Richard had to leave early. Mary was alone in the living room, 'standing by the fire, when he came in ready in his great-coat to await the car that was to take him to the station. He came and stood silently before her, assuming the attitude of an over-conscientious guard at a lying-in-state, his expression so irresistibly comic that she laughingly took his head between her hands and kissed him on the cheek. She felt his whole body stiffen . . .' Then in an instant he was responding passionately, his arms round her, his lips on hers. 'The earth seemed to fall away under her feet, and suddenly with no word spoken he was gone.'

She heard the sound of the car driving away, sat down, closed her eyes, and tried to think how this plunge into a relationship she had neither expected nor intended had come about. Her gesture had been amused, affectionate, lighthearted. Like a far-off small wave that turns out to be a seventh, and later was to prove tidal, it had surged into a passion between them both. 'She searched back over the past few weeks, and could recall no hint from him – except once. Once, some time back, he had said, "I feel happy today – dangerously happy." Only that; and she had not asked him why.' She cursed herself for an impulse that had come so naturally, knowing the dangers so well of crossing that frontier between a perfect friendship and falling in love, and fearing the loss of that gay and easy time, which had brought so much laughter into her life and had held no complications. She made up her mind that, next time they met, they would laugh it off 'as a momentary madness', and reassured herself by recalling their detached exchanges about sex. 'For a time, they did try to recapture that easy and harmonious past; but in vain.'

From that time on, there was to be less of *Gone With the Wind*, of Proust, even of Shakespeare. Would they have been more prudent, one wonders fruitlessly, instead of *Hamlet* or *The Taming of the Shrew*, to have read *Much Ado About Nothing*? This Benedick, this Beatrice, of the mid-twentieth century had fallen; the pupil–preceptor relationship had not ended, but been transfigured; the course of love had begun, and for them both.

Two days' silence from Richard followed that weekend encounter, and then, on 2 February, he wrote from his parents' flat in London.

My darling,

. . . I suppose it is surprising how little we have said about our feelings for one another, and for me everything happened so naturally it was not necessary.

But Mary, I love you . . . It must be love when one feels suddenly that one is no longer self-sufficient, that someone else is more impoitant, and that it is only when with her that one is happy. For me that in itself is an entirely new experience, and one by which I am still a little bewildered.

What your feelings are, Mary dear, I can only guess. That you should feel just as I do would be too much to hope, for I am not really arrogant enough to assume it. For I know very well there must be several men who, to a greater or lesser extent, fill a place in that very warm heart of yours. But of course, when I write that 'it is too much to hope for', I am only deceiving myself, for I do hope, oh so much, that you should, and once or twice I have almost persuaded myself that it's true.

Will you forgive me, I wonder, if just for the purpose of this letter, I assume that it is?

Well there are one or two unfortunate facts that we must face up to, aren't there? I'm not trying to run away from them, but I can do a little to set your mind at rest on what I believe to be the main one.

He meant Merle Oberon. Merle had asked Mary to take Richard 'into her fold', in other words give him a place among her admirers. Richard went on:

If I'm right, what is sticking in your throat is that . . . I should then go and fall in love with you. There are questions of loyalty on both sides which, to say the least of it, are ticklish. For myself I will say only this. I am always honest with myself. (It's one of those principles you were asking about), and after much thought I find that it worries me not at all.

For one thing, letter or no letter, I should have met you on my return. [Through Rosie Kerr, or a number of other mutual friends, this would have been true.] But that is not the point. It is this. I love you, and do not, nor ever have loved Merle. Basically she knew it, knew that while I was amused and intrigued by her, I should be quite unaffected by parting. The result you already know [presumably from their earlier conversations], recurring scenes and my final flight (for it was that). My dominant emotion on arriving back was one of relief. It is, I suppose, a beastly thing to say, and I don't enjoy saying it, but now I feel I must.

I sat down several times to write 'finis' to it all, but I could not find the words, and so partly from weakness, partly from a desire not to hurt her feelings, I refrained. But what I am trying to say, Mary, is that this has nothing to do with meeting you. It was over before, but I could see no particular reason for facing up to it.

Oh, Mary, I am doing this so badly, and I know that it is only now that I'm getting to the real crux of the matter.

That is, what you think, which is going to depend finally on how much you care, or whether you believe as I do that this is the most important thing for two people (or rather, specifically for us). For I must admit, although in this instance I think we are clear, even if we were not, I don't think I should be able to stop. For this reason, perhaps oddly, I want to make you happy. Probably you imagine that to be only natural, but I'm afraid that I have always been so selfish that for me it is something quite new.

I wish that I could have seen you before writing this. It does not read well and there must be a million things I have left out. For one thing I have taken no account of what a complex person you are. For another, this sounds so frightfully egotistical, but I have tried to write dispassionately, but, by God, I don't feel like that. Please, Mary, help me a little, and whatever you say when we meet I shall not mind. Only don't think all this too stupid – or at any rate say so. It's no use my waffling on, so I will say only this.

If you do think that we two might go on together, along the common road, you will help me enormously. I shall probably help you not at all, being moody and irritable by turn. But I will try with every means in my power to make you happy and in doing so be happy myself.

Richard

Then, on a Saturday, ten days later:

R.A.F. Staff College
Gerrards Cross
12th February 1942

My darling,

I am like a man, who travelling through a dark tunnel and seeing a pinpoint of light ahead, has shouted for joy, then hesitated, stricken for fear that it may be a mirage. Reassured, he presses forward, silent, his heart hammering, and it is only when he stumbles out into the light that he relaxes and, weeping for joy, pours out his heart.

Richard

The next batch of letters from him cover about six weeks until the end of March, when his course at the Staff College ended. He had fixed with McIndoe to go into East Grinstead Hospital for another operation on 10 April. He would thus have ten days entirely free, and Mary and he were to spend them at her cottage in North Wales.

These letters are chiefly about his emotions, but show too that he was not yet by any means physically fit. On about 7 March he had lunch with Mary's cousin Charles Haydon, 'to pick his brains on Air Superiority', about which he was writing an appreciation for the Staff College. 'I was not feeling too well. I went all peculiar-like once or twice during lunch and, on dropping my good host at Whitehall, instead of leaping out, opening doors, saluting, and what not, just sat back in a corner, nodding vaguely and feeling very sick indeed. Then on the way back [to his parents' flat] I quietly passed out, much to the annoyance of the cabby, who had to pick me out at this end.' And on the following Monday, back at the Staff College, he writes from bed, because 'this afternoon I began to feel rather ill, and, choosing the top of the stairs to have a dizzy fit, came rocketing down to the bottom and twisted my ankle . . . I now feel quite well again, and intend to do nothing until I see Archie [McIndoe].'

His emotions veer in a slightly frenzied way between extreme happiness, self-doubting, and uncertainty about Mary. The happiness is that of most requited lovers, ecstatic and amazed.

17th February

Darling darling Mary,

Thank you for two such very beautiful days. So much happened in that short time, so many things that might have gone wrong, but through which we sailed triumphantly, almost carelessly, for I knew as soon as I was with you that together we need fear nothing; together we are somehow *right*. After talking to you last night I felt so tired that I had to crawl off to bed and so this letter will not reach you as soon as I had hoped. This week already seems intolerably long and an appalling waste of time, now that all I want and think of is to be with you, and make you smile that lovely smile of yours.

You fill me with a strange humility, my darling, and I still can't quite believe that you really love me . . . that it is not all a beautiful dream. But on Sunday when I see you again I shall remember these words –

> 'I touch her, like my beads, with devout care,
> And come unto my courtship as my prayer.'

And from now, till then I shall think of you and try to be worthy of your love . . .

(Saturday) 23rd February

My darling,

I called you up tonight to say that I would not be able to write to you until tomorrow because of a simply appalling exercise which greeted me on my return, but oh darling, I love you so much that I cannot possibly wait until tomorrow, and am sitting in my corner of the room pretending to write an appreciation . . . My heart is so full, and this is no place to put all I feel into words, but I am happy and, what's more, I know that I'm happy. It's a miracle in the world today, and I give you thanks for it . . . Each time I see you it is harder to tear myself away . . . write to me very soon please.

March 1

. . . I miss you quite terribly and love you very much.

[From his parents' flat]
[Sunday] March 8

. . . Last night was so lovely that I'm still wandering vaguely around the flat, quite unable to concentrate on the no doubt

highly important, but equally dull subject of Air Superiority . . .
please miss me a lot this week. I shall be thinking of you all the
time, and longing for the course to end, so that I may prove it is
really possible for me to be continually pleasant! . . .

But he was far from sure of himself. In the same letter of 17
February, in which he had announced that 'together we need fear
nothing; together we are somehow *right*', he asked in the next
breath, 'Did I fail you, I wonder? I was stupid on Sunday, I know,
but then this is all so new to me that I pray you to bear with me a
little when I become childish or petulant . . .'
And on 1 March,

. . . we have such a chance, so many things, that we share
already that now I must not fail; for if we do fail it will be my
fault. There will be moments when by being casual or careless I
may almost spoil things, but if you will help me, believe in me,
and not be sceptical any longer, we shall come through.

I have wanted you so much this week-end and I have been
afraid, afraid that tomorrow I shall wake and find that it is not
true, that you do not love me, or that you have closed your heart
to me and gone away.

On 8 March, he wished her a very happy birthday for the 10th,
asked her to believe that he would be thinking of her all the time,
and went on:

I am feeling horribly low at the moment, and very remorseful
that I was so aggressive. I would give so much to curl up in your
lap and go to sleep – but then I am being selfish again. Love
should not consist of running to the woman one loves in
moments of distress. Poor darling – what a horrid little man you
took on in me. I don't wonder that you are sceptical, but all the
childish petty things I now find myself doing are as much a
surprise to me as they are to you. You see this has never
happened to me before, and I'm not quite big enough to cope
with it yet, although with your help I think I soon shall be. How

true it is that one can be loved by a thousand people and yet learn nothing, for then, paradoxically, it is easy to give, when it is immaterial whether one gives or not. All very obvious, I suppose, but new to me.

When I arrived back here [at the Staff College] this morning, I felt very humble and a little frightened. As though for the first time, I thought how lucky I was, that I, yes *I*, should have your love. And for a moment I was exhilarated, but then remembered . . . and I knew that this week-end I had given you nothing, but taken all the time. And at once I wanted to come to you, oh so urgently, and when I called you and you were out, I could have wept.

On 18 March he thanked her for her 'very sweet letters' (none of which have come to us), and apologised for feeling sick during his lunch with Brigadier Haydon, and 'I have hopes that I shall be able to hand you the first copy of the book in this country'.

Two days later,

Have just found this and enjoyed it so much that I'm sending it to you:

> Love me not for comely grace,
> For my pleasing eye and face,
> Nor for any outward part,
> No, nor for a constant heart:
> For these may fail, or turn to ill,
> So thou and I shall sever:
> Keep, therefore, a true woman's eye,
> And love me still, and know not why –
> So hast thou the same reason still
> To doat upon me ever!

Do you?

Richard

As his course at the Staff College finished, he wrote that

it is impossible to move from one room to another without being buttonholed by someone who talks of his hopes and fears, until you shout him down with yours. Learning slowly, darling, I am attempting not to do this. We finish up on Friday afternoon and I will be in town by the evening. I must see you before that awful scepticism of yours gets to work. Don't resent the fact that we seem no longer able to talk to each other. We can and will – & what two people could be better at it! It is merely that I see you now for such fleeting moments that I want only to hold you in my arms and have absolutely no time to think of anything else – but I promise not to be a bore next week.

I made a long speech to Macmillans production manager today, but it looks as though we cannot hope for publication before the end of April.

I hated so much to leave you this time, & I could not even see you at the window, so I had to content myself with the hope that I was in your heart – anyhow for the time it took me to cross the Park.

Are you working very hard with your Warships Week?

Don't please charm too many people, because I shall be jealous, even though it is only general charm you are dispensing.

I'm wondering how you liked the book, & hoping that you did, for your criticism means more to me than all the others, because you are the only person who *can* know what she's talking about.

I'm feeling very stale, darling. This course has gone on long enough, & this last week I find particularly trying. Thank God it's not for long, & that you are at the other end.

It amuses me sometimes to realise that of all the people I know you are the only one who understands me – & as you say not always then.

Will you please not be sceptical and when I see you again I will show you that there is no need. I may be very tiresome, but I know I'm constant (perhaps you think consistent would be better) . . .

26 Rutland Court
Sunday 29th March

My darling,
You have been in my heart all day & I have been very happy.

Across the Park the flowers were in bloom & you were by my side. At the Moiseiwitsch recital I felt a great content & you were there to tell me exactly when he stopped playing Beethoven and started in on Schumann. At tea in Regents Park my hostess remarked on how well I looked & laughingly suggested that I must be in love – & I saw you peek out from over her shoulder and had to laugh. At dinner with some people I had asked out last night and had forgotten, I made adequate & convincing excuses, but I heard you say that no excuse I could make could possibly be as good as the real one, and somewhat to their surprise, I laughed again.

All day I have laughed, darling, and been happy. Have you been happy, & was I with you? Only for frightening spasms of a second I have felt that something might go wrong, & that you would say no to next week, & I have been miserable . . .

All these were expressions of his inner doubts about himself in relation to an experience, a kind of woman he had never come across before. He had also practical exterior reasons for impatience and uncertainty. What was he going to do when the course (the one at the Staff College) came to an end? If only there was no war, if only he could work at nothing but his art! His book had now been published in America, and cables began to arrive about the reviews in the New York papers – 'very favourable'. In the copy he gave Mary he wrote: 'For darling Mary, who sees humanity as it is, but still loves it.' In Britain he had hoped for publication before 28 March, in order to flourish the book at the Staff College. This proved unfeasible. The Book of the Month Club decided to make it its choice, which meant further delay while the printing of a first edition of 10,000 copies was doubled. Richard used Macmillans and in particular Lovat Dickson as a butt. He pretended that they had lost the sheets and were having to print all over again; that they were too wrapped up with their old stand-bys, Kipling and Yeats and Hardy, to have anything but suspicion for a newcomer; and in company he teased Dickson for stuffiness, and made him feel quite uncomfortable.

Suddenly a voice rose out of the book, a loved figure from the past, and cast a shadow across the page. It is in the letter of 1 March.

68

. . . I am writing this just before going to bed, and I feel a little sick, for I heard to-day that Colin Pinckney has been killed in Singapore. You do not know him, but you will, and I hope like him, when you read the book. His death makes an apt postscript, and it raises in my mind yet again the question which I have put in the book, and have attempted to answer, of what is the responsibility of the man who is left. I say man, and not men, for I am now the last [of 'the triangle of friendship']. It is odd that I, who always gave least, should be the one who remains. Why? I wonder. Tomorrow I shall go forward again, but to-night I have my head turned over my shoulder a little.

And that is why I come to you, Mary, and I suppose always shall (I wonder if you are stronger than I). For I want so terribly to convince you that I love you (I haven't completely, I know) – that out of all this death and destruction, not only of bodies but of sentiment and feeling, we may make this love of ours a beautiful thing.

Apart from that note of foreboding after Colin Pinckney's death, his letters of that time are nothing very exceptional; not especially well-written, nor meant to be; certainly not strikingly lyrical, nor 'great love letters'. With their cries of happiness, his self-doubting, and his anxiety about a career, they are what is to be expected of anyone at all articulate who has fallen in love; all the more when for the first time, all the more still when from a young man who has been more or less issuing manifestoes over a number of weeks that he is not going to let it happen until he is ready.

It had happened, and he was far from ready; sure only of being in love, of his dedication to honesty, and of a gift, soon to be on the stalls at home, for dazzling observation, and flashes of deep feeling not always disciplined by art, which one day he was passionate to develop into something more.

But the ghosts had not been laid.

And what about her, the older woman, the *femme inspiratrice*? Why so many references from him to her 'scepticism'?

She had by now read his book, and been able to collate it in her mind with their weeks of conversation. The book's kernel had been the deflation, through acquaintance with suffering, of an egocentric who had proudly flourished his egocentricity like a banner, to have it dramatically thrown to the ground in the last chapter by something called Humanity. In their conversations he had picked it up again, mocked her own kindly view of humanity in order to provoke her, and talked a great deal about himself. Now that he had fallen in love, he might seem merely to be airing the experience as a second challenge to his selfishness, and a means of making himself more attractive. How sincere was the love?

Regret for selfishness is one of his principal motifs and recurs throughout the correspondence. Later, when it becomes more muted, it is in earnest. I have wondered if, at this stage, he played the tune too often. People who delight in exposing their shortcomings sometimes imagine that they have expiated, even eradicated them; but, just as often, these ultra-frank confessions have the effect of alerting their hearers, who might otherwise have taken them less seriously, or, if less percipient, or not good listeners, not even noticed them. His lamentations may have seemed to her only another aspect of the thing lamented, and these protests, to one of the most beautiful women in Britain, that he had never really loved one of the most beautiful women in America, not entirely authentic. He was rather macho; later she called him 'pure Blimp'. In January he wrote to someone in America, 'Have you seen Merle at all? We still cable and write, in great excitement. I still have a weak spot, absence gilding the memory.' Mary and Merle corresponded, and for weeks no letter from across the Atlantic reached Mary without a reference to Richard. What finally happened between the three of them can wait until Merle's return in the summer.

Richard's letter of 2 February, declaring love, had been followed, Mary wrote in her notes, 'by much that indicated depth of thought and feeling, which moved her strangely. Yet there remained a fear in her heart, of losing something infinitely precious that had grown up between them . . . and of being hurt'. Each of them had this fear of being hurt. She was not a woman just for an affair. She knew how much she had to give, and he was beginning to demand it. From experience, she detested possessiveness at least as much as infidelity, and must have recalled her marriage, when, very young, innocent, and quite certain, she had been proved disastrously mistaken. That wound had been dealt long ago, but it had left its scar.

The cypher in the text, which may only need to be read carefully in order to provide an answer, may be in Richard's letter of 8 March. He had spoken two days back of some lines of poetry, and now sent them to her, because 'they are so much what you believe'. They come from Kahlil Gibran's *The Prophet*:

Love one another, but make not a bond of love.
Let it be rather a moving sea between the shores of your souls.
Fill each other's cup, but drink not from one cup.
Give one another of your bread, but eat not of the same loaf.
Sing and dance together and be joyous, but let each one of you be
    alone,
Even as the strings of the lute are alone, though they quiver with the
    same music.
Give your hearts, but not into each other's keeping,
For only the hand of life can contain your hearts.
And stand together, yet not too near together.
For the pillars of the Temple stand apart,
And the oak and the cypress grow not in each other's shadow.

'So much what you believe . . .' and, he had added, 'what I shall shortly believe and practise also.'

They went away. Beside the Croesor stream, at Llanfrothen in North Wales, where before the war Mary and her friend Peter Lindsay had restored two quarrymen's cottages, they had their 'immortal holiday' together, in what is to this day enchanted ground.

There they lived out his leave, as Mary later wrote, 'in such happiness as neither had dreamed possible. For that brief spell she discovered a different man. Gone was that overstrung nervous tension that always lay below the surface; gone too was the restlessness of spirit. The peace of nature released him from human conflicts, and he would lie for hours watching the cloud-shadows pass across the hills, drinking in the beauty and the silence as if his soul was striving for such things . . .'

71

They walked across the hills with the silver sea-gleam on the western horizon, and returned to the tiny white cottage glued to the side of a hill, with the stream running past it, that cottage 'with the face of a cheeky child. Lying on the sofa before a great fire they planned to make something beautiful and lasting of their love, a completeness not to be marred by jealousy or possessiveness and which would never affect their individual integrity apart. He was not content with the thought simply of a perfect relationship, static in its own selfish happiness, but believed that the luck granted to two such people should mingle to create something which would help mankind. Truth, however ruthless, should always be the keyword in their relationship, and this prevailed throughout their span of life together . . .'

Typed-out words, so different from the liquid spontaneity of her letters, where her handwriting starts upright, then sprawls, then steeplechases across the page. The gaiety of his youth and her timelessness should soar more vividly from this story than they are likely to. This is primarily a record, that lacks the gesture and the spoken word. One can only imagine all that was happy, humorous, carefree about him, as with countless others in this century, bursting out on leave, and brings into the record his lighter moods.

He mocked the devastation of the war with a personal mockery of the damage it had done to him. 'His sensitiveness', she wrote or was edited as having written, 'was greatly increased by his accident, which made him terribly conscious of his appearance. He seldom passed a mirror without making a face at himself, or without putting his hat at some comic angle to raise a laugh. He was terrified of being hurt or made unhappy and put up a strong barrier of invulnerability. He would also take great trouble not to hurt others; and if he found that he had offended, would go to great lengths to put the matter right . . . No, he was not a good hater, for as soon as an outburst of fury had died down, he felt that it was not worth while. All the same he never forgot and in the case of a wrong done to a friend did not forgive . . . His gay spirit and sense of humour enjoyed a ridiculous situation . . . equally enjoyed a joke against himself . . . had an irresistible desire to break up a pompous situation or deflate a pompous person . . . sarcastic and ironic, with a keen appreciation of intellectual wit, but fully aware that this was not his genre . . . His insatiable love of discussion would lead him to turn any gathering into a cauldron. Then suddenly he would turn the whole thing into a joke against himself in such a disarming way that no one could bear him ill-will. His gift of comedy got him into awkward situations, from which he extricated himself with a lightness of touch that took away one's breath . . .'

He was extremely generous. Though far from rich, it may not have been much of a sacrifice for him to hand over to McIndoe all the dollars earned by his broadcasts and articles in America 'to help the boys in the wards', and could have been done as an act of gratitude by many. But this, said of him by Denise when, a stranger to him, she first came to visit him in hospital, belongs to someone of a rarer nature:

'How badly burned he was I had no idea until a pair of piercing blue eyes stared at me from a sea of bandages. His hands lay heavy in cages of gauze and cottonwool. He spoke with difficulty and had to be fed, which he hated. Yet he never talked of his own suffering, but only of other people's . . . he was in pain of every kind, but as I began explaining who I was and talking about Peter I felt a most amazing wave of understanding and interest sweeping over me from that figure on the bed. By rejecting his own suffering completely he compelled me to forget it, so that when I left I remembered only his indomitable spirit . . .' And after later talks, carried on day after day, 'He was kinder to me than can ever be conveyed in words. He let me talk for hours about Peter . . . always when I left him I felt indescribably happier . . .'

If this was how he was in pain, what must he have been during those days in Wales with Mary! Once as they were lying on the grass together a light aeroplane came overhead, making slow lackadaisical circles as if there were no war. 'Circles of peace' they called them, and it became a saying throughout the correspondence. She went back without him for a weekend during August, and wrote to him, 'I find you here in the cottage. I hear your voice and in spite of the blazing sunshine I expect to see you come in at the gate in that absurd black sou'wester . . .'; and she remembered how a cow had jumped over a hedge in front of the car that brought them from the station.

Back in London he wrote in his diary, 'Perfectly glorious holiday . . . rained most of the time, but went for long walks, wrote a little, and became very domesticated doing the cooking and fetching coals. Returned completely refreshed'; and to Mary, when he was about to go into hospital, from his parents' flat:

April 10 1942

My darling,

Your very lovely letter arrived this morning, and I have read & re-read it with a full heart and a deep gratitude that this thing has been granted us.

Those few days in the country, I can say quite honestly, are the happiest I have ever spent. We seem, my darling, so dangerously complementary the one to the other that with each day a separate existence seems more unbearable.

Wales already seems an impossibly lovely dream – waking to hear you singing as you pottered about downstairs; wanting you so badly that at times I felt almost ill; walking with you on the hills, your hair caught by the wind & your face impossibly beautiful; laughing together . . . & the knowledge that for those few enchanted days we would be together & nothing could separate us. It was all so perfect. I feel almost guilty that such happiness should be granted us in this unhappy world. You give me such a feeling of strength, that I am frightened of becoming too dependent upon you. I can see you working away on me to make me a better citizen, you sweet darling, & while I may smile, I love you for it.

I am writing this with the sun streaming through the window & I'm now going to walk in the Park, and feel sorry for those poor people I see who have not a love like ours to make the sun twice as bright & the flowers twice as beautiful. You will be in my heart & by my side, & I shall look across the grass & the trees & blow you a kiss & tell you so. Will you hear me, I wonder?

They were never to be so carefree again. Almost immediately afterwards, more notes of the tragedy begin to be heard; and what was light, was funny, was tender, loving and impulsive, recedes as it has throughout history under the apparently inevitable onset of an early death, like poor relations who 'know their place'.

Chapter Four
April-June 1942

Reviews of the American edition of his book began to reach him. Praise from the *New York Times*, the *Sun*, the *New Yorker*, the *Herald Tribune*, the *Chicago Tribune*, the *Boston Herald*. Chosen by the Book of the Month with his boyhood model Steinbeck's *The Moon Is Down*. Abridged for the *Reader's Digest*, quoted, recommended. Mrs Warburg wrote: 'All the Australian pilots here have read it. They started by disliking it, then couldn't put it down, because it made them so mad, then couldn't put it down because they loved it so. It has had the most enormous success . . .' Laurels in America, more on the way in Britain. He was in love, and was loved in return; and yet he had no peace.

Mary wrote of the time after their return from Wales: 'He went into hospital and difficulties began to appear. Friends had come to share my flat, which meant that it was no longer mine.' These friends were a married couple and a relative of theirs. Mary had known them a very long time, was very fond of them, and had a financial arrangement with them about the flat. She was extremely loyal and not the kind, even for Richard, to move out suddenly and let them down. 'Richard', she went on, 'had to make up his mind what he was going to do when he left hospital. What he needed at that time was to be able to come in and sit by the hour and talk, as he had been in the habit of doing. He got such nerves about the lack of privacy in the flat, that it amounted to a phobia.' For weeks this 'lack of privacy' comes close to dominating the correspondence, and is always in the background. It drives Richard into frenzies, and Mary near despair of calming him; sends her out of London for three weeks in June–July 'to make things easier for him'; and contributes to the letter from her to him in early October which almost brought about a final break. The 'circles of peace' were fragmented to a few broken arcs.

How can this have happened?

On the stage, even in the most skilfully constructed drama, there may arrive some episode to ask of the watcher's commonsense a practical question, crucial to the plot, which, swept temporarily aside by words and action, returns in tranquillity to reinstate disbelief. Why, for example, did Hamlet not stick a knife into Claudius sooner? How was Othello so easily gulled? All that business about Desdemona's handkerchief – ludicrous, incredible! And in this drama of real life – was it really so impossible for Mary and Richard to find somewhere to themselves? In 1975 someone who had just read their letters wrote to me: 'The generation under thirty would find incomprehensible what kept them apart. It is very much a story of the thirties'; implying that, apart from the practical difficulties of finding somewhere, nowadays the social and moral objections would have much less force.

Mary was a woman of strong principles, not lightly discarded, and discreet by nature; she respected discretion about other people's private affairs, and hoped for it about her own. In July, when she went away to Dorset, she confided in the friend who accompanied her, Mrs Dorothy Toye, 'because for one thing she guessed, and for another we know pretty well everything about one another, as we have been through every joy and sorrow together since the age of 10. It is a very rare friendship, and I trust her as I do no other.' But in another instance, when Richard had suggested meeting her at lunch in the country with mutual friends, she felt differently: '. . . It would look bad if I suddenly suggested coming down to them after this long time. I am really devoted to them both, and they are the most loyal and devoted friends to me, but secretly they bore me! I am ashamed to say this, but they are so factual and nice that I fall fast asleep. For this reason I hardly ever go down to them, so it would look too fishy if I suggested it now . . .'

Discretion was not for fear of Richard's parents' disapproval, even at that early stage. He was twenty years younger than Mary. She might have been 'that woman'. She never was. They had already met her, and very quickly came to love her. A few days after Richard's death Edwyna Hillary wrote to her: 'You and your loving friendship to me in these dark hours have been more than wonderful . . . I love you very dearly. You were so much, so very much more than loved by Richard . . . our home is your home always.' And sixteen years later, on Mary's birthday in 1958, Michael Hillary wrote: 'Many are born, and live and die, without leaving any imprint on the sands of time. You on the other hand are a continuous source of inspiration . . . and a constant paean of thanksgiving goes up for the happy event that brought you into the world.'

Discretion was for the sake of Mary's children, and also for its own sake. Then, as surely also today, a love affair was still something precious which, like silver, may tarnish if exposed to too much light. The privileged society within which they moved harboured as many *mauvaises langues* as any other. K. did Richard damage enough; and in July some gossiping 'friend' was to drop him a groundless hint that threw him into a transport of jealousy, and caused Mary intense distress. There are always people envious of happiness, and ready, even if unconsciously, to pick away at it; this she knew, and Richard also knew.

As for practical difficulties: I have not gone into the availability of undisturbed accommodation in London during the war for an unmarried couple, but imagine, and those who remember have confirmed, that during those months when Americans were beginning to arrive in thousands, it was not abundant; unless for the very rich, and Mary and Richard were not among them. Some time during July Edwyna Hillary, while adoring her son, her only child, had grown so fearful of becoming too possessive that she suggested Rosie Kerr should take a flat with him, where he would have freedom. Rosie was willing, but thought Edwyna should ask approval of her own mother. (Here we are indeed in the thirties. Such filial deference is hard to imagine in the eighties.) Admiral Kerr's formidable spouse, a pillar of the Girl Guides and by then in the Censor's Office in Liverpool, gave her blessing, and Rosie too began a search. She too failed to find anywhere.

All this seems to me sufficient explanation of the perpetual crisis about 'somewhere of their own', which may seem to have an irrational, at times almost dementing influence on the story. It will at least be understood by any of the 'generation under thirty', married or not, who have spent months and years in our own age on a waiting list for homes. Delay may merely inconvenience. It may put a strain on a joyful association, may even come near to destroying it. But such unfortunates, of whom there are still hundreds of thousands, can be patient in some kind of assurance that sooner or later their names will be reached, or a mortgage available. Time is on their side. Not so with Mary and Richard. As early as 3 July he writes of 'an appalling sense that time is closing down, events moving in, suddenly we shall be wrenched apart . . .' By the time Mary had at last found somewhere, it was too late.

Why, one may also inquire, was it necessary for this *affairé* youth to 'come and sit by the hour and talk'? Talk about what? Himself? Hadn't he done that enough? Could he not make up his own mind what to do? What was the matter with him?

'Lack of privacy' did no more than exacerbate what Mary called 'his inability to compromise, even for a time, creating a bitter resentment in him, which threatened to turn on me'. The trouble was with him.

His stint at the Staff College had ended at the end of March. The Commandant asked him what he wanted to do. The College had proved to him that, although he had passed, he could never become a Staff Officer; 'I am no organiser, but they have made a brave attempt.' He suggested return to America. The Commandant, opposing this on the grounds that he had been there once and now needed responsibility, offered Combined Operations. '"Think it over,"' he said, as recorded in Richard's diary. 'I did. For three hours I walked up and down, and I knew he was right . . . when I analysed it, I had to admit that, enchanted as I was with the Americans, and eager as I was to do a real job this time, it was the possibility of collecting material for another book, of making contacts for after the war, that had really made me plump for America. Having decided this, I felt much better. I should very much like to work for Charles Haydon in Combined Operations . . . and told the Commandant. A very remarkable and understanding man. What a pity there are not more like him in the Services.'

Haydon was another such man. Richard had met him through

79

Mary. He was a Regular soldier, an Irish Guards Officer, now in charge of the Commandos on Lord Louis Mountbatten's staff. A letter in *The Times* of 6 November 1945 said of him that 'he successfully joined the experience of a Regular with unorthodox imagination and enterprise and so gave a classic example to those under his command. He had to keep the experiment alive against the prejudice of those who thought it a waste of time and against the impatience of his own volunteer force, who were constantly keyed up to raids cancelled at the last moment.' The raid on St Nazaire took place on the very night Richard's course ended, and Richard noted it with enthusiasm in his diary. Haydon had taken to him. The Commandos were after his own heart. His injuries would limit his use, but use there might be; and a project was set afoot that he should accompany raids and, if he came back, write for the newspapers about them. Such a job would bring him lodgings of his own in London, and the prospect recurs now in letter after letter. While waiting, he tried to write.

He had two passions: for writing and for flying. *The Last Enemy* had been a fusion of the two; one had served the other. Flying seemed to have been closed to him; as for writing, his lack of self-confidence returned. He knew his failings, which were those of most beginners. Emotionally, wrote Mary, he longed to romanticise, and on such occasions his only help was a streak of sentimentality, which he detested. In his diary he put: 'I know I am not a great writer. I can write good prose, and I have a certain feeling and some wit, but the feeling is not strong'; and noted his besetting ailment: 'I am lazy all through. I shall never write anything until I have cured myself of this.' In Wales he had 'written a little'. About this time he finished one short story and planned two others, undistinguished exercises in the macabre. Eric Linklater, to whom Lovat Dickson introduced him, advised him to drop this genre and stick to 'the straight lines of reality'. But what reality? He was learning the reality of love, but was nowhere near mature enough, nor sufficiently distanced, to depict it. What other reality could he draw upon, which had not already been consumed by *The Last Enemy*? America? Not enough to make a book. He was no chronicler of society, no Proust or Jane

1   Richard at Oxford, 1939

2   Mary in her twenties

3a Michael Burn (left) on the morning of capture after the raid on St. Nazaire, March 29, 1942. German newsreel photograph

3b The 16th Annual Reunion of the Guinea Pig Club at East Grinstead

4   Richard before the Battle of Britain

Austen; as for Virginia Woolf, he tried one of her novels, *Jacob's Room*, and 'could not stomach it'.

His forte was reportage of exciting events; for him reality meant action. Combined Operations would do; but as this new outlet for his gift and unrest delayed, the old one opened up again. At the end of March he put in his diary: 'I wish to Heaven I knew whether Archie's next operation will make me fit for flying again, and whether, if it does, they will allow me to function again.' In hospital he soon learned that he would have to pay further visits, and on 20 April, his twenty-third birthday, made his first mention in the correspondence of what earlier he seemed to have dismissed. 'I shall have to come back here if I am to become operationally fit; and even if I am finally passed, it will be a good six months before I am back again with a Squadron – all rather depressing.'

Geoffrey Page, another terribly injured pilot, was with him in April at East Grinstead, and together, as described in Page's book *The Tale of a Guinea-Pig*, they discussed the chances of return. Richard thought that night fighters were the only answer for the likes of them. 'In a daylight dogfight your hands might not be able to cope with the speed, whereas at night you can creep up behind your target and shoot the bastard down.' Although Page disagreed, on the grounds that night-fighters were too heavy for their crippled fingers, they both went to see McIndoe. McIndoe told them they had 'not a chance in hell of getting back. Not only do I disapprove, but the Air Ministry would not allow it.' They learned that this was an excuse. In truth McIndoe considered that they, and others like them, had had enough; Page had already had fifteen operations, and spent two years in hospital. But the two went on at him, and after weeks of being nagged he gave in, telling them, 'If you're determined to kill yourselves, go ahead. Only don't blame me,' and wrote out medical certificates for them. After three months Page was finally passed operational, and went brilliantly on until the end of the war, winning the DSO and DFC with bar. Richard was not given the later operational category, but had to be content for the time being with a Board, which classified him as fit only for light aircraft, and for daylight flying. He seems to have accepted refusal of the operational category, for on 17 May he wrote to McIndoe to thank him for his letter to Air

Commodore Standford Cade, at the RAF Medical Board, and went on:

> I am very glad in a way, as now I know I can settle down to this Staff job [perhaps in Combined Operations]. I am not feeling too fit, and my eyebrow is still mucky. But I must be in this job within a month, so suppose I must forge ahead with being operated . . .

Exterior frustrations about lack of privacy, about a job and the need for copy; inward frustrations about his own laziness; ardent physical desire – these are the background to the letters during April and June which follow; to which add health not yet recovered and two bouts in hospital, playing upon a passionate intransigent nature, subject to moods of 'black depression', and in so much of a hurry, so impatient about everything, that the tranquillity of Wales was soon forgotten. He returned to East Grinstead on 15 April, five days later than he had expected. Geoffrey Page described his first sight of Richard, introduced to him in the ward by another burnt pilot, Richard's great friend and drinking companion Tony Tollemache:

> . . . one of the queerest apparitions, in a long loose dressing gown, with the head thrown right back so that the owner appeared to be looking along the line of his nose. Where normally the eyes should be, were two large bloody circles of raw skin. Horizontal slits showed that the eyes still lay behind. A pair of hands wrapped in large lint covers lay folded across the chest. A cigarette in a holder was clenched between the ghoul's teeth, and a condescending voice said, 'Ah, another bloody cripple. Welcome to the home of the aged and infirm.'

In his first letter to Mary after returning to East Grinstead he was working himself into a fury against his old antagonist, K., and with some reason. Through her money and influence she had done much for the hospital. In *The Last Enemy*, especially in the chapter called

'The Beauty Shop', he had not minced his words about its shortcomings. She had powerful friends, and he was in a panic that she might try to get publication in the United Kingdom stopped.

> The Maxillo Facial Unit of
> Queen Victoria Cottage Hospital
> East Grinstead
> 15 April 1942

Darling Mary,

I have just read your letter & I'm on the trolley waiting to go in. It promises to be quite a party except that I have a spot on my nose, so they may not touch that . . .

I'm afraid I'm really worried about —— [K.] having a copy of the book sent her from America. Pray God it does not arrive before May 1st, because she will do all in her power to stop the publication [in Britain], 'in the name of the Hospital'.

I feel so helpless now. If only I could get hold of Rache Lovat Dickson or a lawyer or something – there is nothing you can do.

I fear I'm being rather silly, but that woman is *EVIL*.

I love you,

> Richard

> Hospital
> East Grinstead
> Friday night, 17th April

Oh darling, how I have missed you today. I'm afraid I allowed myself to get a bit down in the dumps, as the fingers are a bit of a bore.

Will I be able to convalesce with you in Wales, I wonder? And will you want to, even if I can? I don't know how I'm going to wait & see you. More I think about it, the more advisable I think it is for me to be out of here before the book comes out.

Please take care of yourself, & remember I love you.

'A bit of a bore'. If ever there was an understatement!

Years later, in another description of East Grinstead, more detailed than Richard's, Geoffrey Page gave an account of himself as he underwent the same kind of operation on his hands as Richard: '. . . they would wheel me into the operating room to have the mass of scar tissue removed. Skin grafts taken from the inside of my leg would then be sewn into place to cover the raw hands . . .' He was wheeled in, and Dr Hunter injected him with the anaesthetic. As it wore off, 'Now I had a glimmering of what Christ must have felt as they drove the nails through . . . hammered inexpertly through the same hand, only to be withdrawn agonizingly with huge pincers. The hammering torture came from a distance, or so it seemed, but it was there nonetheless. Wildly I tossed my head from side to side on the sweat-damped pillow. "No . . . no . . . n . . . n . . ." The moan came as a disbelief that such things could be, were allowed to be . . .' He was given morphia. 'The prick of the needle was unfelt in the sea of pain. Soon my head stopped its senseless rolling and torture disappeared over the horizon as the drug began its calming effect.

'Hillary paused at the end of the bed and stood silently watching what he thought to be my unconscious body.

'"You're not as tough as you try to make out, are you, Mr Hillary?" There was something near to triumph in Sister Hall's voice.

'Quickly recovering from the surprise of being caught unawares, the tall figure gave a contemptuous snort. "Bloody fool should have worn gloves."

'She did not even bother to glance down. Hillary's hands had been equally badly burned, and for the same reason – no gloves.'

In his next letter to Mary Richard went right back to the cynical egocentric he had been before he wrote his book.

> In hospital
> In bed
> In anger
> April 19

My darling,

Your two adorable letters have been the only bright spot for the last few days.

The bug has now spread to my eyebrow graft, where it is doing its work. I suppose I should accept this as all in the game, but I cannot. I know it is due to negligence & the inevitable carelessness which results from too much familiarity with filth. I do not particularly care for myself, for if the eyelid falls off it falls off. I don't expect anyone here to understand that, but it's true.

One of Mac's minions asked me if I was not 'browned off'. I said, 'No.' A year ago I should have been angry to have come in perfectly healthy, to have the wrong eye-lid grafted, & to be presented free with a streptococcus. Now I am resigned & find it fairly humorous. He of course thought I was being sarcastic, which I was, but I meant it. At the same time it infuriates me that the patients sit here with a dumb acceptance of things going wrong.

I know Archie does a magnificent job (although even if he didn't, they wouldn't notice), but the wards are full of infection even now.

Humanity is irony from the neck up. I guess that's the first thing you've got to realise, if you want to fight for it. You'll get nothing out of it, & if you don't find virtue being its own reward sufficient, you have to be human enough to be amused by it, otherwise God help you.

As you see, I am in grave danger of returning to my belief in the survival of the fittest. ME, R.H.H., and to Hell with the rest of the snivelling half-witted bums that surround me.

I'm the split personality you think me all right, but it's not the poet that's uppermost.

I'll champion lost causes after this war. I'll write & I'll make people listen, but I'll make damn sure the sponsoring of them takes me to the top.

I was wrong when I wrote in my book that the mass of humanity leaves me cold. It doesn't – it infuriates me.

For example: I know (don't ask me how) that if I could get back to flying, I wouldn't get shot down again. I'd go on knocking Germans out of the sky until I was one of the country's heroes, covered with medals and written to by soft old women. But I wouldn't be doing it for them. I would be doing it for the sheer lust of killing to get something out of myself. It's no good, Mary. I don't want to fool you. I just don't believe what I wrote in that book – sometimes I do. I meant it when I wrote it, but now I don't. It's only when I'm with you that all the tenseness, the anger goes out from me and I'm at peace. And you know, God bless you, how long it sometimes takes you.

I must come to London soon, I must come to you. For that is now the only good destruction, with you, in you. The rest is vicious.

Bear with me. darling. This is madness, but it must come out.
Richard

Hospital
East Grinstead
April 20
Monday

Today & tomorrow will pass for me all too slowly. But on Wednesday I shall be happy. Do you really think you can stay over for the night?

The dressing on my eyelid was taken down yesterday. The graft is neat & admirable and I think it therefore a pity that McIndoe has done the wrong lid. It was the lower one that was raw (& for that matter still is) & pained me. However, I cannot work myself up greatly about it. He is on a tour at the moment, but returns tomorrow. Perhaps, as he takes down my hand & eyebrow dressing, I shall ask him gently, 'Why?' – but then again perhaps not. One does not like to be too inquisitive.

Reading at the moment is a little difficult, but today I have started Eastern Religions & Western Thought, although I only concentrate with an effort.

He had charmed K.'s secretary into arranging for any parcels coming from America (and which might contain his book) to be intercepted and held back until 1 May. He thanked Mary for forwarding a letter from Merle Oberon, containing Press cuttings of reviews.

Today is my birthday. I always feel that something should happen on a birthday, but so far it has been characterised by a conspicuous lack of incident.

There are some terrible cans in at the moment. They should of course be inspiring, but succeed only in making me feel slightly nauseated. Such is familiarity with filth. I can notice it even more in the nurses. If So & So is troublesome, it's because that's the way he is – they no longer think of people in relation to what they're suffering. Ah me!

I love you,
Richard

Sunday, April 26
Hospital
East Grinstead

I hated so much leaving you yesterday, & very nearly changed my mind & missed the train. It was lucky that I didn't, because when I got back my eye was in a pretty bad state, and today I am feeling a bit low. The eyebrow promises to be a great success, however, & the stitches come out of my hand tomorrow, so with any luck I shall be on a few days leave before my next incarceration. If only my eye would heal I would come tomorrow.

It will be so lovely if I do work in London [with Combined Operations] and can have a place of my own for you to make attractive & come to always. The sooner I get out of here the better! I find it quite impossible to concentrate on anything . . .

Otherwise no news; only an increasing irritation with myself for being unable to concentrate on anything *sauf toi*!

His next letter was written after a furious row with K. In front of other people she had called him a coward to his face, and accused him of being afraid to go back to fight; and Richard had lost his temper.

Hospital
East Grinstead
May 21

My darling,

Tomorrow I come to London until Monday, when I return here for a new arm splint for my hands, then go to Torquay for a fortnight [the RAF convalescent home].

I will tell you all about the strife & turmoil when I see you, but as always you are right. By losing my temper I put myself in the wrong, & said things which though true were better left unsaid.

McIndoe had pointed out to him that K. had been out of control of herself . . .

and I should have realised this . . . & kept my sense of humour.

I felt quite sick afterwards & had to ring you up at once . . . I feel completely drained of vitality & long only to be with you.

There is so much beauty in the world that it seems quite pointless to let oneself be dragged down by pettiness like this. I must not let it happen again . . .

But he did let it happen again, almost at once, and with Mary. It is unfortunate that her first letters to have survived show her in moods not at all typical. In the first out of the brown paper envelope, written from her flat, he had come to London, and his confusions, his operations, the expectation of more soon, and his aggressiveness against pretty well everything (including even the untidiness of the patient in the next bed) had reduced her to tears.

Mary to Richard:

> Tuesday night
> 27th May
>
> My darling,
>
> I just needed the sound of your voice to-night, since all day I have thought of you and wondered if everything was all right. I feel ashamed for having cried, and so tired, for when I cry my vitality drains away from me with my tears. I know that you are right, and I am glad you said what you felt. It would be unthinkable for either of us to bottle things up. It did good, for in the end I was much happier and all to-day I have felt nearer to you than ever before.
>
> I seem suddenly to know you better and love you with a new love born of a deeper understanding.

Be happy darling in Torquay, and don't worry about anything. Just concentrate on getting well. You have been through a difficult and nervy time, but I feel it is all behind you, and with your new job [Combined Operations] you will feel happier and more settled in your soul. Apart from this you and I must make a perfect life – a world of our own framed in a frame of peace. We have all the qualities – dependence with independence; attachment with detachment; together yet apart – and with all this we share the gift of laughter, the quick communion of the mind and the sudden ecstasy of passion and desire which rises up between us and shuts out the world of reason. All this we have and more, and as I write I hold my breath not daring to believe it.

Goodnight, my love. I see you sleeping next to that very untidy man, but I will put out the light and in the darkness I will hold you close.

I love you,
Mary

R.A.F. Officers Hospital
Torquay
27th May Wednesday

My darling Mary,

I did not realise as I came away just now how much I was going to miss you. Already a fortnight seems an impossibly long time, although I shall do my best to get really strong & well for you, so that I need never make you cry again. I know we must say what we feel, but I could have been nicer about it . . .

Please, darling, get well too. Don't stay out so late and don't see so many people. You see, I pretend to think of your health, but I suppose you think I'm jealous – well, you're quite right. I AM. I love you so much that it hurts.

Richard

In their second surviving interchange, Mary, in her role of bird of Paradise trying to calm a caged lion, though normally extremely healthy, had proceeded to get ill.

Richard to Mary:

R.A.F. Officers Hospital
Torquay
28 May

Oh Darling,

I feel so helpless all this way from you when you are ill and I should be by your side to love and cherish you back to health.

You really terrified me talking so lightly of diphtheria. My heart nearly stopped beating and for one terrible moment I knew what life would be like without you. It was as though a shadow were passing across the sun.

I shall come up on the 1st whether you are well or not, as I must see you and hold you in my arms; whisper that I love you and bring the warmth back to those ivory cheeks.

Last night, having dinner at Shaldon with people I had not seen since the war, grey, factual people, eager to please in their own dull way, I felt suddenly very old and tired. They were so far away and had never known and now would never know what it all meant, what it was all about. How could they, as they didn't realise there was anything to know?

This morning I walked out along the cliffs until I could go no further, and the sea lay directly below me. There was not a soul in sight, and I lay down, closed my eyes, and was happy . . .

Darling will you please be sensible over the next few days and nights and not attempt to get up before you are really well again? . . . You have been racketing around lately and I feel that I am largely to blame. Just lie in bed, think beautiful thoughts, and do nothing, and then when we come together again we shall be perfectly blissful and cured of all our ills.

Last night I dreamt of you . . .

Richard

Mary to Richard:

Thursday/Friday/May 27–28

I don't know what I would have done last night and all today if I had not had you to think about. Last night was the longest night

I have ever spent. I would drop off to sleep and wake thinking I must have been asleep an hour at least, and it was never more than 5 minutes.

To take my mind off the pain of my throat and ear I have thought of you all the time. Turning up the past and present like a kaleidoscope and dwelling on all the incidents and pictures that I love best – and gathering all the pictures together I was struck by the extraordinary contrasting and many-sided qualities of our love. The lightheartedness covering up depths that neither of us admit even to ourselves. Trust and generosity running hand in hand with the capacity for wild and passionate jealousy.

Once or twice in moments of almost sacrilegious flippancy on our part I have been struck, in mid-heart as it were, by the seriousness of our love. It is the strangest feeling – rather frightening mentally and giddy-making physically

I feel this letter reads very disjointedly as I have written it in tiny bits in between my 5 minute sleeps. Now it is Friday morning and I am much happier having two letters from you . . .

I am a bit better this morning too. Everything less painful. I'll stay in bed today and possibly tomorrow as I feel very peculiar when I stand up. By Sunday I'll be able to leap up like a young gazelle, and on Monday I will be cured by sheer happiness of seeing you.

Last night, about 20 minutes after we had rung off, the Torquay telephone operator rang me up and asked me how long I thought my call had been. I said I thought about 5 or 6 minutes after your 3. 'Well,' he said, 'to all intents and purposes you are still talking to Flight Lieut Hillary as he has not put down the receiver!' I had to talk to him in my most seductive voice to get him to reverse the decision of the clock from 19 mins to 6 mins . . .

I am so glad you are determined to spend this fortnight really getting well. I will too, and even when I am all right again I shall use it as an excuse to go to bed early and never do the things that bore me. You are quite right, we do too many things that are abortive. One's vitality and life's blood is drained by the uselessness of it all. On the other hand it is difficult to make rules, draw lines, and generally be utterly selfish.

I know exactly how you felt after your walk alone on the cliffs. No human being can give you just that rich peace, and very few people actually know the experience exists.

I think your typing is very good. How do the fingers feel? All the same I prefer your scrawly writing – the machine too impersonal.

Give me all the strength of your love to make me well. If it weren't for you, I wouldn't make any effort. I feel too tired and with too much pain. I love you my darling

Mary

They met in London on Monday in distinguished company. A date had now been fixed for publication of *The Last Enemy*, and Rache Lovat Dickson had introduced him (as well as to Eric Linklater) to Storm Jameson, Elizabeth Bowen, and Arthur Koestler, especially famous by now for his novel *Darkness at Noon*. Richard much admired Koestler, and after he left London they continued to correspond. Mary took to him less: too much intellect, too little heart.

She wrote to Richard, back in Torquay, next evening.

3rd June

I wonder what you are doing on this very beautiful evening. Looking out on the trees tipped with gold in the setting sun, I have such a longing for your presence – and as always when we are together there crops up an element of comic tenderness. It appears even now in the picture before my eyes.

All the hundreds of [barrage] balloons in the sky are turned towards the East, fat and friendly porpoises and each one with a shiny nose! I wonder why our hours so blissful and so treasured, always turn out not as expected – never as planned in our minds. To begin with you are never in the mood that I had arranged for you to be in. Do you find the same with me?

As viewed from the point of view of an outsider (very difficult), we are the most extraordinary couple that ever loved. There is no getting away from it, we are *both* still afraid of being hurt. We seem to watch each other with slightly bristling fur and at the least sign from the other up it goes like a streak of lightning. Too highly sexed to stand the wear and tear of artificial society, I suppose, for in Wales we lost none of the excitement, cut off in paradise from the rest of humanity.

I know that apart from that time I see you more clearly when you are absent, and yet your absence takes so much of me away, and I am left with this tugging of the heart. It was *so* lovely to see you yesterday, and yet how unexpectedly it all turned out. With our terrible colds, the icy dynamite Mr Koestler, your many-too-many drinks, and the conversation dashing somewhat wildly from world economics to Mr Fry [Roger Fry, the art critic]. God help us if either of us loses our sense of the ridiculous.

It is 10.30 and the balloons are one by one being brought down and put to bed. I too will follow my darling. Hold me close in your heart and take me with you in your dreams.

Mary

Richard to Mary:

R.A.F. Officers Hospital
Torquay
5th June 1942

I have just been reading through your last letter, & thinking how stupid mine was by contrast.

It is true that we still hold back from one another, but for me it is no longer from fear of being hurt, but from an exasperation that amounts at times to frenzy at the people who surround us, kind and amiable, but cutting as surely through our private life as a plough through a field, inexorably, furrow after furrow, till I feel I must scream.

And then finally we are alone; but by then it is no longer any good.

O darling when I have my flat, I'm sure we shall be happy again, free from a thousand pettifogging little worries . . . it will be like falling in love all over again . . .

Darling get well very soon and don't hold back from me. I do love you most deeply and hate to see those moments of doubt in your eyes, though often enough it is my fault.

Good night,

Richard

Mary to Richard:

Friday,
5th June

My darling,

I promise to try to get well, so please don't worry and concentrate on getting well yourself. I'm furious with myself for not being all right already, but I don't seem to get on and every morning I wake no better – or rather cured of one thing and developing another. No matter, I'm taking lots of care and since I'm not feeling too good I'd rather be in the comfort of my own home, so I don't think of going away to stay. When you come back to London, I'll be well again as I will be gay and happy . . .

I forgot to tell you that last week I cabled Merle to announce my promotion to being the grandmother of a Yugoslav grand-daughter [one of Mary's daughters had married a Yugoslav], and had an answer of congratulations saying that I must be the youngest grandmother in captivity. First communication of hers without mention of you . . .

My little sweet – I've just been talking to you on the telephone and feel *much* better. Perhaps it is the picture of your 'furious' face trying to turn itself into one of don't care a damn, but I feel amused for the first time for two days.

I hope you will have peeled by the time you get back as I don't like the feel of peel.

I know suddenly that I am going to get perfectly well, and anyway a slight tinge of frailty won't be unattractive to your new virility, and I'll be doubly impressed. In spite of your bullying, you sounded to me infinitely attractive, and if you were here I'd be very sweet to you, and you would love me beyond thought or reason.

I'll post this now and go to bed and sleep and rest and wake up all the things you want me to be. My love surrounds you and keeps you safe.

Mary

Richard returned to London and on Friday 19 June *The Last Enemy* was published.

All that week he had been extraordinarily tense. Some absurd misunderstanding arose whether or not he was to dine with Mary. He came up from hospital and the misunderstanding reached a 'climax in Victoria Station'. The same evening Mary wrote to him:

There is no doubt but that we are not only too exaggerated in our individual make-up, but also we are too exaggeratedly alike . . . Both of us are drifting further and further apart in a dense fog of obstinacy born of too much sensitiveness and much too much pride. Ever since that moment of parting I have not been able to think of you as apart from myself, but only of 'us' as one colossally absurd person.

It was such a sudden and unexpected relief to know that you had been feeling the same way about 'publication Friday', and had been equally hurt and refusing to mention it, that the whole station started buzzing round and I had to lean against the rail near the ticket hatch for support. Now it no longer seems to matter that it has to be Sunday instead of Friday and the hurt is all healed up again. But please darling never more must we be so IDIOTIC. You know that at rock bottom I want to be with you always. That airy performance of casualness is in part a defence and in part a sort of respect for individual freedom. If you had said that you felt that you should have your 'publication Friday's' dinner with Denise, I should have understood in spite of being passionately jealous – [in minuscule letters] as anyhow I am . . .

I am thinking of you in such great tenderness tonight and

wishing you all success in the coming-out of your book. I am almost as excited as if it were mine – the *almost* being made up for by my great pride in your achievement . . .

P.S. You have just rung up and my unselfish side is happy that you had a nice evening and sounded gay! I wish you were here now to talk to me. As this cannot be I will remind you that . . . I will meet you at Hatchards at 3.30 [where he was going to sign copies of his book].

They met on Sunday, when his tension, and consequently hers, became so much worse that she decided to accept Mrs Toye's invitation to the country, and left London next day 'thinking it might make things easier for him'. She went to a cottage near Corfe Castle, got a telegram from him the same morning and wrote him two letters.

22nd June
Monday

My darling,

We have made a sudden decision to go down to the village, so I'm writing you just a line to tell you that my heart is with you; that I was happy to receive your telegram this morning; that I wanted to write to you last night and instead fell fast asleep . . . Tonight I will write again and tell you all about our outward life here and what is in my heart to tell you.

I miss you frightfully and only hope I shall be able to 'stay the course', as it is best for me to be away as things stand at the moment. Our nerves were pretty well at cracking point and in London I could not sleep any longer without you. I wish you could hear some news about Combined Operations. It would give us something to build up and get busy about. Think of me my darling, and work hard. You feel very near to me all the time and you are very loved.

Monday night

It was lovely my darling to hear your voice on the telephone this evening. I shut my eyes so that nothing should disturb the sound and now I have it still in my ears. I feel that half of you does not understand that I could leave you just at this moment, but you know the artificiality and frustration of our life in London was breaking my nerve in a way that I have never experienced before. I felt desperately unhappy Sunday night and could not sleep, as every time I dropped off something happened inside my head, and I woke up with a jerk and my heart pounded away in my ears.

All the time you were too near and yet always out of reach. Somehow here I feel more at peace with you – in love and in perfect understanding. In the worst moment on Sunday night – when I was in the taxi – you said 'Somewhere deep down I suppose something is straight'. It was the first thing you had said that evening that came from the heart – from deep down where everything is straight. If it weren't so fiercely straight, we wouldn't get so desperate about the jaggedness of present conditions.

Chapter Five
June -July 1942

The Last Enemy had an immediate success, and by September had gone into a third printing. Millions had been roused by the events of the Battle of Britain, as they read of it or heard of it on the news or in Churchill's speeches. A few had witnessed episodes from the ground. Very few, even in 1942, knew anything of the young pilots' atrocious injuries, or of McIndoe's and his staff's prolonged and exhausting fight to heal them. Now that Richard's book had brought all this so unforgettably to light, hundreds of readers sent McIndoe cheques, and notes arrived at East Grinstead in many denominations, including a few rupees from an Indian peasant. H. G. Wells wrote Richard a long letter, 'of which I could not understand a word'; but from the novelist Storm Jameson came one he described as 'enchanting', and really embarrassing in its humility. 'You've written the best book of this or the last war. I've managed a fair share of physical agony in my life, and I've never seen it written about with your – it seems natural – power to make one word or phrase do the work of fifty. I guess now there's nothing you can't look to be able to do in writing.' Like Byron, whom in character he resembled, he awoke to find himself famous.

Little of this is reflected in his correspondence with Mary, which during the months from late June to October put one in mind of two high-tension cables endeavouring to touch without exploding; what earths, insulates, and saves them remains 'deep down, where all is straight'. Success had revived his self-questionings about his responsibility as a survivor, which help to explain his chronic vehemence against K. When she wrote him 'quite a pleasant note', suggesting that they should forget their row, he commented to Mary: 'I suppose one should pity rather than dislike her, as one who has lost the life of the body and failed to reach the life of the spirit.' When a little later Tony Tollemache saw her and reported that all the old accusations against Richard had been dragged up, 'using my friends, etc', his anger returned, and he could not resist the gibe, 'I personally have not seen the old witch, as she has been up in London – getting satisfaction, I hope.'

He could not forget that she had called him a coward. To all who knew him the barb had been so obviously envenomed by jealousy, and the target aimed at, his courage, so impregnable, that he would surely have been able to dismiss it had it not opened up some neighbour wound. Perhaps he *was* afraid? But afraid of what? Of what 'people', not just 'the old witch', would say if he did not go back to flying, as he and Geoffrey Page had agreed they would? Geoffrey Page had gone back, almost forced his way back; and so had others. Perhaps he, Richard, was not resolute enough. Perhaps, now, he knew all too well what war really meant, and what could become of men not fortunate enough to be killed outright. McIndoe had a cottage near the hospital, and there he would turn up, much as he had once turned up at Mary's flat and questioned her about life, to question the surgeon about the end of life. Did dying men foresee it? Sometimes, McIndoe replied; but in hundreds of other instances he had no evidence that they did, and was sure that men who had suffered dreadful maiming had neither premonition nor pain. 'Their physical agony affected their mental condition, and they slid into death without awareness.' It was something this restless hunter after truth in all her shapes had to know, if he was to write about death; even more, if he was to risk facing it again himself.

It was on his mind that he had done so little. He had missed 15 September 1940, the St Crispin's Day of the Battle of Britain, when the RAF had thrown the Luftwaffe back for ever. A photograph from the *News Chronicle* on the second anniversary shows Lord Dowding, bowler-hatted, in the centre of a row of his ace pilots. All have medals on their left breasts. Richard lurks behind figures who mask the absence of any DFC on his. Only five planes downed! Others had ten, twenty, thirty, to their names. But for his book, he would have been a mere candle among stars.

And the book? Perhaps he was still 'a sham'. Perhaps he had not really meant that peroration. The war was indeed for civilisation, it had become truly a crusade; that much he had learned. But what about his own part? At the end of March he had put in his diary: 'One must write sincere books. One's emotions afterwards may be those of an old tart counting her money the morning after; but at the time one must mean everything one says.' And what had he said? 'If I could do this thing, if I could tell a little of the lives of these men, I would have justified, at least in some measure, my right to fellowship with my dead, and to the friendship of those with courage and stead-fastness who were still living and would go on fighting . . .'

Well, he had told their lives sincerely; according to many, superbly. The messenger had made all haste and delivered what he had to say; his narrative had been masterly, but now that he had got his breath he had grown doubtful of his message. V. S. Pritchett, in a slightly patronising review in the *New Statesman*, disconcertingly observed that 'Mr Hillary conveys the impression that he likes the spectacle of himself believing, and not that he believes . . . he remains egocentric, busily self-conscious in defiance and remorse.' Yet more transfixing, because it came from a fellow pilot and fellow patient, was the reaction of Geoffrey Page. He had been reading the book in the hospital, and Richard had asked him what he thought:

He had an unconcerned air about him, but I knew my criticism was awaited eagerly. 'I think it's beautifully written, Richard. In fact I'm surprised a supercilious bastard like you could produce something like this.' Richard grinned. 'However, there's one thing I don't quite understand.' The author was now alert and tense. 'You write,' I continued, 'of your being an irresponsible undergraduate before the war, then, as a result, you change, and, presto, here you are, a different person.' I shook my head before continuing, 'In my opinion, you're still as bloody conceited as ever.' The grin returned to Hillary's face. 'Perhaps you're right. Anyway, that's the way I felt when I wrote it.'

McIndoe remarked of him, 'There goes a *very* unhappy young man.'
Many writers have treated as an expiation a book which may in

fact have been a fresh self-indulgence and continued afterwards as egocentric as before; if accompanied by success, often more so. But Richard was too honest and too self-observant to make this separation between life and work. On the only occasion he had a public audience, he said, 'I ended my book on an emotional note. It is easy for anyone to have an emotional experience; it is the application of it that counts.' In answer to the emotional challenge, he had applied himself to write a book; and the book had boomeranged. Was more demanded of him?

This fierce and continuous self-scrutiny extended into his relationship with Mary. In so many of the letters that follow, the words of intense longing are haunted by a fear that, despite her 'Oh so vulnerable sweetness and understanding', he may lose her through his 'offhandedness' and 'working off of frustrations'; and by resentment that he has become dependent on her. Alternatives loom up: either more frustration, or 'a complete break'.

Something similar was happening with her. Her role hitherto had been to offer counsel, help him to unwind, encourage him to write, talk of serious things jestingly, with that 'airy performance of casualness', and, beneath it all, give him the security of her love. But by now the lightning-conductor, which had failed her that evening in March when his *coup de foudre* had swept her off her feet, was beginning to re-instal itself, and her great power of detachment was coming into play. To go away cost her much effort of will. A conflict of head and heart was being waged within them both. With one side, she could not do without him; with the other she looked back not only to the idyll in North Wales, but to that uncommitted time in her flat in London. Her letters during her three weeks of absence grow more passionate, but also sadder, as there dawns on her the lugubrious possibility that it was not his crash which had 'exploded his ego', not his injuries nor the months in hospital, not his humiliation in America, but, through the strength of a love hitherto beyond his ken, herself. Had he fallen for a termagant, sure to ignite in retort to his ignitions, the attachment would soon have ended; if for a meek hero-worshipper, content to squat at his feet and change his bandages, whether of hand or heart – but he never would have fallen for such a person. Famished for experience of life, he had

101

stumbled on and had his love returned by a woman of spirit more than equal to his own, and of far greater tolerance and wisdom; one who, in the words of his own inscription, 'sees humanity as it is, and still loves it', the principal item of humanity she was now seeing 'as it is' being Richard.

To defend herself against the 'Oh so vulnerable', irony creeps into the 'sweetness and understanding'; particularly when during July he gives way to a fit of jealousy. She warns him, in the midst of great tenderness, that 'your position is very dangerous', speaks of an iron hand beneath the velvet caress, and of surveying him from 'an icy chamber'.

Lack of privacy continues to exasperate. They go on hoping for a job for him in Combined Operations, and the flat that will go with it. He still talks of writing. But the empyrean does not cease to summon. His second bout at East Grinstead becomes crucial to the question whether or not the condition of his hands will permit him to become operational again.

Mary's letter of Monday 22 June, quoted in part at the end of the previous chapter, continued:

> I was thinking last night before I went to sleep how, when we first knew each other, and used to talk and discuss everything under the sun, I thought to myself that you had been through an experience from which you needed me or somebody like me to help you to readjust your life. I realise now how far this was from the truth, as it turns out. In reality it seems to me that in your life everything has always gone the way you wanted and that suddenly the path is strewn with thorns, and I, who could give you peace within and happiness and moments of ecstasy all rolled into one, seem to be the cause, at the same time, of those thorns in the path of your happiness.
>
> It is as though the gods had chosen us as the two people most spoilt and in need of character-building, and to have thrown us together to show us undreamed-of possibilities of happiness and then put in the way just the sort of obstacles most frustrating to our particular natures. Just to see if we could take it, or destroy the gift.

And so I am here to gather strength in the thought of you, away from that crazy passion that your presence evokes, and which unfulfilled threatens to destroy the gift. Please write and tell me that you think I am right, as I hate so much being away from you . . . oh darling, I would so love to see you now, to have you with me for days and nights of perfection. There is too much I want to talk to you about . . . there are not enough days and nights to satisfy me.

Mary

Richard answered the same day, from his parents' flat:

23rd June

. . . Somewhere, somehow there must be an answer that is not a frustration or a complete break, but I'm damned if I can see what it is. Anyhow darling, have peace in the sun . . . I feel you beside me all the time you're away, & as when we're together in the flesh we are never alone, this spiritual awareness is really more satisfactory.

He had called at her flat to know if any news of his job had come. 'No news as usual. I was so tired that I didn't even have the energy to enjoy the irony of being able to enter with impunity, instead of having to crawl in at two in the morning if I want to see you.' He had dinner with Mary's friends, inwardly venting his rage on them for daring to be so much at home, '& afterwards in your room'. He talked of going to Oxford to 'be utterly magnificently alone, at peace & able to write. Why didn't I think of it before, God only knows.'
Mary to Richard:

25th June
Little Woolgarstone
Corfe Castle

Most dear and best beloved,
    Your letter arrived this morning and I have read it many times, finding in its economy of words so much more wealth of

103

life than in the many volumes of books around me at the present time. I was happy to know that you not only understand, but feel the same as I do about being away from one another at the present time . . .

The worst of it is that I find that the high sophistication of spiritual communion, in all its beauty and pure white line of truth, is not enough. I am not happy without you. I need the feel of you beside me. I want to talk to you, to make you laugh, and when I wake my arms feel empty – a need that has lost nothing of its urgency by the fact that it has so seldom been fulfilled. I feel sad, my darling, sad amidst all this beauty and the sun. I feel restless for you and hate not knowing where you are and what is going on at this very moment in your enchanting mind . . .

The relative of the friends with whom she shared had just undergone a dangerous operation. Richard had disguised or overcome his inward fumings, since, when Mary telephoned them, they told her that 'Richard was wonderful, and helped us all so much . . . especially nice to the patient and gayed her up a lot'. He had also written the patient a warm-hearted letter of sympathy. 'You shouldn't hate them or be bored,' Mary rebuked him, 'as they do offer you real friendship. All the same I should have been equally maddened by the whole situation . . . I cannot feel that there is no circle to embrace us both, and yet at the moment I feel as you do and see no light. I woke in the night last night and lay awake for some time thinking of us, and as I lay in the darkness the thought came to me that it was I, not your accident, that "exploded your ego", and that, this being so, by all the laws of average, cause and effect etc., it lay beyond the bounds of possibility that I should give you peace – and yet – and yet. I felt desperate and sad and finally slept in sadness. Write to me as often as you can. Don't leave me in great silences. I am not so strong alone.'

He cannot have got on far with his writing at Oxford, since he was back in London two days later.

Richard to Mary:

June 25

Still no news . . .

He had been asked to broadcast and to write an article, and had been on the town with Tony Tollemache, 'but even with him I had to come home early. I just can't bear it any longer . . .'

I miss you most frightfully and am sick to death of everyone. We can of course do nothing until some decision is forthcoming, but at night I have nightmares and wake in a cold sweat. Why do you do this to me? Tomorrow I am all day at the B.B.C. & end my London season chez Colebox [Lady Colefax, hostess and interior designer]. A fitting conclusion, I feel.

If Combined Operations do finally decide that Hillary is invaluable on the Claridges front, I shall move into the flat at once & never stir save to come to you . . .

There are many things which I have to say to you – nice things – which tonight I cannot – maybe I never shall – and finally you will get tired of my offhandedness and decide I just am useless. Please don't! At the moment I'm in a mess & it's better that you should be away than that I should work all my frustrations off on you, simply because you are so sweet and understanding and Oh so vulnerable.

When I'm settled I shan't behave so badly. I love you very dearly. Please bear with me.

Next day he went off with Rosie Kerr, who had a few days free from the wards, to Lady Sylvia Combe's cottage in Surrey, and spent his time answering questions about his book, and 'mumbling', a word he used for his conversations with both Denise and Rosie. His relationship with her was similar to that with Mary at the beginning, but much less 'psychological', less *exalté*. He was more 'like' her than he was like Mary. She was nearer his age. They shared two years' experience of McIndoe's hospital. He had been burnt, she had had her face smashed in, and was still under treatment. She was without Mary's religious convictions or flights of poetry, and in tune with Richard's cynicism. To her he remained that 'rather jolly creature';

105

and with her he could cheerfully work off his dislike of some nurse, or some other moan about the hospital, and get a sympathetic, drily humorous response. This association made no difference to Rosie's friendship with Mary. Mary's visits after Rosie's car crash had helped to give her back the will to live, and they remained devoted to one another.

Richard to Mary:

> Yew Tree Cottage
> Lingfield
> Surrey
> June 26 Friday

Darling,

Such an utterly lovely letter. I read it through twice for sheer enjoyment, and then again critically. It is high time that you wrote a book; but then again, perhaps not, for you might cease to care about letters.

You are right, & we must somehow rise over this thing; it is crucial for us & if we fail here we shall always fail – surely we are intelligent enough to get what we want, if we really want it.

Our fate was still undecided today, but Charles [Brigadier Haydon] is pressing for a decision over the week-end. Today they said that they 'were giving the matter their consideration', and I have told Charles that, if by Monday there is no decision, then I go to the Air Ministry & ask what the hell they do want me to do. He agrees . . .

I miss you most horribly although I hope, probably quite erroneously, that in the country air I shall cease to wake in a cold sweat after a nightmare of frustration.

I am going to attempt to outline two broadcasts & finish 'the children' short story, though how far I get remains to be seen.

Oh darling, come back to me soon. I long to hold you again in my arms, for I have no life apart from you. Let us pray for a pleasant decision before the week-end.

Richard to Mary:

Yew Tree Cottage
Lingfield
June 27 Saturday

Charles Haydon rang up this afternoon advising a further sojourn
in hospital on Wednesday & promising to have a definite answer
within a week of my incarceration. Oh darling, now I shan't
even see you on Wednesday. I suppose there must be an end to
this some time . . . Please don't get used to being without me. I
could not bear that.

I see in the papers to-day that Sir Alex [Alexander Korda, who
was in America] intends returning to the Fatherland with his
wife [Merle Oberon] as soon as he can get on a plane. Their
arrival should be quite amusing. I really do feel as if half of me
were not here. It is the most peculiar sensation, and not at all
pleasant.

Sylvia is away today & Rosie and I have the place to ourselves.
She is agreeably unobtrusive & I am struggling away at a story,
but I find it very hard to concentrate. All I want to do is write
you one of those obvious love letters one should never write.
Why should it always be Rosie with whom I can spend days &
days of undisturbed peace – & never you? I can see you now
reflected back at me from the paper & it is your second & secret
face – the passionate one; the one I only see now in dreams.

On 1 July he went back to East Grinstead for what was to be his
final crucial operation. Although, in letter after letter, Mary left him
in no doubt how much she hated being away from him, he resented
the peace into which she seemed to be settling with Mrs Toye in
Dorset. She wrote him descriptions of her life there, in order to
entertain him with some subject other than the strain between them.

The cottage, grey stone and thatch, sits in a garden of rampaging
flowers on the edge of the sloping downs. The interior is cool
and self-possessed with its stone floors, shining furniture, and
rows of books offering to you all the civilised thought of the
world. It is owned by two fairies, both professional singers who

107

have spent the last thirteen years of their lives between here and America. They live in a large studio not far from the cottage and cherish us in the most endearing manner. Being fairies, we do not have to bother about our personal appearance at all, which in itself is a complete rest. They look at us with great interest but surprising detachment. Nevertheless they light the fire in the morning, get the coal, do our shopping for us, and make us feel we are their sole interest. Ideal! . . .

I sent your book some time ago to an ancient intellectual of great wisdom. The answer contained some interesting things about your writing – about you as presented by your book. 'At the time of writing we would tend to infer that he was a charming egoist – that there was in fact too much ego in his cosmos – courage there is, a power to experience and high hopes of achievement. So far, when he wrote, he had not "lived" – Life indeed eludes those who seek themselves. The law runs that they find what they seek, and the "find" often makes for disillusion' . . .

Suddenly Richard was seized with panic.

The cottage had been rented from its two gay owners by Dr T., a gifted Hungarian who was Mary's doctor, and for whom all her life she retained great confidence and affection. He had never seen the cottage, and the two women had undertaken to get it ready for him. Without warning, he decided to arrive, and Mary sent Richard a happy letter, little guessing the effect it was going to have, which described the bustle for his arrival, how they had invited the owners to dinner, and afterwards (Sunday 28 June):

We went round to their studio and they sang for us. It was perfectly exquisite, and they sang early 14th century songs and negro spirituals, all equally beautifully. I looked into the loveliness of the fading day and felt you beside me all the time . . . I think we may stay till Thursday as the weather is so lovely . . . and I don't suppose I shall see you & my flat seems to be unusually crowded and all and all. It is hateful not knowing what you are going to do. I suppose it makes character. I feel I have never done anything so strong-minded as staying away from you all this time. All of me longs to be with you, so that it has become a physical pain.

I have been reading aloud to Mac [her name for Mrs Toye] – Gertrude Stein's *Paris France* – enchanting – you must read it. A new American book by an authoress called McCullers 'The Yellow Light In The Eye' [presumably *Reflections in a Golden Eye*] – pornographic and utterly incomprehensible. Eric Gill's autobiography which got such wonderful notices and which to my mind reveals him to be the most crashing, smug self-conscious bore . . .

I had a very amusing letter from Rosie. I suppose she is with you now and wonder what her face has unveiled like . . .

Two days later she wrote, still quite lightly, that they had decided to stay on, because

since no decision has been reached, and you have to go into hospital anyway, it is really best that we do not just meet once in unsatisfactory circumstances, and *then* have to separate again. It would just be an agonising strain and fray our nerves to bits again. So as things are it is perhaps best so, and since I feel I cannot be in London without you I would rather stay here, where I am so alone and with you in spirit . . . In London I would only know restlessness . . .

I'm sorry you had a shock about T. I did not know you were ignorant of the fact that this is really his cottage . . . I thought I told you this, but perhaps I didn't. Certainly our conversation these last days was very limited to one topic . . .

We have made great friends in the village. Mr Cooper, the grocer, took us into his back parlour and talked to us about the immortality of the soul. His faith in the afterlife put us to shame, as he believes even in the reunion of individual spirits. A thing I should like to be sure about.

So Sir Alexander and his lady wife are returning to England. Somehow that makes me uneasy.

. . . I hate your going into hospital. More operations, more pain, more discomfort. I shall be separated from you by silence, and you will not be able to write, and I will imagine all the time that they are not looking after you properly . . . Rosie will be able to pop in and out, but never me . . .

The same day a letter had arrived from him:

I awoke this morning with the feel that you had gone from me; there was no contact. All the way up in the bus I felt that something was wrong & then I got your letter [of the 28th, about the gifted doctor's arrival], I did not like it.

. . . I have to be in hospital this evening . . . I feel sick and alone. I am afraid I am too dependent on you. But I love you. I need you quite horribly . . .

Next day, Wednesday 1 July, there followed a telegram from East Grinstead to Corfe Castle:

WRITE HOSPITAL STOP A LITTLE HURT AND VERY UNHAPPY BUT I SUPPOSE ITS ALRIGHT LETTER FOLLOWS LOVE RICHARD.

One of those ever-busy ever-curious 'friends', always ready to pour a little more oil on waters already smouldering, had met him and asked him, 'oh so sweetly', if Mary was staying with Dr T.; to which, not knowing it at the time, he had answered with a sinking heart, 'No.' He had then learnt of the gifted doctor's arrival; next, that Mary intended to stay on; and finally gone in to hospital, where there would be no fourteenth-century madrigals, no spirituals, and no interesting tradesmen to mix immortality with the shopping and take his mind off things. Jealousy had flared up, he had put two and two together, and made them at least seven. She wrote to him at once:

Little Woolgarstone
Corfe Castle
Wednesday 1.7.42

Oh darling I do not understand and I am unhappy. You are so wrong to say that I have gone from you, and if you did not like

110

my letter it was because you read into it the reflections of your mind at the moment. All your hurt and unhappiness giving into it a warped sense of insecurity . . . I partly understand because I suffer in the same way. We are both frightened. Frightened at being swept so unexpectedly into something stronger than ourselves. Both of us at heart so arrogant and secretly revelling in the possession of ourselves – now finding no happiness apart – no longer in control of the Heaven and the Hell of it all . . .

It is absolute Hell knowing that you are being operated on to-day, and that I do not know how you are, only that you are unhappy and feel yourself alone. I too feel empty and sick at heart. Why should it be like this? I am trying my best to be grown up about this time away, to look upon it as a cure . . . Write and tell me that you are no longer unhappy and no longer feel alone. I will never again go away from you like this. It is too hard, and life seems so terribly short to be thus cut in half . . .

She tried to ring him at the hospital, but was not put through, and sent a somewhat acid reply to his telegram:

Little Woolgarstone
Friday July 3

I was afraid that your 'letter follows' would remain just that, but I gave it until this morning before admitting to myself that you too employ that old 'gag' together with the rest of human beings.

Having reached this point, I put a call through to East Grinstead 666 to find out if you had had your operation and if you were all right. The nurse in No. 3 first said you were very well *indeed*, and then said 'Hold on'. After a pause she came back to say you were improving. I can only hope that this statement is all-embracing.

Perhaps you will like this letter better than the one you complained about. It is, as that one was, a sincere reflection of my mood at the time of writing, the difference only being that of head and heart.

Now I can only imagine that your eyes are bandaged and you

cannot write, and so my head must start unaided on its In Search of a Heart. I think you have often experienced this difficulty yourself, so you will sympathise and understand. To add to the encouragement of head over heart, a cold-blooded wind has sprung up and driven dark clouds across the sun with accompanying rain. Your position is a very dangerous one. I cling to one single hope – 'Flight Lieutenant Hillary is improving'. I hope God gives him every help and encouragement.

Your old friend

Softie

Misunderstandings were cleared away; the storm in the tea-cup subsided.

Richard to Mary:

> Telegraphic address: Quvichos
> Eastgrinstead
> Queen Victoria Hospital
> Plastic Surgery and Jaw Injury Centre
> Holtye Road
> East Grinstead
> 2nd July 1942

. . . your Wednesday letter arrived. It made me happy again . . . Stupid, isn't it. But it all seemed so unlike you . . . not to tell me, I mean.

I don't feel very well as I am full of M and B, but I gather from Rosie, who watched it, ' that the operation was a great success. She tells me that my lower lid lay for about half an hour on my stomach, ere McIndoe seemed suddenly to remember it, when he stitched it on again.

I slept all yesterday, knocked cold by Dr Hunter, for apparently on coming back from the theatre I terrified the wits out of the ward sister. She had visions of 'Author of Hospital Show-up Dies in Ward'. For some reason or other I could not get my breath, coughed violently, went purple in the face, & caused general alarm and despondency. After getting me on my side &

112

making generous use of the oxygen cylinder, things improved however & anyway here I am. I'm rather sorry I missed it all . . .

Last night I had a series of most peculiar halfwaking dreams, mostly concerned with you. One often has that feeling when one knows one is dreaming & yet remains conscious. Last night the process was reversed. The reality was the dream & consciousness, though present, was weak – most peculiar.

I have needed you & longed for you so much these past few days – with the body as well as with the mind. But now they are wearing me down with these filthy drugs. I simply won't let them near me with a hypodermic.

I don't see why, because through you I have exploded my ego, I should not also through you find peace. If I cannot, so be it. But at least we can find peace from the stupid outer nonsenses which at the moment block the path of our happiness, even if spiritually the future is strife.

Anyhow I realised last night, it is you & you alone who mean anything to me; & that anything is more than the whole world.

Richard

And next day:

Darling,

Those fools only told me that you had rung me a few minutes ago, & I could so easily have spoken to you.

The dressing is down now, & I shall probably go out over the week-end, although the stitches will not be removed for a week or two.

I am really quite happy in bed, reading alternately *War and Peace*, *Heloise and Abelard* . . . Meanwhile the idea for the second book is maturing & I have roughed out the children short story. So I should not complain.

And yet I have an awful sense of time closing down, events moving in – suddenly we shall be wrenched apart & all the while we might have been together . . .

I am now putting the M and B under my tongue & throwing it out of the window, so feel better.

My darling, I'm sorry if I have caused you distress these last few days, but I resent most fiercely you being with somebody else. The desire to hold you in my arms is becoming wellnigh intolerable . . . Please darling don't have a crisis, and if you do surmount it. I think it may be important . . .

Mary to Richard:

> Little Woolgarstone
> Saturday July 4

My darling, it was lovely hearing your voice this morning and all my heart is back with you. I hate so much being away from you, and then I heard nothing, and was unhappy and finally I felt that you had gone away and left me alone, in silence, and I in turn shut myself up in an icy chamber . . . I had to steel myself in discipline not to worry about you and not ring up until yesterday, but of course it was no good. I have slept in jerky starts and dreamed unpeaceful dreams all night.

Thank God they pulled you through in time, the silly careless idiots . . . Why do you say that I try to make you jealous? Goodness knows, it would be as easy as pie for each of us to make the other jealous – hideously jealous and unhappy.

The only lovely dream I had – a dream all heart – was one in which I came to you in hospital. Your eyes were bandaged. I took you in my arms and kissed your lips and told you that my great desire was to make you happy. You turned to me and with your lips against my cheek you murmured, 'Stay by me. Stay by me.' I woke to find the day already there and lay still to recapture the beauty of the dream, but it had gone and I could sleep no more.

Richard was released from hospital and posted to Fighter Command HQ at Bentley Priory near Stanmore with the sedentary job of re-writing the secret Pilot's Order Book. Mary returned to London.

114

They had dinner together on 7 and 9 July, and spent the following weekend at Mrs Toye's house near Beaconsfield. On the 15th she began a letter with the last sentence of a much loved quotation which, long ago, she had copied out into her bedside book. It was said at the Mass after her death, and reads in full as follows:

'O my beloved, remember me. I shall be yours in life or in death. And even if some other place is destined to hold my body, yet I think that my soul shall find its rest with you; and though diversity of merit shall have one life more blessed than another, yet the equality of eternity shall have them all live happy. As one sun shines on all, yet is seen by some eyes more clearly than by others, so shall the Kingdom of Heaven be.

This is the blessedness of life, that that never is absent which always is beloved.'

For years I tried in vain to find out who had written those exquisite lines. I took it for granted that they must have been sent from a lover to a lover, until at last I came on them. They are from the hand of the great eighth-century scholar and ecclesiastic Alcuin of York, saying goodbye to the Chapter of York as he returned to the court of Charlemagne.

'And so,' Mary's letter went on,

because of this I have felt great happiness today . . . a lightness of spirit that, in spite of your absence from my sight, has made me walk the streets on air. You have been beside me in a different way ever since that absurd and lovely last night. Even my hair has stood on air again in a gay and challenging rampage. Was it only me living in fools' paradise, or did you share it with me? Your voice this morning told me nothing.

Goodnight, my darling. Sleep happily, and remember me in your dreams.

Mary

Chapter Six
July-September 1942

Lodged near Bentley Priory on Fighter Command staff for the next two months, Richard was at last able to report the news he and Mary had been waiting for:

> R.A.F. Officers Mess No. 2
> The Cedars
> Stanmore Common
> Stanmore
> 21st July 1942

> . . . John Simpson, a friend of mine here in Operations, dined with the C in C [of Fighter Command, Air Marshal Sir Sholto Douglas], gave him my book to read, and told him that I wanted to go into Combined Operations. S.D., after reading it, sent for him and asked to see me when I arrived. I meet him tomorrow at 11 a.m. He has agreed that in two months time I shall go to Combined Op as a Squadron Leader . . .

To Mary this was 'very exciting news' but the next day, without mentioning the interview, Richard wrote:

> . . . two months is not too long, assuming always it is only two months. One never knows with these slippy narks.

It was not to be two months. It was not to be at all. The project from which they had both hoped so much disappears entirely from the scene, the official reason being that, since Richard had been

116

through the RAF Staff College, he must remain at RAF disposal. Weeks later, writing from the aerodrome to which he was finally posted, he blamed this fatal disappointment on a certain high-ranking official. 'I must hand it to ——. He has certainly done his work well. This is the worst-organised, over-little-Caesared, and most disagreeably-peopled station that you can imagine . . .' A few days later he reiterated the name, but took back the appalling implication. 'On one point I'm thinking that I have not been quite fair. Old —— Certainly he did the mischief about Combined Operations, but I really was exaggerating when I suggested that he wanted to write me off. In fact he could not have chosen to send me anywhere else but here . . .'

So now there was to be no place of his own in London, and it was left to Mary to find somewhere.

Now and then, in the letters that follow, Richard still speaks of writing. Eugene Reynal, his American publisher, was 'glad to hear that you have started on your second book'. Richard had summarised the idea to Charles Morgan the novelist, who had liked it. He informs Mary that he is getting on with the short stories, which Linklater had recommended him to abandon; but all these efforts seem to have been abortive, for on 1 September he is writing, 'I am in a black depression and must make some decision what I am going to do very shortly. I haven't written anything for a year.'

With Combined Operations closed to him, he could not but return to the old spell, the old obsession, the air, to him as to St-Exupéry, as the sea to Conrad, the West Country to Hardy, Paris and Balbec to Proust, the fountain of his inspiration, and almost of his being. He did not even regret the drudgery of re-codifying the Pilot's Order Book 'and issuing it as a Command publication. This entails reading through some 4000 orders, deciding what is obsolete & what is relevant – re-type the whole bloody lot – collect everything under an appropriate heading – to be decided upon by me! & plan, yes plan! the lay-out of the whole thing. The Pilot's Order Book is the thing every pilot has to sign as understanding the rules & regulations that apply locally. And I have to standardise the whole bloody lot. I suppose this is secret, so say nothing. It's certainly secret to me.'

All the same, 'although any hope of writing anything appears to

117

have vanished completely for the moment, in a way I am not sorry. If only I had not been landed with this horror, I should feel quite happy to be back.'

So his life at Bentley Priory appeared to him. To someone else, vastly more important to the RAF than Richard, there was another side. It illustrates the extraordinary effect Richard had, even on the very high-up indeed, that twenty-four years later the C-in-C (by then Marshal of the Royal Air Force Lord Douglas of Kirtleside), should have given him two pages in his memoirs.

Douglas starts by saying that

> for all that one might mistakenly expect of them, we found that the young intellectual was well represented in our air crews. One of these bright young men with whom I came in quite close contact was Richard Hillary.

Douglas felt a strong initial sympathy for Richard, since Richard had been at Oxford when the war broke out, as he himself had been at the outbreak of the first war. He too had been a keen oarsman and stroked his College boat.

> Richard Hillary was typical of the intellectual who becomes a fighter pilot. That in itself sounds formidable enough, because the qualities of both must produce in a man obsessively strong traits of individuality. By the time that he arrived at Bentley Priory, the whole force and expression of Hillary's character had become excessively individualistic. It was known that he was exceptionally talented and highly-strung. That was clear enough from a reading of his remarkable book *The Last Enemy* . . . He had also been a handsome young man; but by then his face was disfigured by scars, and his hands were like claws. But it was not this physical disability that caused him to have what appeared to many to be a chip on his shoulder. He was too intelligent for that. I found him charming, forthright, and with a tart· sense of humour. My liking for him might have been because I have always preferred that a man should have some bite in his character.

In Hillary's case there was some devil goading him on which none of us could really quite understand. He never spoke about it, but the result of that goading was to be seen in his manner. From the moment that he arrived at my Headquarters he started nagging at everybody about being allowed to return to operational flying. He had been through a hard and trying time, and many people went out of their way to help him; but Hillary simply could not reconcile himself to having to stay on the ground. He spoke to me several times about getting back to flying, and each time I told him that I simply could not recommend it. But he kept pestering me, and in the end I gave in with a rather foolish suggestion.

'If you can get the doctors to pass you,' I told him, 'you can go back on ops.'

I said that because I felt certain that the doctors would never pass him as fit for any sort of operational flying. But I had not counted on Hillary's pertinacity and persuasiveness . . .

Of this promise by the C-in-C, Richard said nothing in his letters.

On 21 July, taking advantage of his permit for light aircraft, he flew a Vega Gull to the coast to collect some information for the Order Book, and met an old friend of his out of *The Last Enemy*. 'Raspberry', the Yorkshireman he had first known as a Pilot Officer, was in command of a Squadron. 'It was great to be up again.' Jauntily, off-handedly, he telephoned Mary that he had nearly had two accidents. 'I somewhat rashly took to the air in a Master and scared myself out of my wits. However, apart from it failing completely to start when I wanted to come back, nothing untoward occurred . . .'

He was back again among that exclusively male camaraderie of souls simpler than his own, with whom troubled and highly sensitive men have often taken refuge. The hearty in him was beginning to enjoy it, as once he had enjoyed bump-suppers at the University, the rough-house at the end of the Staff College course, pub-crawls to Limehouse from the hospital, drinking sessions with Tony Tollemache. More important, everyone at Fighter Command was vitally occupied with the war. Half in his element, half the writer–looker-

119

on outside, he had once written to Mary: 'What is the particular quality of the Air Force?' and had answered:

> . . . it has something . . . which sets its members very distinctly apart from the other Services. To say that it is an ethereal quality is both whimsical and untrue, yet I can think of no better word. It is something, some knowledge, not understood if you like, which can only be born of the combined humility and supreme self-confidence which every combat pilot feels. Perhaps in the end it is this. Any human being lies closer to the unseen than any organisation, but as an organisation the Air Force leaves more scope for the human being than any other. And yet if they do feel this thing, it must be unconsciously, for they themselves are strangely disappointing. Too often the theme is sublime, but in the attainment of it something is lacking . . .

So, mockingly, yet also in sympathy, he wrote of his immediate chief at Stanmore:

> . . . very charming and a complete Hollywood version of the English silly ass.
> 'Good show, old boy, good show!'
> 'Wizard!'
> 'Terrific, old boy!'
> and so we go on all day. I'm catching the habit myself.

He flies a Spitfire again, the first for nearly two years, and this gives him a great boost. The tone of the letters alters. Although in July he could still tell Mary,

> In my sane moments I miss you terribly – and when quite insane I nearly jump the next tube back to you.

By mid-August the endearments have grown less fervent, the sub-ject-matter more practical. She asks him questions, and he does not answer them. He mocks her 'extravagance' of language. As a boy he had taken his decisions alone. He had joined the RAF because in action he would be 'as free from outside interference as possible [and have] total responsibility for his own fate. One either kills or is killed, and it's damned exciting.' All this excitement is now over. He has not been killed but, what he had declared he would never be, maimed. Ahead, if he goes ahead, lies the ultimate 'outside interference' of the Medical Board, whose powers set a limit to his 'total responsibility'. Meanwhile, fortified now by the C-in-C's promise, he determines to carry that responsibility as far as he can, weighing the arguments by himself, steeling himself to demand that he be passed; so that, if finally rejected, he will know, and others will know, that he has done his utmost.

In order to gather together his strength of will, he withdraws into himself. Medical Boards, according to his biographer, 'fended him off as long as possible'. It is not clear how many times they rejected him. He was obviously not fit to fly in combat, but from the sole hint we have of his conduct with doctors (other than McIndoe) later in the year, he was utterly refusing to admit it.

Lovat Dickson states that he and Richard's other friends, by whom he meant principally Eric Linklater and Arthur Koestler, understood his desire to return, and did all they could to dissuade him. 'But when we opposed him, he withdrew behind a bitter mocking mask, and turned the subject aside with a joke . . . He became moody and truculent . . . spiritually frozen . . . as if his closest friends were not to be trusted . . .' They fell completely under the spell of this armed and ramparted personality. 'Something bigger than us was at work on this boy; some power had seized him, which never entered our calm and negligible lives.'

I doubt that Linklater, and still less Koestler, thought of their lives as either calm or negligible. 'Yet I was one,' Linklater said in a broadcast after Richard's death, 'who tried to make him change his mind. I was alternately rough and plausible. I wanted to keep him out of the sky and make him earthbound. And then, one evening, I was frightened I might succeed; and said no more. It was strange and disquieting when news of his death came, to think how many people there were who, though they could not have argued him out of his desire to fly, might have restrained him from fulfilling it in those icy Border clouds; but had in fact done nothing to prevent him. But if my experience was typical, their acquiescence and passivity can be sufficiently explained. I remember very clearly the night when I discovered that I could no more try to dislodge him from his resolution, for fear that happened. In his character – in his mind, his spirit, his personality – there was a quality like something with a sharpened edge and a fine surface, and I was suddenly frightened that my argument would dull the edge or tarnish the surface.'

Lovat Dickson includes Mary among the would-be dissuaders. This sounds to me extremely unlike her (although as she wrote to Richard she was bound to be *with* Linklater'). It is contradicted by Richard's letter of 19 November, in which he thanked her for never questioning his decision, as he also thanked his mother. He and Mary met only about a dozen times during August and September. He wished to involve least those whom his decision could hurt most. He had written in *The Last Enemy*:

I didn't believe that a man with something important to do in this war wanted the responsibility of a wife, especially if he loved her. She was a distracting liability and he would be far happier with her out of the way. Then he could concentrate his whole mind on his job . . .

Mary was not his wife, but he appears to have been treating her very much on this pattern, and in her letter of 2 August she as good as says so.

Her 'cluttered' life continued. Meetings, appointments – an Ambassador, an Air Commodore. The demands made on her 'serenity' throughout her life were sometimes in conflict with her private inclinations; the demands so often won that they seemed to be identical with the inclinations. Mostly she saw people she really wished to see: her mother, living just outside London, her children, her new grandchild, family, and old friends. Pretty well every evening is occupied. The same names recur: the ever-faithful Dorothy Toye, Rosie, Gerry Morel, who had been dropped in France and returned terribly injured, with his Brazilian wife, Dr T., Kitty Bruce, who had been at school with Mary, Edward Hulton, David or Michael Astor, the Director of Naval Intelligence. Two new names appear, Miles and Blossom; Miles was the former pilot and now designer and manufacturer of aircraft to which he gave his name, and Blossom was his wife, Sir Johnston Forbes Robertson's daughter, who had taken a degree in aerodynamics and eloped with Miles. And always, evening after evening, and sometimes at weekends, the Right Reverend Monsignor John Gabriel Vance MA, DPhil., her friend, spiritual counsellor, and a man of many parts. He was both worldly and devout. A secular priest, then in his late fifties, he had a cottage in the country, and always arrived with flowers. In youth he had passed all his exams at the University of Louvain 'avec la plus grande distinction'. He wrote reviews of books on philosophy for *The Times Literary Supplement*. He had studied psychology, and written a book about it. He was also a trained accountant, and at one time had had charge of the finances of the Roman Catholic Archdiocese of Westminster. A true scholar, if you wanted to know what Plato or John Scotus Erigena had said, he, in a measured lapidary style, could tell you. His conversation, *sub specie aeternitatis*, above the war, above Richard, above everything, meant much to her.

With her too, in order to prepare herself for a possible return into solitude, the withdrawal continued towards detachment of mind and, more profoundly, those sources of spiritual strength which enabled her to survey both herself and Richard as might 'some god', or, in another letter, 'some humorously-minded chemist'. The romantic and the witty, veiling a heart at moments near despair, mingle in phrases whose poetry and poignancy would surely have appealed to her mother's two Yeats cousins: to the exuberance and gaiety of the painter, and to the melancholy of the poet who had once, from experience, advised, 'Never give all the heart'. At her lover's insistence she had given all hers, to find now that he was going away from her, beginning an armadillo retreat inimical to 'excess of demonstrativeness' and ill at ease with all emotion. Several times she sends out premonitory signals that she is capable of 'slipping away'. No more than he wants romanticism or emotion, does she want his 'inability to compromise, even for a time', his 'literary frustration', and interminable malaise. A bad time comes, though only briefly, with the return to Britain of Merle Oberon. We are treated to a play within the play, an intermezzo, almost comedy, as the famous star, not apparently with much reluctance, allows the wagon to unhitch himself.

Mary to Richard:

Tuesday night
21.7.42

My darling One, I suddenly realised today that I have given up trying not to love you too much.

It probably happened some time ago, as between us there runs a curious strain of the inevitable. Something that in spite of our gay-hearted awareness is yet beyond our control.

It makes me smile when I think how diabolically clear-headed we both are – so determined to be complete masters of our own emotions and to run the course of our lives with light-hearted cynicism – and looking back to our first meeting it seems as though some humorously-minded chemist had thought fit to take two cool still fluids and gently pour them into the same cauldron to watch the result. If the said chemist had expected an instant explosion, he would have been disappointed. But he had a more subtle mind, and the gift of waiting. On the surface, and to a less trained eye, the fluids would seem scarcely to merge, but rather as oil and water to remain apart. Yet the chemist remains absorbed, for at the very base of the cauldron evolutions of the strangest nature are taking place, and he smiles to himself as he watches.

My heart fell three feet into space this evening when you said you had almost had two accidents in your plane today – and then to tell *me* that you had no one to show off to. I have never seen you show off to anyone but yourself, and that you do constantly and get a *jolly good kick out of it too*. I find it endearing when you have both your feet on the ground, but *not* when you are away from me – not when you are up in the sky. Please promise me not.

Walking along the street today it suddenly sprang to my mind, as it has once or twice before, what a very amusing companion I am to myself; and then I thought that I have that same sense of

124

absurd enjoyment when I am with you – only better. I feel the same about you as I do about myself, only better. Very amusing we are to ourselves and to each other. For me this is something new. This does not mean that we are necessarily alike, or that we think alike, but our thoughts and reactions act in perfect complement one to another, as you once said, and produce that unbelievable harmony of being by oneself with the joy of not being alone . . .

He had given her Koestler's *Darkness At Noon*, with an inscription

> For Mary of the lovely hair
> Who now will realise that there
> Are men, their eyes perhaps too close together,
> Who yet write books both great and clever

on which she commented,

I have to admit that I am very impressed and agree that everyone should read it. It is a great contribution to enlightenment. I am reading it with great care and thought, and with the full awareness that I am adding to my education. He could do so much to influence thought if only – but alas – alas . . .

I believe I set out to tell you something in this letter. If I have lost the trend and have not said it, I say it now – that I love you Richard more completely than I ever dreamed I could, and that I am happy that it should be so.

Mary

22.7.42
Wed.night

. . . it was lovely to get your letter this afternoon . . . It must feel very strange to be flying again – strange and exciting. I see that till you are back in London you will not write a word. All that surface talk in the Mess over drinks is very insidious and easy to fall into. Without noticing it I am sure one can easily get

125

into the Wizard class, having no privacy, and nowhere to read and write in peace . . .

I would like a photograph of you to keep in my bag. If I leave all my culture to you in my will, what will you do for me? This letter is definitely not worth taking a copy of, so tear it up. I am asleep . . .

Richard to Mary:

> R.A.F. Officers Mess No. 2
> The Cedars
> Stanmore Common
> Stanmore
> 23rd July 1942 Thursday

Darling Heart,

I shall be with you tomorrow – possibly before this reaches you.

I am off to bed somewhat exhausted, but I just wanted to thank you for the very lovely letter & to tell you that I feel you a very part of my bones.

> Richard

They spent the 24th together in London, and she wrote on the following night:

> Saturday night
> 25.7.42

My darling One, it was hard to believe my waking eyes this morning when I saw a letter from you on the hall table. So few words, and yet it brought back the man I write my letters to.

It is strange that your presence could not do it, for I slept and woke beside you with a searching and despairing heart. I realise that we have a great disadvantage in not being of the 'Wizard' mentality. If we had been, last night would have been so different. We would both have thought what a 'jolly good show' the party was, and, whatever our moods during the day, all

126

gloom would have been dispelled by the very fact of being together after so long. Instead of which I was nervous and exhausted, and bitterly resented those voices that I did not want to hear, while you obstinately became more and more Comus [i.e. lecherous. I once said to Mary that Comus was the alive character in Milton's masque, and the Lady rather a boring symbol of Virtue; she was indignant: she had played the Lady at school and by acting her 'with fire' made her a true heroine].

If I had been in a bloody mood (which I don't put past myself), I would have understood you not giving an inch, but I was really low for once, and you knew it. I viewed your reaction with great interest, but the interest was cold . . .

A chance had come of moving out of the flat into one of her own, since her landlords were thinking of putting up the rent to a figure neither she nor her friends would be able to afford. She went on:

. . . I wish you were here tonight. The flat is at peace and in utter silence, and I have come to bed at 10.30. I feel the need to find you again. I need to be comforted and reassured in my jealousy of the air. I want to hear you say that when you leave the ground you take me with you, that I am *never* left behind. I want you to quiet a restless and searching heart. I am asking too much, aren't I? It was better before, when I did not feel so much. Yet it was you who wanted me to feel with no holding back. It was definitely better before. Take care of yourself my darling for ME . . .

Mary to Richard:

Sunday
2.8.42

Darling one,

With no reason to expect you to come up today, I nevertheless found myself so disappointed that you were not in London when you rang up.

Somehow it had been an empty day, and I needed you. I

needed you in a different way from any other day and I can't explain. After you had rung off this evening, all the feminine in me smiled and went on smiling at the colossal male in you. It had never struck me as forcibly before how very male you are. I don't believe you have even a gossamer streak of the feminine in you. Even that surprising awareness you have for things unseen and unspoken (here I speak as between us) is nothing to do with what is usually termed 'feminine instinct'.

She had found a flat and was going to try to strike a bargain.

I am mad to get something fixed up soon and have an oasis to fly to where I can see you and talk to you in a world that belongs to us . . . I look forward very much to Tuesday . . . My inner self feels very happy again after last Thursday. It marks for me again something new. The memory holds a strangeness of great beauty, and something I did not have before, and which can never be taken away.

Think of me my darling especially in the air, so that I do not have the feeling of being left behind . . .

in love
Mary

Richard to Mary:

R.A.F. Officers Mess
The Cedars
Stanmore Common
Stanmore   2nd August

My darling,

I feel rather tired & depressed to-night. It is my own fault for not being firm about these drinking sessions.

I had lunch with Cavalcanti [Alberto Cavalcanti, the film director] – the meal prepared by his mother, a charming old lady, & what a cook! She spoke French, & I found mine had become very ropey.

Cavalcanti is very anxious to make the picture [of *The Last*

Enemy] . . . He wants me anyhow to help him make a documentary about Air Sea Rescue. I don't know whether to ask for the time off or not.

If only this bloody war were over & we could go away somewhere, where the sun never set, where we saw no one who spoke English, where the flowers were heavy as a drug.

I have taken the skin off my hand playing tennis . . .

I feel very near you to-night. The other evening solved a lot of problems & released something in us again. It might so easily have gone awry, but you, bless you, made everything come right . . .

He had dinner with Mary on the 4th and went off to stay the weekend with Lord and Lady Astor at Cliveden. Bernard Shaw and his wife were among the guests. 'America was represented by Bullitt, & a large genial and slightly odorous female by name Miss Bonnet, who took endless flashlight photographs. She has covered every war front and been practically lynched twice. Now she is off to Sweden. The only hope I could have offered her was to assure her that she would not be raped. I resisted the temptation . . .'

One would expect Richard to have had something to say about Bernard Shaw. Sixty years before, the great man had been present when his own great man, Henry George, gave his first address in London, and been enraptured. 'Hearing him', Shaw had written afterwards, 'had fired me to enlist . . . as a soldier in the Liberative War of Humanity'; and later, in a message to America, 'my ambition is to repay my debt to Henry George by coming over some day and trying to do for your young men what Henry George did for me.'

But Richard wrote little more about the company at Cliveden, except that 'there were several violent arguments, all very friendly, and I enjoyed myself'. Perhaps they had talked about Henry George, because, he told Mary, 'arguing tonight I found that Jakie [the Astors' youngest son], of all people, had SEEN THE TRUTH. [This, with Richard, nearly always meant some aspect of George's teaching.] He actually talked in terms of bakers and blacksmiths, if left alone, producing and exchanging. Unfortunately he rather spoilt things before we went to bed by asking if an anarchist was someone who wanted a King's Party . . .

Apart from that (in the same letter, of 10 August):

Please don't be miserable or let down. Is it me, or your conditions of living that are finally proving too much of a good thing? Does it now look impossible for you to move out, or is there hope? so much depends on it. Let us meanwhile pray that by Friday you will have cleared up some of the traffic a little, & that we shall be together and alone.

You were with me all the time over the week-end. Michael [the Astors' third son] asked me what I thought was your particular quality, to which I replied that, apart from being very attractive and *very* intelligent, you saved one the trouble of defining what one meant by 'good'. He agreed.

I too am feeling very low. I have only been back about four hours, but already the place is on my nerves. My revered Wing Commander simply cannot sit still for two seconds . . . Oh God, how I wish all this were over, and that we two might find some peace.

Mary to Richard:

Tuesday
12.8.42

My darling, your letter arrived this afternoon and brought with it all that I love in you. You ask me if it was you, or the state of my life, which got me so down over the week-end.

Between us alone there is nothing but happiness, but the fact that we can never be alone together becomes at times so distorting that I am capable of imagining anything. In this you help me not at all. You seem to have no power (or is it no inclination?) to reassure me at such times. On Friday I put down the receiver on our conversation in sudden despair. A note; a telegram; a postcard just saying – darling don't be silly – would have brought me through the tunnel. Instead you left me in silence and went off gaily to your weekend.

I have no sad resignation in my make-up. Automatically my blood turns to stormy petrol, and my heart closes down with the thought that you do not care, and that therefore it is not a thing worth while.

With things as they are at present, we have only Wales and some moments spent together above the stars to remind us that in our togetherness lies perfection. Because of this, and because I understand that the present situation must at times be almost more intolerable for you than even it is for me, I do try to make you feel that your faith in my love can lie unshaken in your heart. I find in my love for you so many qualities hitherto unknown to me and seemingly so contradictory – that gay unpossessiveness of spirit; that happiness in your happiness; and with it something strangely uncivilised, that in moments of doubt would become quite ruthlessly destructive rather than compromise.

It is not easy to have patience, but we *must* help each other, as I cannot arrange things differently all of a minute. Please let us try and discuss it quietly when we meet . . . the telephone has never been my best medium of expression.

I am glad I did not know you were going to take up a Spitfire this afternoon. At the same time I feel proud you did, and as I expect you are feeling rather grander than usual, (if poss), I'm feeling rather grander with you. Your weekend sounds great fun, and I want to hear every detail. Michael told me B.S. [Bernard Shaw] was staying, and I wondered what you would think of him. I am very fond of Michael – such a queer mixture of sacred and profane. He thinks a lot, which adds not a whit to his stability.

Why do you think I'm 'good'? Is it not as difficult to define as 'normal'? Anyway don't let's start all that again. I only hope that over my pigeon-hole in your mental filing system the label is not 'GOOD', or even 'the GOODS' (a dreary smile from Hillary). Well, anyway, I'd like a straight answer to this question . . .

My darling goodnight. I love you and need you.

Mary

There had been more 'cluttering'. She had been dining at Admiral Godfrey's with him and ——, a well-known writer, when an American journalist arrived late with some friends and insisted that they should all sit on the floor and play a game with matchboxes:

18.8.42

. . . One never can tell. Here I am at 2.30 a.m. and only just got to bed . . .—— tried for ages to retain his dignity, but finally had to get down to it . . . the conversation became so incredibly silly that I got exhausted listening to it, and when I rose to go —— gave me a look of profound gratitude and offered to escort me home. I found him interesting and attractive to talk to, and would have liked to engage him in more conversation than was allowed by that sort of party. I could never get *fond* of him. I agree that this is not important, but it means that basically he has nothing to get fond of . . . 'I like that one', he said about you . . .

The H.O.M. – this is for you to work out [possibly and jokingly, due to jealousy from Richard, 'Horrid Old Man', i.e. Admiral Godfrey] – was at his nicest, though he looked exhausted and obviously had something on his mind. Certain activity seems to break through the repose of this flat too – the telephone etc. I pray to God that whatever is afoot is successful.

Are you asleep, I wonder? I wish we were together.

That natural interchange of thought.

Those world travels of the mind.

So sad,

Not shared.

It is strange to miss so much that I have never had with you. I must sleep my darling. Take care of yourself. My thoughts are with you, and I love you.

Mary

Thursday. Cold Morn.
20.8.42

Darling Goof,

You with your hair parted on the wrong side.

You with a cold.

You who accept my love with gay nonchalance, but definitely *try* (*and fail!*) to damp down any form of what *you* consider excess of demonstrativeness.

You the flirter with life.

You wishing to be pollen flitting from flower to flower of life.

You whom I love, but with my eyes WIDE OPEN.

Your back view disappearing down the road in the sun held great charm in my eyes.

I wonder if you know how much of yourself you leave with me each time we meet. I think you fondly imagine that you are wrapped up tightly in hermetically sealed paper, and tied together with yards of resentful string. That at any given moment you can gather up tidily all those pieces, that carelessly may have strayed away through some word or gesture flung out in a moment of abandon. In short that, whatever happens – you Richard Hillary remain intact – the great invulnerable – the hard nut – the Tiny King of Self-realisation – all arrived at with the minimum effort.

I feel I would be more good for you if I didn't find even your monstrosities so absurdly endearing. Our early relationship, so critical, intolerant, and hardheaded, would serve better one who seeks after *true* self-realisation. However, don't lose sight of the fact that behind each velvet caress is the iron hand.

The part that matters is all around me in this room. I leave the windows of freedom open wide and you remain beside me.

Mary

Richard to Mary:

No. 2 Mess
The Cedars
Stanmore
21 August (Friday)

My Darling,

Both letters greeted me on my return; I loved them both, but that written in the morning was really a masterpiece. I smiled over it all the morning. So you have your eyes WIDE OPEN, have you?

My darling as soon as we can be together you will see that I am not refusing to give – but I must have time & peace.

It was a very lovely surprise to find you at home – & in such a very endearing mood, & to be able to stay until 8 o'clock!

I flew up to Duxford to-day for lunch, and back in appalling weather for dinner. I saw London lying below in the mist & wondered very tenderly, where you were, who you were with, and whether I was as much in your mind as you were in mine.

I opened the roof and blew you a kiss. I wonder if you felt it.

I am away to my billet now to try and write a little. If I feel you beside me, perhaps I shall find the inspiration I need.

Richard

Three days later came Merle Oberon's expected return from America. Alexander Korda had already arrived, to receive the order of knighthood from King George VI. Merle had a right to share his honour. She had raised large sums of money for British causes in America, and arrived, after a very dangerous and uncomfortable flight across the Atlantic, to co-star with Al Jolson (whom she detested) at the head of a troupe organised to entertain American and British armed forces in Britain.

'I loved her,' Richard had written. 'No one could help loving her,' but that had been all. 'I was never in love.' His departure from America had been 'a flight'. He had meant 'to write "finis"' to the affair , but had not had the pluck. Nonetheless Mary, in her letter from the cottage in Dorset, had expressed herself 'uneasy' about Merle's impending return, and it is clear from a letter to him on the day of her arrival that uneasiness was an understatement.

Monday night
24.8.42

My darling, just at this moment I need your presence more than I have ever needed anybody or anything in my life. It was only when the telephone bell rang that I realised fully the tension of nerves and the sickness of heart that had hung like a cloud over my day.

My heart bounded with happiness that you should telephone, and yet when I heard your voice I could no longer communicate what I felt. I could only have done it by taking you in my arms . . . Only that way would I have been able to make you feel all the strength of my love, and the infinite relief you gave me in confirming my faith and belief in you as a grand person.

If it had been otherwise, I should have understood, since there is nothing you could do that I would not understand – but all the beauty would have gone and left me disenchanted. Instead, through that infernal machine, we said things that meant so much in a flippant nerve-wracked way that hurt. If anything you were worse about this than I, taking into account my day – torn with passionate jealousy, immense pride and terrible fear of being hurt and losing my faith in you. I would have had no doubt of you yourself, but I know something of what you would have to face; and, once, you had said that, if it came to it, you would rather hurt me than her, as I would know what it was all about. With the circumstances reversed, you would have felt rather rocky about me!

Darling please don't go away from me. It makes me feel so terribly sad. You think I don't care enough about all this. I hate it more than you could possibly imagine . . .

The phrase 'what you would have to face' is a reference to Merle's tempestuous nature. The phrase 'you would rather hurt me than her' implies that he had considered temporising with Merle, since of the two women Mary had the stronger, more stable character and would have understood what, out of weakness, he was doing; and the sentence beginning 'With the circumstances reversed' in self-defence invites him to consider how sure he could have felt of her, had she confronted him with a lover, not yet broken with, of her own. He, evidently, was trying to treat the whole matter light-heartedly and assuming the same of her; in which he was mistaken.

There is a discrepancy here between the letters and the biography of Merle. According to the biography, Merle told the singer and actress Patricia Morison, who was one of her troupe, that she and Richard 'would be leaving for the whole week-end [of 28–30 August]; that she wanted to give him two days and nights of complete happiness'. The letters seem to indicate something less ecstatic.

Mary dined with Richard on the 27th and went to the cottage in Wales on Friday the 28th, presumably to leave Merle and Richard free. From there she wrote him a long letter:

> Tan-y-clogwyn
> Llanfrothen
> Penrhyndeudraeth
> 29.8.42 (Saturday)

My darling,

This coming here without you just now is playing strange tricks with time and memory. I find you here in the cottage; I hear your voice and in spite of the blazing sunshine I expect to see you come in at the gate in that absurd black sou'wester . . . and yet you are missing all the time, and with the need of you I no longer have the content which before has never failed me. It is nearly five months since we came here together. Yet with the charm of every detail imprinted on my memory it seems like yesterday.

If we had not had the other night before I left, I should have been very unhappy. I shall always remember, as one always does remember those rare moments of life when one is fully aware of real happiness.

It wasn't only that I felt you had come back to me after a long time, but also that I felt that you gave me something new that you had not given me before. I was wide-awake with happiness, so that it seemed a waste to sleep and perhaps miss a moment of the consciousness of it all.

The next night was pretty strange and equally sleepless, as I left Albion Gate at 10.30 p.m. with Vera [Mrs Gerald Barry]. Olde Walter Moyne [Lord Moyne, British Colonial Secretary, assassinated in Cairo in 1944] took us to the station and saw us off. The first part of our journey I slept fitfully next to an American officer, whom I found gazing at me every time I woke.

At 2.10 we fell out at Crewe and finally arrived at Bangor at 5.8 a.m. As I am really at my brightest at that hour, I was able to fully appreciate the beauty of that drive, with its famous landmark of our encounter with the cow. Gerald B. [Barry, Editor of the *News Chronicle*] was at the gate to meet us and we all had breakfast in the sun. The garden is blazing with flowers, all giant size, and the garden is full of charm and you . . .

Since you are dining out on Wednesday, maybe I won't return until Wednesday night . . . It all depends what I feel like as the days pass. Will you please think *only* of me, and when I say only, I mean *even* to the exclusion of yourself, and let me have at *least* one letter here and two telegrams saying you are all right, *and* (*this is important*) think how *lovely* it would be for *me* to have a letter to greet me on my arrival home. Always remember that what to you may seem the MAXIMUM is to *me* the [in minuscule letters] the minimum . . .

There are always such millions of things I want to talk to you about. Once you wanted to take in the whole of my life in 24 hours like *Gone With the Wind*. Years passed and he got no further. Now he doesn't even keep up with what is going on in the woman's life at present. I know that, as things are, it has been hopelessly difficult, but you have systematically made the worst of it, hoping no doubt that by a role of passive resistance you would finally galvanise me into doing it all [i.e. finding a flat]. In this particular case we all agree it had to be me – but I suspect that this technique is a steady routine, which you have always so far got away with, and hope to continue equally successfully for the rest of your existence.

Therefore, I say, concentrate on reflecting *my* jolly old ego, and you will get a glorious come-back. It might even be that it is the shortest cut to your great ambition of self-realisation.

I wish you were here. It is so wonderful to get away from all the pettiness and disillusionment of the life in London. It renews all my hope and inspiration of life. I think of you so much and find it exciting [big sprawly handwriting] that you are different *from* [four underlinings] the rest, and with me in all the things that matter. All my love goes to you darling

Mary

She got her letter on her return to London. Richard wrote her his own version of what had happened with Merle. Unless he was a gigantic fraud, it does not read to me, and surely would not have appeared to her biographers if they had seen it, like the letter of a man who had just returned to Mary after two days and nights of bliss with someone else.

> No. 2 Mess
> The Cedars
> Stanmore
> 1st September (Tuesday)

Darling,

Your wire arrived last night just before I went to bed, so that I slept happily. The 24 hours previous had been somewhat hectic, but finally I think everything is cleared up, in spite of one or two unforeseen tactical disasters.

As you know, Merle wanted me to dine with her on Sunday, but seeing very little future in it, I determined to ring her up from here, saying that I was in Peterborough and would not be back.

I rang up; got through to the pub where they [the troupe] were staying, and her voice answered. I started breezily on my explanation that I was calling from Peterborough – only to be cut short by her saying – 'what do you mean, you're in Peterborough; I have just been put through to you at extension 263!' A chance in a million that we should ring at the same moment, but there it was.

I finally convinced her that she could not have got me, had I not been ringing her – & that as I was ringing on a service line my call had to come through the Command exchange. A tall story, but I made it, only to find that the whole subterfuge was unnecessary as Alex had returned, & she was calling me to say she would be unable to dine. Ah me!

I had meanwhile however written to her & explained fairly clearly that I felt we should really call it a day. I did this as nicely as I could, & she rang me up yesterday to say that she quite understood, & to thank me for the letter. She was very good about it. I think now we will find that everything is settled.

My darling don't be miserable about this. It had to happen – you or no you – and now it has and very satisfactorily too.

I have thought a lot of you in Wales – mostly tenderly, but once or twice with furious jealousy – me sweating in the office in this glorious sun, and you lying out by the stream.

I am writing this to the flat to await your arrival.

The news from here is dull. I am in a black depression & must make some decision what I am going to do very shortly. I haven't written anything for a year.

I must see you. Please dine Wednesday.

She did dine Wednesday, and met Merle several times during her brief stay in London. All references to her in the correspondence are affectionate. The expected drama reads as something of an anticlimax. Richard had been fearful, he had told Mary when first they met, that Merle might want to marry him. Great as his charm and physical attraction were, one gets not a twang, not an echo of a twang, of Merle's heart being broken by his 'calling it a day'; and no trace of a wish to change her name into Mrs Hillary from the Lady Korda she had just become at Buckingham Palace.

Merle, her biographers write, was on location in Hollywood when Richard was killed. 'She left work for several days and remained in seclusion, hysterical and inconsolable. Hillary', they consider, 'had touched her more deeply than any man; he had worked his way through the vanities and self-satisfactions of the star in Merle and brought out the tenderness, givingness, and impassioned romanticism that lay at the heart of her nature and represented the best part of that nature. There was no hope of her going to the memorial service in St Martin's-in-the-Fields in London,' or, they add, 'to the funeral in Buckinghamshire, where he was buried close to the spot where she had spent that last unforgettable week-end with him.' Memorial service at St Martin's-in-the-Fields there was, but no burial in Buckinghamshire, or anywhere else, which makes one wonder afresh about the 'unforgettable week-end'. Richard was cremated at Golders Green, and his ashes scattered by the RAF above the Thames estuary.

Mary and Merle continued to meet whenever Merle came to London and they went on holiday once to a spa in Germany. Soon after the war, when I was with Mary in Budapest as a foreign correspondent, we read in a newspaper, or, it may have been, heard on the radio of a tragedy that had befallen her. An Italian lover of hers had said goodbye to her at Cannes airport, taken off in a hired plane, crashed, and been killed before her eyes. A day or two later the telephone rang. It was Merle, distraught. She and Mary had a long talk. Merle had wanted to know if Mary believed in an afterlife. She needed her company, and Mary went at once to be with her, and tried to comfort her. She was impulsive and generous-hearted as well as seductively beautiful. Later, when I was more than usually broke, she lent me money which, when I could pay it back, she would not accept. Whether or not she ever knew about Richard, it made no difference to a friendship which lasted until Mary's death.

That too was a sad event for her, although they had been out of touch for a number of years. She wanted to know all the details, which I wrote to her. She replied, saying that she had lately sent Mary a long letter about her own troubles, which Mary never received. She explained the reasons for the breakdown of her third marriage, to Bruno de Pagliai, and her happiness in her fourth, to Robert Wolders. 'I was quite sure I'd never fall in love again, & more sure that no one would fall in love with me – much too old for that sort of thing. [It was 1975, and she was sixty-six.] Then lo and behold, I met Robert, & if I had put in a request and specified my preferences he could not have been better! I suppose I should worry about the difference in our ages [he was some twenty-five years younger], but neither of us are aware of it. He's kind & good – kinder than anyone before – he's intelligent & perceptive . . .' and she was happy with him the remaining four years of her life.

Her biographers tell us that all Richard's love letters were destroyed in a fire in one of her houses, 'whereas those to his English girl-friend Mary have been preserved. It would be correct to assume', they go on, 'that his correspondence to Merle was of a similar character: filled, despite his condition, with the lust and joys of youth.' His 'condition', if his injuries are meant, never mattered to Mary, who scarcely mentions them. The 'lust and joys' are present in his letters to her, but I think it most unlikely that all his correspondence with Merle was 'of a similar character'. Both women were enchanting, and entirely different. In separating from Merle in that autumn of 1942, Richard had exchanged a sultry imperiousness, prone to storms, for cooler latitudes, where an ironical word could be more devastating than a flying saucepan. After Merle had left England, he wrote to a friend in America that she had 'raised scarcely a ripple on the surface of my existence'; and one can suppose that she might have said the same of him.

Some time about now, he received a crucial message. Max Aitken, one of the most renowned of fighter pilots, whom he had known at the outbreak of war, and speaks of in *The Last Enemy*, offered to take him into his squadron of night-fighters, if he could pass the medical.

Chapter Seven
September - October 1942

Cavalcanti indeed wanted to make a movie of *The Last Enemy*. His colleagues, Richard wrote, thought it 'too pacifistic. They compare it to *Journey's End.*' Sherriff's play about World War I had exposed the disgrace and the comradeship of war through the fear, barbarity, and boredom of the trenches. Richard's book had narrated the comradeship and excitement of aerial warfare, and the true horror afterwards in the hospitals and in the silences of the dead. He had never desired war. At Oxford he had reckoned that it was something inevitable, which he calculated on using as a short-cut to experience. He had taken the short-cut, and it had robbed him of his friends and of his hands. His portrait, in the book, of the pacifist David Rutter had been a sympathetic one of a man whose integrity he respected. When a woman pacifist who had read and been shaken by it sent him a rather aggressive letter, he wrote to Mary, 'My God, I never thought I should be pushed into a corner with the militarists', and Mary wrote of him after his death, 'he hated war more bitterly than any young man I have met.'

Leaving *The Last Enemy* until peace-time (it has still not been done), Cavalcanti asked him to help with a short film about the Sea Rescue services, which he got leave to do in mid-September, when his stint at Stanmore came to an end. He wrote and worked on a script about the men of the Margate lifeboat, who had saved his life. It took him into October, and he did it conscientiously and well; though Charles Crichton, who directed it, found him 'not particularly keen on a small propaganda job', especially since it entailed conferences with Government officials at the Air Ministry, the Admiralty, and the Ministry of Information, against the last of whom he had

142

nursed a fierce grudge ever since the ignominy in America. He thought of it as a test, and talked of using it to get leave from the RAF to write another book. He did a broadcast for the BBC, mainly a re-hash of passages from *The Last Enemy*, and wrote an article for a propaganda magazine, published in German in London, to which Arthur Koestler had recommended him. That too was mainly re-hash, but with a passage added about the arrival at East Grinstead of two German pilots:

. . . The one so badly wounded that he died without regaining consciousness; the other, burned and in need of morphia, stretched on the casualty table, sheer terror naked beneath the braggart façade of his Nazi bravado; indeed a terror that was a very part of that Nazi teaching. For he believed that he was to be killed. It was for that reason that I, being able to speak German, had been summoned. And when, taking the needle from the surgeon, I came up to him, he cried out and drew away. For surely here was a man, himself a victim of the Luftwaffe, to whom had been granted the privilege of finishing him off.

It took me ten minutes to convince him that we intended him no harm. Slowly the terror left his face, and such was his exhaustion that tears of relief ran down his face. For a moment he looked what he was, a simple, probably kind-hearted boy, caught up in a system which he would never understand, and now lost, wounded and alone, amongst a people he had been taught to hate, bewildered to find himself not tortured, not killed like a dog, but taken in, cared for, and nursed, like any other human being.

Articles, broadcasting, a script; such were Richard's activities after leaving Stanmore. In the intervals he went to pubs, was invited out, asked to stay, was admired, played the part expected of him, and exercised his charm. He refers in one of the letters that follow to 'that appalling London existence'; and from the aerodrome he wrote to Mary, 'My London period sapped my will', and to Mrs Warburg in America that he had 'lost touch with reality'. The script was

leading to nothing. Nothing was coming of a book. From his parents'
flat he writes, 'I have sat and sat and thought, but with little result
so far . . . I have an awful impotent feeling. Time is rushing past and
I am doing nothing – nothing; not even reading.' It was in answer to
this that Mary sends him her long letter of 25 September, rebuking
him for laziness and lack of mental discipline, and encouraging him
to read and write.

September was a critical month for them both. The offhandedness
he had displayed about Merle Oberon seems to have extended
towards Mary. At the beginning he 'may' be in London of a night,
when she will be able to come and 'give him inspiration'; he and
she 'may' be together, when he will spoil her, just as she has spoiled
him. He means 'spoiling' literally. He considers that she has been
disastrous to him. Her tolerance has been bad for them both, since it
has stimulated not his writing, but his selfishness. There is a good
deal about his selfishness. He is ashamed of offloading his 'innermost
problems' on her, but continues to do it, and at the same time is
scared of losing her.

Mary to Richard:

5.9.42

My darling, as usual it is late and I should be sleeping, but you
keep coming to me in a strange restlessness of spirit. I have the
same feeling as when you flew over the house at Beaconsfield,
except that then it came from me – a thousand strings stretching
out to you pulling at my heart. Now it seems as if your spirit
were reaching out to mine unable to express itself.

I feel you are asleep and yet you do not rest. I minded parting
from you this afternoon more than ever before. I cannot account
for it, but I had a deep down desperation to keep you with me.
I expect it is all imagination on my part, and that you went to
bed at 8 o'clock with no restlessness of spirit, and only a vague
cursing against Fate. Yet it is in your sleep that you have
revealed yourself to me, as at no other time; and so perhaps it is
natural that you should come to me so vividly now, when your
consciousness is no longer putting up the barriers against

5 Richard in uniform after plastic surgery

6a   Mary at window, late 1930s

6b   The Cottage in Wales

7   Mary, 1941

8 Richard, 1941

vulnerability. I will take your restless spirit into my arms to sleep.

Mary

Sunday 6th

Darling, having written this last night, or rather in the early hours, I find myself tonight in a different mood – so take no notice. All day I have ranted internally that we could not be together – but in a mood that you would appreciate better than that of last night – the throwing of the hat over the moon – gaily and recklessly – You probably would have tried to damp me down, as your affectation is to avoid violent changes of temperature (especially in others!). Emotionally – if one did not see beyond – you are pure Blimp. Luckily I have the volcano on my side. I think I shall build him a tiny Anderson shelter to keep him safe.

Tonight Rache rang up and asked me to go round and talk to him and C[harles] Morgan. I felt very unlike it, so I didn't go.

You would not find me 'yellow-skinned' to-night. A warm light shines underneath it from the sun, and my thoughts of you go hand in hand with that same light.

Mary

Richard to Mary:

Mess No. 2
Stanmore
Saturday 5 September

My darling,

It was so refreshing to see you to-day. You do me so much good & all I do is mock you.

This evening I played squash & in doing so discovered the real reason for my inability to concentrate on anything. It is simply that I am completely out of condition. After two games I had to sit down, I felt so sick.

You were looking very lovely to-day, Mary dear – that's why I walked you a bit after lunch. I wanted people to look at me with envy – then I had a silly little fear (I hope it was silly) that I might lose you, so I popped you into a taxi to have you all to myself.

I am away to bed now when I hope to dream of you & hold you in my arms. Maybe in a week I shall be permanently in London, & then you will be able to come and give me inspiration.

The volcano is subdued, passive, cunning, waiting – how long, I wonder. Also feeling a little ashamed for being so selfish; very selfish. Please forgive.

I love you
Richard

Richard to Mary:

Thursday 10.9.42

My darling,

How right you were! Please try to forgive me for being so utterly thoughtless. I have come so to rely upon you, for it to be dangerously near taking you for granted.

When you were so far away from me on the telephone I realised how near I was to throwing away Oh so much the most precious thing in my life, purely through being so concerned with my own innermost problems as to be in very truth an emotional Blimp.

Will I see you this evening, I wonder; anyway tomorrow, & if you are nice to me (which I don't deserve) I shall wag my tail off with joy and relief.

The wheels have finally turned, and as soon as my replacement arrives I am off.

Then darling we may really be together, and I will spoil you as badly as you have spoiled me. But you it cannot hurt; me, it has nearly ruined.

More 'cluttering' in the West End, while Richard went off to sea for the filming of his script.

Mary to Richard:

Friday night 18.9.42
After the party

My darling,

You have been in my thoughts so much during the day. At times so close and then at others so far away, that the remembrance has brought a pang. It was sweet of you to ring up last night. I took the words and the sound of your voice to sleep with me to take away that unreasonable sadness. Somehow the day had worn away my party spirit and only you could have given it back. None of the things the others said could gay me up. However, I realise it was me and no one else's fault.

Practically the whole party met this morning at the Ritz before lunch (some by accident, and some by appointment). Amazing revelations – everyone pulled to pieces – your name bandied about with the rest. I found myself wondering whether I had been there at all, and decided that certainly even in my earliest school days I had *never* been so immature. At any rate they all seemed to agree on one point and that was your hideously bad manners. Also they all hated ——. Miscalculation on my part, as I thought they would all think him fearfully intriguing without quite knowing why.

You will be glad to hear that Merle has taken your hint about the bedroom hair and is doing it as she used to do. Consequently she really looks lovely again, and at least five years younger.

She told me the other day that the only thing for you would be to fall madly in love with some glorious woman – you need a good influence in your life, it seems. I thought to myself that what you *need* and what you *want* are conflicting elements in your life.

I find myself disturbed sometimes in my thoughts of you that you have so little inner happiness. I do not quarrel with your restless spirit, because that will achieve great things, but what about that perpetual grouse & cynical outlook on life? Is it a pose, or is it from within? It shouldn't really be, that the very memory of the few occasions on which I saw real happiness in your face should strike me each time in wonderment, as if a

147

miracle has happened. You talk a lot about yourself, but on the whole you tell me very little, don't you?

Richard to Mary (telegram, 19 September):

PUT THE RECEIVER BACK LOVE RICHARD.

Evidently she put it back, as witness:

Sunday night 20.9.42

It is wonderful what just your voice on the telephone will do for me. I had missed you so much. London is not the same . . . I had made up my mind to go to bed before dinner and *sleep*, and after your call I was persuaded to fling myself into the social whirl once more and dined at Quaglino's with Patrick and the Fitzgeralds.

The planes to America are all held up and Merle and all the Americans at Claridge's pack and unpack and sit about disconsolately and moan. The joy of your heart, old Godfrey, came in to say goodbye. Ian [Fleming] is going too. All this going and coming across the ocean makes me restless.

I have thought of you so much on the sea. What thoughts did you have? I always find it changes one's perspective. Mine at this moment is in one straight line with you at the other end – all the barbed complications between do not exist . . .

Richard to Mary:

25 Rutland Court
25th September

My darling,

It is now half past six, & the day seems to have gone very slowly. I have sat & sat & thought, but with little result so far. Merle came along, as you know, & was really very sweet. Otherwise the day has been gray. You have been much in my thoughts, & sitting alone I realise how badly you spoil me.

Sometimes I am very horrid to you, but you are so tolerant that it is bad for both of us.

Sometimes I feel it is almost a pity that you see me so clearly & understand my motives so well. If you did not, you would be more exacting and I would, perforce, be less selfish.

When I carp and complain, it is really at myself – for you are so really all right that by contrast my own selfishness stands out. But I hate to admit it; so I pick on you.

If one could only keep still for a moment in this appalling London existence – still for long enough to see oneself as one really is, how differently one would run one's life.

I have an awful impotent feeling. Time is rushing past & I am doing nothing – nothing; not even reading.

This script is really the big test. If I cannot do that, then I certainly shall not feel justified in asking time off for the book.

Have a good week-end, my sweet, but take me with you, & bless you for your wonderful long-suffering.

Richard

Mary to Richard:

25.9.42. Friday,
continued Saturday night
26.9.42

Your roses are so lovely, my darling, and I have been happy to have them by me all day. To me they seem to be more beautiful than any flowers I have ever had, and if you smile at this 'extravagance', my retort is that only once before did you send me flowers, and their message then was more of politeness than of love . . .

. . . For once I am in bed the same day as I got up . . . my thoughts are re-possessed by last night, when you lay beside me and slept. I feel that, if I had not known you in sleep, I should have missed a great experience. It is difficult to explain, but you have an almost stronger personality in sleep than you have awake. Most people fall asleep, and they have gone and left one

149

out in the cold. One feels lonely, and out of sheer boredom one falls asleep too. You, on the other hand, fall into what is known as a 'dead' sleep, and immediately become alive. You do not even *look* asleep. All cynicism drops from your face, which assumes the look of a very cheeky little boy with his eyes shut. Your hands and your body become caressing in a way utterly different from your waking hours, and you mutter a good bit, which always sounds very amusing if only one could catch the words.

The only sign of aggressiveness is shown in moments of fierce possessiveness.

Apart from feeling so ill last night, I was happy to lie awake. I felt loved and strangely entertained. It came to me that, if I had not already fallen in love with you awake, I should certainly have fallen more deeply in love with you asleep. There have been other nights too when your sleep has been haunted and restless, and you have sought quiet in my arms as you would never do in your waking hours. Meanwhile it makes tonight, and all the nights apart, seem even more wasteful than the days. But in my secret head I hold the certain knowledge that this unique communion in your sleep belongs to you, and you alone, and will never be experienced by either of us through any other.

You talked a lot of sense last night at dinner, and I understand and entirely agree. No two people could have had worse circumstances to contend with in the matter of their daily lives. Mine is certainly the most cluttered up, and, if it were not for the fact that I do see a remedy in the new flat, I should be very desperate.

I have had times of deep depression about it all on your account, because I have felt that I was no help to you. Besides happiness, I want to give you a sense of peace as a background for your unpeaceful and restless mind – not that you should have to rely on the 'trappings' of peace, which in our case could not be more conspicuously absent but which I have tried to make up for by giving you great inner peace of mind as regards myself. You worry too much about not being able just to sit down and rattle off literature without sweating blood. No creative artist has ever achieved anything without the sweat. Laziness and a positive lust for short cuts are your downfall. Apropos our dinner conversation, Bacon said it all when he said:

'But little do men perceive what Solitude is, and how far it extendeth. For a crowd is not company, and faces are but a gallery of pictures, and talk but a tinkling cymbal, where there is no love.'

Saturday night

. . . You say in your letter that I spoil you. I am quite aware of it, and I am equally aware that I encourage your self-centredness by being fascinated and occasionally amazed by its enormity. The unique experience of loving someone who is more interested in himself than he is in ME, is one that I find absorbing. When I think that I might have died without experiencing this salutary phenomenon, I go cold all over. The moment for *you* to go cold all over will come when I suddenly tire of it – when the novelty wears off.

Doubtless you will be too nippy to let this happen. The technique of surprise is the one best employed with a woman of my spirit. I assure you that no one who hadn't a colossal core of self-confidence could swallow you whole with such delight.

The question of unselfishness is a different one. What you think is my unselfishness is very often pure selfishness. You arrive to fetch me for dinner in a feeeelthy mood of drink and literary frustration – *Determined* to have a disagreeable evening. My fighting spirit is up at once. I immediately call into play all my feminine instincts, which automatically play the role most suited to enable me to enjoy my dinner. The fact that I do usually enjoy my dinner feeds my ego. Q.E.D. Finally you end up by making love to me with all the passion and tenderness that matches mine.

Deep down I know that I could always count on you in matters of 'epic' unselfishness. I believe that, if I rang you up in tears and begged you to come round at once – even if it was before breakfast – I believe you *would* rush madly across the Park.

Think it over, and give me a straight answer one of these days.

I have been thinking very much about you in your work on the script and willing you to give it birth. With your originality of ideas and positive genius for expressing them in vivid language, I have not the slightest doubt that it will emerge with the same alive quality that characterises everything you write. Someone once defined genius as 'seeing everything anew', and, whereas *I do not go so far* as to say you are a genius, I do think you have a new and original view of life, and of expressing yourself. This makes it impossible for anyone to help you, except by inspiring you with faith in your own achievement. This I do, with all my heart, adding the advice of discipline of the mind to work to time.

There is no reason, except idleness, that you do not read, as you can force yourself to read in bed in the morning, or at night, also in bed – no effort at all. When I have my new flat, we will read all through the meals, and afterwards too. We will form a night school, and educate each other. I used always to carry a book about to read in taxis and buses and waiting in restaurants, but finally I lost too many books that way.

This was meant to be a small letter to thank you for your lovely roses, and' to tell you I was thinking of you, and then somehow I found myself having a conversation with you at different times during the day. All in different moods, you will observe.

I wonder how your day has passed. Perhaps you will call me later, and tell me nothing in a very gloomy voice. Very unsatisfactory you are in many ways – and yet – and yet –

Anyway, I have enjoyed my day without you, as I have been able to imagine you as you were in Wales, and I have been happy.

My room is a mass of flowers from all my admirers, and I have just given yours (still my favourites) a dose of sugar to keep them going. Just before dinner the bell rang and I opened the door to my ex-husband, who handed me a chicken and 12 pears. I was so astonished that I hurled it straight into the oven and [one of the lodgers] and I fell on it for dinner . . .

I hope the Bottums are beastly and that you are bored. [He was going to stay with the writer Phyllis Bottome and her husband.] I resent them with all my heart and soul and all the fire of my blood.

[In very strong emphatic handwriting.]

Mary

'And yet – and yet'. There is always this 'and yet – ', at the root; with, on the surface, his nagging at her 'long-suffering', and her 'very unsatisfactory' about him. Something had to happen. Either she must tire of him, of that unique experience of loving someone who is more interested 'in himself than in ME', or he will meet someone, some new person will appear, as Mary had appeared nine months earlier, to steer him on to the next stage in his life. Both happened, and simultaneously. She did tire of him, and he did meet someone; this time a man.

'He was always searching for what he termed "the complete man",' she wrote of him. 'By this he meant those who, having discarded life's trivialities, lived according to their principles, with a proper adjustment to things that mattered. He was always probing into the secret of this achievement. He felt that he himself lacked the integrity and serenity for being a complete person, and was especially drawn towards men who seemed to possess it.'

A few weeks back, Eric Linklater had introduced him to the friend of T. E. Lawrence, the painter and sculptor Eric Kennington, who had just finished an officially commissioned series of portraits of the RAF. Richard decided that he needed a portrait of himself; Lawrence too had gone to Kennington because he had 'wanted a face', in order to assist him to learn about himself. Kennington had a farm in Oxfordshire, and there Richard spent a short time at the end of September and beginning of October, free as he had been in Wales.

This visit, following the C-in-C's promise, and the message from Max Aitken, was decisive for him. At the same moment, Mary made her own decision that Richard was becoming too remote from her, and that she could no longer accept the tensions of their relationship. I mentioned earlier his resemblance to Byron. The famous lines from

Don Juan, the classic text for male chauvinism, seem worth quoting at this point:

> Man's love is of Man's life a thing apart,
> 'Tis Woman's whole existence.

She was emphatically not that kind of woman. She very seldom included comments in her diary, which for 1942 consists almost entirely of names, times, appointments. But against the date Tuesday 6 October she put the words 'Dismissal R.H.', and the same day sent him the following letter.

Monday night
5.10.42

Darling, I don't know when I shall see you, and anyway it would be impossible to say – I'm better at writing.

It is just that I feel miles away. I don't feel that I *know* you any more. When you ring up I have nothing to say, because I feel we know so little about each other's background, that there would be too much to explain.

I realise that I've been nervous and restless and not happy for quite a time. I don't seem to belong anywhere, as I am no use to you in serious matters, and cannot ever give you that care-free relaxation in contrast to hard work, and I'm no good at fitting into that middle pigeonhole.

If I had never known those moments of oneness so startling and unlike anything else I have ever experienced, I would have written this letter before. But I know I can't go forward having to look back to recapture an illusion.

I suppose we are neither of us big enough to have survived all the difficulties. I would rather just be friends with no kind of responsibility or expectation from either of us to the other. Surprising though it may seem, on the face of things, I too have work which relies on tremendous concentration, and of late I've been fuzzy-minded. My mind wanders about in restlessness, and I find no inner peace to get me through the outer chaos.

I feel that I'm explaining badly, but if I did not expect so much that you are not able to give me, I would not burden you, and I myself would be less unhappy.

All this has nothing to do with your going away, seeing other friends, or whenever you can meeting people who can help you in all you want to achieve in life. All this is right.

I cannot write any more. I know you will understand that it is not my love that has failed.

Mary

A letter reached her next morning from Richard, written before he had received hers:

Darling,

I have quite lost my heart to Kennington. He has the most extraordinary personal magnetism of anyone I have met – a great man I think. Certainly his sculpture of Lawrence is a master-piece. His farm is so restful, that I feel the life in me stirring and the writing is beginning to come.

I return to-morrow until Thursday to sit for him. He is no longer with the RAF, so it must be a private arrangement. He is being very reasonable however.

Now I really shall have something to leave you. As soon as it is done, I will make my will & set my family's mind at rest.

All love
Richard

After reading this, Mary added to what she had written the night before:

next morning

Your letter arrived this morning. I had looked forward to it so much, so I read it through 4 times to try to place it. Finally I find it the letter of a man to the woman he has been married to for 17 years, and is in the habit of writing to every day! I never achieved being married so long, so I feel that my heart is at the bottom of the sea.

155

It shows my darling how far away you are from me. There is no blame, but I am right in what I say at the beginning of this letter. You and I must never pretend. I know that as friends we are perfect for each other. But I must have a little time to adjust the heart, which you always complained was too big anyway.

Mary

Chapter Eight
October 1942

Eric Kennington, whose portrayal of Richard coincided with Mary's 'dismissal' of him, was an artist accustomed to depicting men of strong will trained to war. He first became known through his drawings of the infantry in World War I, with whom he served. Lawrence invited him to illustrate the *Seven Pillars of Wisdom*. In World War II he painted many leaders of the Armed Services; personnel of the Royal Navy after the battle of the River Plate; and anti-aircraft batteries of the Home Guard in action. His works made the British war effort known by exhibition as far afield as Russia and both North and South America. His portraits of the RAF, executed in spare forceful strokes, have the girdered, iron-jawed, slightly unnatural look of men who have subdued their weaknesses. His long association with Lawrence, of whom he did the bust now in the crypt of St Paul's and the marble effigy on the floor of Wareham Church in Dorset, had made him the confidant of one of the most sensational and self-conscious heroes of this century. Kennington recognised Richard as in the same tradition, possibly also of heroic potential, and had himself been recognised as that 'complete man' for whom Richard had been searching. 'A great man,' Lawrence had written to Robert Graves, after his first meeting with Kennington; and Richard now said the same to Mary.

Painter and sitter, guru and chela, had many conversations. They had much in common. 'I like the race of men,' Kennington wrote to Mary after Richard's death, ' – if they are rough, tough workers – not so much those that sit at desks.' More important than either talk or portrait, Kennington brought out his private copy of Lawrence's *The Mint*, on Lawrence's instructions not to be published before 1950,

157

and Richard read it. 'I have a decision to make,' he told Kennington. *The Mint* made up his mind. 'Had I not stayed with Kennington,' he wrote to Mary from the aerodrome on 25 November, 'I should not have read *The Mint*; and had I not read it, I should not have come back (perhaps).'

The Mint is Lawrence's account of his escape from world renown and the verge of mental collapse into the ranks of the RAF in 1922; 'a step forced on me', he told Robert Graves, 'by an inclination towards ground level, and by a despairing hope that I'd find myself on common ground with men; by an itch to make myself ordinary in a mob of likes; by a little wish to make myself more human . . . All these are reasons, but unless they are cumulative they are miserably inadequate. I want to join up, that's all.' Richard wanted the same. So did countless injured pilots. Other impulses drove Richard which were similar, in all save degree, to those driving Lawrence. Conscience had forbidden Lawrence to draw any profits from the part he had played in the Arab war. Richard had given all his royalties from his American broadcasts to McIndoe, but was now gathering both money and fame, though of course on an incomparably lesser scale than Lawrence, out of his book about the Battle of Britain; and it disturbed him. Lionisation is for lions, and Lawrence had been a lion in flight from it. Richard was barely a lion-cub, but he too was in flight; in flight from that corrupting facility for 'being charming and saying witty things'; in flight from the temptation to play a part; in flight from what he called 'cleverness' and Lawrence 'intellectuality' (witness Richard's disgust with Virginia Woolf, his disregard of H. G. Wells; even, during that weekend at Cliveden, of Lawrence's mentor Bernard Shaw). Richard too wished to re-discover himself among 'ordinary people', by whom he meant men like the pilots he had known before his crash, as Lawrence meant the squaddies and mechanics at the Uxbridge depot. Arthur Koestler, one of the few 'intellectuals' whom he listened to and corresponded with, gave him a French phrase for this not uncommon aspiration of a clever man to lose himself among the supposedly simple. He called it '*l'espoir de la fraternité*', and said it was a wild-goose chase.

Yet, though Richard came to *The Mint* with much likeness of mood to that other author-warrior who had written it, a chasm of circumstance divided the two which might have given Kennington pause before he put that, of all books, into Richard's wounded hands.

Lawrence had enlisted into the ranks. But Richard, if ever passed fit, would be returning as an officer. Lawrence wrote from Bovington, after he had been transferred to the Tank Corps, 'I have to answer here only for the cleanness of my skin, cleanness of clothes, and a certain mechanical neatness of physical evolution on the Barrack square. There has not been presented to me since I came here a single choice . . .' How different the prospect before Richard! He would have responsibility for himself, for his plane, and for whoever was flying with him. There had been no flying at the ghastly Uxbridge Depot, about which *The Mint*'s first sections are written, nor later at Cranwell, where Lawrence at last came somewhere near happiness. As for aerial combat, in 1922 it was either all over for the time being, or in the future; meant either the crates of the old Royal Flying Corps five years back, or the Spitfires and Hurricanes of twenty years ahead. Richard was the finished product which those twenty years had been preparing, the doomed flower of the seed Lawrence's hero Trenchard had sown. Richard going back would be going back to war, with broken hands and weeping eyes, and, night-fighters being his only hope, to war by night. What Lawrence sentenced himself to face (those 'horrors of institutional life', that 'agony', as David Garnett termed Uxbridge), meant square-bashing, clearing out pig-swill, noise, dormitory fights, bullying, the humiliation of fatigues. He stood no major risk. Indeed his enlisting had been the life-saver for his broken nerve. What Richard would have to face would be the probability of death.

It seems appropriate here to quote what Sir Sholto Douglas has to say about *The Mint*. He liked Eric Kennington, who had spent some weeks at Douglas's HQ at Bentley Priory doing portraits of Fighter Command. Kennington had brought his copy of *The Mint* with him, 'one of the rare manuscript copies of the original unexpurgated script' and not 'the emasculated pallid edition that was published in 1955'; the copy therefore which Kennington had handed to Richard. It was passed by one of his staff to Douglas, who read it and 'could not bring myself to tell Kennington just what I thought of it . . . I found the book thoroughly poisonous. He [Lawrence] was masquerading as a

159

raw recruit in the Air Force, and naturally the routine and the physical training and the drill and the coarseness of the life were distasteful to him. But he had deliberately chosen to live a life designed not for a highly educated man who was approaching middle age but for young men of nineteen or twenty, many of whom were by no means bright . . .

'The way in which T. E. Lawrence wrote about the RAF Depot at Uxbridge in *The Mint* was mean enough in spirit; but what I found quite inexcusable was the spite and the vicious unfairness of what he had to say about the Commandant of the Depot at that time . . . In the long run, many of us came to feel that T. E. Lawrence, so far as the RAF was concerned, was scarcely more than a nuisance . . .'

It was this nuisance, or, to others, genius or hero, who now had, through Kennington, so decisive an influence on Richard.

Richard received Mary's letter of 'dismissal' while still sitting for Kennington, and replied at once. His reply is, he tells her, not premeditated, and in places it reads confused. Yet one wonders how many men of his age could have written anything so honest, so adult, and so strong.

I have reproduced it exactly as he wrote it.

6.10.42

Darling,

It was a shock, though not entirely unexpected.

You're right, of course, and the deficiency has been mine. It's not that I love you any less; in spite of this I feel you a very part of me. It is not even a question of being big enough to rise above the difficulties. The difficulties have become a very part of us; they have made the present situation intolerable, because, by their very nature, they have made all spiritual and mental contact – except through the act of love – impossible. I should have seen this before: a purely physical relationship is a thing which could never be for us, and yet almost – by the very fact of

160

our only contact being physical – we are suffering from an animal frustration. Yet these difficulties are transitory; they cannot destroy us. We *are* too big for that.

As you say, we must never pretend. I never have. My letters reflect my mood exactly. You are there. It is on you that I depend, but at the moment contact is impossible. This letter must seem ordinary enough, and yet I strain to be a part of you as I write it. I am not much good at straining.

I must give all of myself or nothing. Before I met you, it was always nothing. I had so little to give, and I did not want to waste it. (No, that's wrong. I had a lot to give but not then.) Now I cannot give you everything – so I give you nothing. It is quite simple. At this moment I can give nothing to anyone. It is bad and yet it gives one power – immense power, and that's bad too. If I took a woman now (other than you) I think I would destroy her – for though when confronted by small things, I am lost – chaotic – inside I'm frozen, hard, but powerful. Is this nonsense? I don't know. This is not a premeditated letter so there must be something here of what I'm trying to say.

It's funny that I should get your letter after three days of such peace sitting in that room of Kennington's which is not Kennington's but Lawrence's really – not only because of all L's things there – I felt such a wonderful surge of peace & potential creation as I have never felt before. Kennington knew it I think. He has an uncanny second vision – you can see it in his portraits – they are all of the subjects as they may be in five years time. I just sat there and let his words flow over me. He remarked on it finally. 'Funny,' he said, 'you sit there and hand over your mind for me to play with and yet you have the power – not I.'

I was really distressed at leaving. Had I been able to stay – something would have happened – something good. More I cannot say.

But enough of this! It is irrelevant – or is it? No I think not.

I can make nothing of this letter. (You perhaps will) and yet in some way it seems an explanation – an explanation of why we can never talk now. It is those circles of peace again. They must return – they must. We are too important to each other to fail.

I will not apologise – or say I have treated you badly. I have not. It would be in some curious way an insult to say so – insult to you I mean.

In three weeks this triviality comes to an end. Then what? A momentous decision I know. And yet now it does not affect me. I shall go back I think. I can rationalise no further. I must let instinct decide. Maybe it is for this that I have withdrawn into myself. I don't know.

This I do know – you are right. We cannot play down to circumstances. We must accept them – forget them, and wait. Need it be long?

Richard

He wrote to Kennington next day:

26 Rutland Court
Knightsbridge S.W.7
7th October

Dear Kennington,

Two immensely important days for me; thank you for them. Lawrence, I wonder, or you? T.E. to some extent, certainly, for The Mint helped to clear up something that had been worrying me for months. To fly again or not? I had got to the stage when I could rationalise no longer, but relied on instinct to tell me when the time came.

The answer I can see now is simple. Does one wish to write for power – or success – call it what you will, or because one has something to give? Again I have despised these men I have lived with in messes – pilots too – despised them above all drunk, and have felt a longing to get away from them and think. But Lawrence is right. Companionship such as this must depend largely on trivialities (the wrong word), ordinary things is perhaps better . . .

But it was not all T.E. There were moments when I wished you would not speak of him; he got in the way. How glad I am that I had nothing to hide from you . . . I can almost find it in me to pity those poor unfortunates at the Air Ministry.

162

Forgive this letter: it is not saying what I intend. (I can almost imagine Buchman looking over my shoulder and rubbing his hands.) It is simply that for those two days no one was being 'clever' and the issues for once were almost simple.

I appreciate your doing the portrait very much. I also like it. Whether it's 'good' or not, I suppose we'd better leave to Kenneth Clark and posterity.

Yours sincerely,
Richard Hillary

Dated possibly by Mary 'Oct. 8th' and headed by her '26 Rutland Court' came the following note:

My darling,
Something has gone wrong with my eyesight & I am retiring to bed, but I want you to know that my last thoughts are of you, that I love you, & that when I saw you to-night my heart turned over.

Richard

She answered his long letter of 6 October next day:

9.10.42

My darling, Thank you for writing as you did. It is a wonderful letter, and no one but you could have written it.

As I read it, all my generosity of heart opened up again and brought you back to me, and nearer than you have been for months past. No other letter could have given me back my faith in you. I wrote my letter in the light vein that we are wont to do, but in my heart I had ceased to understand or even want to understand. I just wanted to get away and be alone, as I was before you came.

I found your letter so mature in parts – so much more mature than my attitude – and when I read the part about your present complete lack of human contact, the hardness, and that feeling of immense power, I held my breath, for you describe *exactly* a state which, three times in my life, I have myself experienced. I have never before met a living soul who had ever experienced it, or could even remotely understand.

It is startling at times how alike we are. I look back now with horror at those 'pagan interludes', and the effect they had on people who then came in contact with me. That great sense of power, coupled with perfectly inhuman detachment, can be very destructive. In your case perhaps it will release itself in something creative and good. It must, it must.

Another thing your letter has done is to have opened up a gate of my mind to yours, which I wasn't really aware was shut. It is very absorbing and exciting to discover you bit by bit, and learn that fundamentally you possess all the qualities I most value, and have never found. There are so many things I want to talk to you about – hours and hours with long silences and peace.

We are both too highly tuned to stand this particular type of frustration. Yet of the two you are the stronger, and don't plunge about, as I do, between Heaven and Hell. I am in a prison of soft hands, so much more difficult to escape from than the barbed-wire variety. I have a strange faith in you – that you will get me out.

For some reason I feel uneasy about Kennington. I can't think why. I had it very strongly when you said you were going back for your portrait. I have absolutely nothing to go on, but the thought is always disturbing. (How I hate women who have vague 'feelings' about things!)

Do you realise how lucky you are to be feeling so little with your cold fossilized heart just at this time? I wish I wasn't so alive.

All the same, now that I have your letter and understand, I am no longer unhappy. The strength of our combined wills will give us our circle of peace.

Hold my heart closely against yours always. Don't let me slip away.

Mary

It is no wonder that she felt uneasy about Kennington. Richard must have spoken of her. Whether he did or not, after his death Kennington wrote of him: 'Too critical, too truculent, and too assured, was the verdict of some of our household. I defended him against these charges (of which he was unaware), saying he would probably use others for a time to rid himself of a load of suffering . . .'; exactly the use, in those moods styled alternately 'careless', 'thoughtless', 'selfish', 'off-handed', and so on, that Richard had been making of Mary, hated himself for making, but refused to extenuate or ask pardon for. Uncompromising, total, absolute for love or absolute for action, here was another difference between him and Lawrence. Lawrence had many anguishes, but Richard's confused crescent love for Mary was an experience he lacked.

Nor does one wonder at Mary's comment when Richard suggested bringing her the portrait (19 October):

I am looking forward tremendously to seeing it, and wonder if I shall like it. I probably won't be able to tell at first glance, and it is bound to give me a shock, as I realise I see you utterly differently from anyone else. Whatever it says to me, I shall be happy to have it because of your thought, which was for me. I will, apart from sentiment, study it carefully, and give you a full report on what it says to me.

She did not do so, unless verbally; not anyhow in any writing that has survived. He did leave it in his will to her, 'the most complete woman I have ever known'. After his death she lent it for their lifetime to his parents. His will had not been witnessed, he died intestate and it passed by the wish of all concerned to the National Portrait Gallery. I do not think she greatly cared for it. She could have sympathised with the thought behind Lord Portal's foreword to Kennington's gallery of the RAF: '. . . the trouble with a Kennington portrait is that it gives one too much to live up to . . . he draws us as he would have us be . . .' Richard's, for her, was too self-consciously heroic; she had known him better, and preferred him, in other moods. But there, for the public, it will stay: his bequest to his 'complete woman', the work of his 'complete man', done while he turned those pages of *The Mint* without whose influence ('perhaps') it might still (today he would only be sixty-eight) be his.

That interchange of letters between 5 and 9 October is the most remarkable of the correspondence. It broke through the ice that had been forming round the relationship, into a warmth that had almost been lost, and led the two of them on in mutual understanding.

.

We now have many portraits of 'our Mr Hillary', quite apart from the one in the National Portrait Gallery. We have him wilful and loyal in childhood and adolescence, done by his biographer; the happy disillusioned egocentric athlete at Oxford, done by himself; the Battle of Britain; sketches of agony and mockery in hospital; Denise's 'whenever I left him, I felt indescribably happier', alongside the tough Philistine pilots in Ward Three, slinging rationed eggs at the slim blond polemical provoker in red pyjamas, and Geoffrey Page's 'you're just as bloody conceited as before'; in America, the embittered reject, alongside the charmer and the lover; Rosie's 'rather jolly creature'; Brigadier Haydon on him, 'full of a glorious glowing confidence that nothing was too big, too difficult, or too frightening for him'; Eric Linklater: 'He would talk, now like a three-quarter running with a ball in his hands; then listen like a priest in a Chinese temple'; Sir Sholto Douglas on him as 'someone goaded' and difficult to understand; and Mary's portraits of the arrogance, the comedy, the 'black despair', the Blimp, the enchantment, and many other vignettes, some of them even in his sleep. It is a rich gallery for so very young a man, with only one book to his name, more than for most people three times his age. Another belongs to October. It was done by Monsignor Vance, who had never set eyes on Richard, though he had read *The Last Enemy*. He was invited to a dinner party to meet him, and sent Mary his impressions afterwards. Most were written the next morning; from internal evidence, some sentences must have been added after Richard's death.

As he walked into the room, I was struck by his stature and bearing. He walked with great alertness and yet there was

something in his poise and footfall that indicated a 'brake' on his
forward movement. He was undecided about something of
moment or had made a difficult or, perhaps, reluctant decision.
(In point of fact, though I did not know it, he had just decided
to return to the Air Force.) It was emphatically not the bearing
of a young man who strode 'breast forward' into life. Later, as
he strode down Piccadilly after dinner, I caught the lightness of
his step, the rhythm of his movements and a certain 'huddled-
togetherness' of bearing. He was, I thought, seeking comfort
within, and finding none . . .

On listening to his voice I recorded the impression of a vibrant
personality, strong in passion, violent in determination, concentrated in self-determination and sensitive to a degree – not only
for himself but, it might also be, for others. There was a plaintive
note, when he spoke softly, which told of great power to
experience inner pain and anguish. It sounded as if he were
accustomed to question himself and his own purposes, unduly
perhaps, and perhaps mercilessly. It had a gentleness, a modu-
lation and a note of compassion unusual in youth; it was the
voice of one who had suffered in body and mind keenly and
terribly. To me it was a most appealing voice.

I was struck above all by the extraordinary beauty of his eyes.
In that particular light they seemed almost of a china blue,
luminous, keen, intelligent, experiencing. I have rarely seen
such wonderful eyes in any man's head: they seemed to scan
one's mind and inward purposes.

As he spoke a few conventional words of greeting, I felt
immediately the impact of his personality; strong to the point of
violence, keen, vivid and, in some undefined way, unbending. I
noticed nothing of disfigurement in his face for at least two hours
and this is, perhaps, the most remarkable fact of our encounter
for, to my confusion, I am painfully sensitive to any physical
disfigurement, which may readily lead in my case to actual
sickness. It often needs no little self-discipline to enable me to
talk to one who is sadly burnt in face or hand. After two hours I
did notice that his upper lip was a feat of surgery, that his nose
had been re-made, that the eye-brows were artificial and patch-

ily inartistic, that his eye-lids had been grafted and that his face was terribly battered and scarred. Yet I ask myself now . . . if one noticed poise and footfall, how fail to observe scar and patch and terrifying disfigurement . . . The fact remains; when I began to notice the marks of his suffering and the heroic efforts at repair, they seemed to me of no significance whatever. The eye-brows slightly irritated me because they were so unnecessarily patchy. Only a maimed hand aroused in me a deep sense of pity. It was this hand which, in all probability, afterwards cost him his life.

I found Richard youthful, argumentative and wonderfully decided. He rejoiced in telling anybody that he or she was wrong, though the opinion was chronicled without truculence. It was not discourtesy nor aggressiveness, nor even forthright-ness: it was just a man quietly thinking aloud. Obviously too he loved to win an argument and felt hurt if the tide of conversation flowed against his view . . . His was a quiveringly sensitive spirit, endowed with a strange alertness and with a passion for experience. He wished, it would appear, to seize life, to know it, to live it, almost, or so it seemed, he wished to wrestle with life and to 'throw' it. This sensitive spirit had developed about itself a number of heavy screens which nothing would induce him willingly to disclose. And what were the screens? They seemed to me principally a fund of robust undergraduate humour and a tendency to laugh at everything, including himself; an unwillingness to take any emotion or feeling of his own seriously (but why should a man mistrust his feelings? They are often the truest things in him); a keen irony; an undefined, to me undefined, sense of humour (those gleaming eyes were too searchingly intelligent not to enjoy the incongruity of things); an occasional cynicism uncanny for youth; a pose of self-assur-ance, a pose almost of defiance, and a masterful self-assertive-ness. The screens were many and I venture to think that none but a select few were allowed to pass beyond . . . Naturally, in order to live, every person of acute sensitiveness will develop harder surfaces and enwrap himself in outer coverings. Richard's wrappings were many and the surfaces were setting hard for one so young.

Apart from a desire to experience life to the full and to share the experiences of others insofar as they might help, he seemed, without being an intellectual, to be possessed by a mighty intellectual curiosity and wonder. He wished to know everything, to glean the necessary facts in the speediest fashion and to form his own rapid judgment with a defiant regard only for the truth of things and – what is rarer still – with utter truthfulness of mind. Was he straining life for his books? I wondered. Again, he seemed to have a passion for beauty and wished to pursue with inner fidelity its many lovely forms. It was of beauty and its meaning that we spoke for some time at our dinner party. What he said was of little importance; it was his zest and a lovable diffidence of approach that gave a clue to the real man.

Let me emphasise, therefore, my abiding impressions. Of an impact and thrust upon life, linked in some intangible way with a sensitive spirit's recoil; of a thirst for experience; of a passionate intellectual curiosity, linked with the rare gift of truthfulness of mind; of a humble but resolute search for beauty. I even wondered if he could ever be really humble in the presence of anything but beauty. I recorded these things at first light next day and sent them to [Mary], remarking that Richard was indeed a striking personality.

Yet there was one other impression not transmitted [to Mary], that I recorded with no lack of vividness soon after we had parted and more especially as I wrote of Richard the next day. I was convinced – how I know not, nor would it be useful to enquire – that in the innermost secret places of his being there had just been waged and concluded a terrible and mighty struggle between Life and Death; that he had passed through a veritable torment of hopes that carolled and fears that hissed; that he had endured, doubtless with high courage and dogged resolution, agonies of apprehension, and that the man to whom I bade goodbye was on his way to keep a chosen appointment with Death. Let me try to be truthfully clear. Of course I had no conviction that he would die soon – if he were still alive the impression would be equally valid – and no knowledge whatever of his immediate return to the hazardous life of a pilot. If anyone had told me of the decision, I should have laid it aside as criminal irresponsibility on the part of the medical men and of the authorities, and as recklessness, utter recklessness, however lovable, on Richard's part. I should have dismissed it as impossible, as a waste of life and as madness, however courageous. No! Of all this I knew and thought nothing. Indeed I was not 'thinking' at all in any ordinary or technical sense, but if the impression made upon me may be put into words – and how otherwise express it unless it be by a symphony of sounds? – it must be recorded that in his innermost heart Richard knew that he was keeping – though for what high motive was not disclosed – an appointment with Death. It must have needed all the moral courage, all the defiance, and all the sensitiveness of his nature to reach this decision.

That is all I knew, and there the record ends.

Chapter Nine
October - November 1942

❧

The remaining letters during October are the last interchange that has survived. There are no more from Mary, apart from her final letter of farewell.

On the 17th Richard had written, 'I shall go back, I think.' Four days later, 'I think' has become 'I am sure.' From the 11th until the 22nd they still did not meet, except twice by chance, although he telephoned her every night. Mary went on seeing friends; Richard was finishing 'the trivialities', and preparing for his final Medical Board in mid-November.

The decision which he says, in his letter of 13 October, he has to make alone, is *not* the decision to return to the RAF; that he had already made. What it was, Mary explained in one of her preambles. Two or three days after the letter,

he rang up to say he wanted to see me. He came and told me he felt he wanted to make love to someone else; that he was puzzled and disturbed by having such a feeling, when he was only really happy when he was with me . . .

Her typescript breaks off here, at the bottom of a page, with no page following. The comment that his 'decision' had nothing to do with the RAF is her own manuscript insertion. She need not have made it, and no one would have guessed what the letter really referred to. One can say that it was not of crucial importance to her; that he was being honest, as they had promised one another they always would be; that it was part of his liberty, his nature, that he should enjoy himself away from her, dancing, chattering, drinking; and, in Rosie

171

Kerr's words in her tape-recording, Mary had always assumed, bearing in mind the difference of age, and now, particularly, his tensions, that he would have a glancing affair or two with someone nearer his years. She had a very big heart, and was prepared for the consequences. But for all that, one cannot pretend that the message did not hurt her, however little it took from their own relationship, the foundations of which were secure. It is not mentioned again by either.

Her long letter of 19 October has the old note of sadness veiled by irony at his offhandedness and her own romanticism, but not of bitterness. It is *'l'esprit très gai'* trying to get the better of *'l'âme sanglante et désolée'*, and written in full awareness that 'you do not want emotion'.

On 22 October he made his speech at Foyle's literary luncheon. After that he was with her almost every evening until the end of the month. Her letter of the 27th, and her diary entry of the 30th, are a recovery of happiness.

Richard to Mary:

> 26 Rutland Court
> Knightsbridge
> S.W.7
> Sunday [dated by Mary 11 Oct]

Darling, ·

You have been much in my thoughts and I have just re-read your last letter [of 9 October]. It is so full of understanding – all your letters are, and I never get over my astonishment, when each is better than the last.

I am now very nearly at the end of the tunnel: my decision is as good as made. Thursday, in fact, will be in the nature of Ave atque Vale to the literary world. Eric Linklater is still at me (I dine with him & the Peter Flemings on Monday), but even him I have half convinced.

After leaving you on Friday I had a completely escapist evening & I must confess, enjoyed myself immoderately. I took —— dancing until 4 a.m. & became progressively drunker and

172

happier. The whole thing was so utterly detached from reality – so unlike me, and she is most attractive to gaze upon, while one listens to the melodious flow of one's own verbiage.

Saturday to Fighter Command with the script & to make arrangements for the nature of my return.

To-day, writing, reading, and seeing no one . . . Enjoy your week-end my sweet, but not too much . . .

Richard to Mary:

26 Rutland Court
13th October (Tuesday)

Darling, please don't get too cold or go too far away. I have no right to ask it of you, but in a little while now I shall be all right. I have a decision to make and I want to make it quite alone – and try to be honest with myself about my reasons. In three weeks time I shall know the answer.

Your letter to me was quite wonderful. How very alike we are, in spite of all these surface differences.

I am just off to dinner with Rache [Lovat Dickson] after a hectic day at the studio. We are certainly working against time.

Think of me a little my darling. I feel you very near to me. Is that illusion? I don't think so. I'm sure I'd know if you shut yourself right off.

Richard

Mary to Richard:

Sunday
18.10.42

My darling, for two days I have had the desire, without the opportunity, to write to you. My thoughts have circled round you in different moods, and there has been so much I have wanted to communicate to you. Yet to-night in the utter silence of the sleeping house I feel shut off and unable to reach you. I wonder why?

I wonder where you are.

173

Last night I dreamt you came and, kneeling beside the bed, you took me in your arms in silence and leaned your cheek against mine. Just that and nothing more. Even in my sleep I must have been profoundly touched by this gesture so unlike you, that I woke to find my eyes were drenched with tears.

Apart from these surface dreams which have no future in them, I *know* we spend our sleep together. On waking my thoughts don't leap forward to you – they are *there* and linger *back* on the wings of recent memory, in the semi-consciousness of waking. So that at the first moments in waking I find my mood sometimes of happiness, and sometimes disturbing, without being able to remember why.

I wish sometimes you answered some of my letters. I don't mean point by point, but often I have suddenly remembered something I have written to you about, and have no idea if you agreed or disagreed. In the end it is mighty like talking to myself, only more boring. I have got bored now and must sleep.

Goodnight my darling.

Mary

P.S. It was extraordinary seeing you suddenly at Yvonne's [Mrs Hamish Hamilton] the other day. It was the very last thing I expected, and as I walked home with your script I felt happy, which again was the last thing I expected. Why? I said to myself, since the only thing you said to me was that my nails were dirty.

Mary to Richard:

19.10.42

My darling, I often wish I did not possess that *'esprit très gai'*, which goes inevitably, it seems, with *'l'âme sanglante et désolée'*. In plain English understatement, I am suffering this evening from melancholia, nostalgia, and what have you.

Last night, after writing you that somewhat uninspiring letter, I proceeded to dream that I had a baby. Very small and fair, who died before my very eyes on the pavement in Sloane Street

174

of spinal meningitis! I still suffer from the memory, it seems, and then you have rung up and told me you are ill.

I know that you are not very ill. I tell myself this, and still it all crowds in on to me that I cannot be of any use to you – that I cannot be with you to share your gaiety or your depressions. Nothing that I have to weigh against all this helps at all. I just feel I am, as regards you, a failure.

All this bores you at present, I know. You don't want to be bothered with emotions. Quite right. I'm bored too now I've written it down. But we did say we would tell each other what we felt.

Don't you have your ups and downs? Are you always so sure, calm, and serene about everything as you seem? Have you really achieved such power of detachment, that you never feel even a sadness at this separation? Did you feel no quickening of the heart when you saw me the other day? Were my jet black nails the only thing you noticed?

When you have thought up some good answers to these questions, I would like to know the *rock-bottom truth*. The answers to perfectly IDIOTIC questions are always interesting.

If I was much in your thoughts during the week-end, what did you think?

All this sounds as though I were 'in one of my moods', as one's Nanny was wont to say. But if I am able to feel like this, and you are not, there must be something wrong somewhere. This is cold reason to appeal to your cold reason.

You always tell me what you want, but how seldom do you tell me what you think? I know you don't realise how little you reveal your heart to me. At rock bottom I understand you can't at the moment, so take no notice of all this. It has to come out, and there is no one else I talk to . . .

I am glad, darling, that you are nearly out of the tunnel concerning your decision [to go back], yet I find myself *with* Linklater. We on the outside could not help finding ourselves on the same side. True justice should not have put the decision on you at all. I love and honour you for weighing it all up with courage to search for the truth and honesty of judgment, but I

175

still deplore the lack of justice that should allow the weighing to be done by you. The camel-driver has his thoughts; the camel, he has his.

I was very happy with you in a sort of crystallised ether over the week-end. It made me feel disembodied and very light and clear in the head. I heard myself from afar being quite brilliant and quick as lightning. I thought of Rebecca West, whom I met for the first time at a dinner and who has no four-wheel brakes to her tongue, and who, looking across the table at me, said 'The *extraordinary* thing about you is that you are very intelligent'.

I shall be awfully proud of you in my secret heart on Thursday [Foyle's luncheon], and my hand will be in yours. I know you will be all right, but if you feel your tongue might cleave, Barnszky [a doctor] has a thing which calms the nerves and clears the brain.

I have turned down the Ministry of Supply regardless of the salary, and am going to the Americans. It suits the general scheme of my life better. After the war I shall retire to an island with you, and write a book in 4 vols, entitled 'Human Nature in the Raw', dedicated to Mr Luce.

Nobody can make me laugh like you do. It's a pity, isn't it?

Mary

Richard's speech at Foyle's was the first and only occasion he had a captive audience; that audience hoped for in America, for which he had been found too repulsive.

He talked about 'after the war'. It is now forty-five years after: and it has been strange, researching this book among his old haunts at Trinity, and thinking about it as I look at Mary's cottage in Wales, with the 'face like a cheeky child'. So much is the same. The waterfall beside the cottage is the same. The stones, the lawns, the catalpa trees of Trinity – the same. Even some of the questions he poses in his speech are much the same. And I am the same, in one respect, as he was. I too am a survivor. Friends of mine were also killed, nearly all of them in one night, that very same night he finished his course at the Staff College. I too thought and talked and wrote about

176

a dream of Britain after the war. Six years older than he was, I had had time to knot myself into the fashionable dogmatic conclusions, and time also, later, to unwind from them. But even if he had had the temperament, he did not have the luxury of that leisure. War came upon him before he had even taken his degree; and though he knew a little of Germany and France, he had seen next to nothing of England outside the University, and not much there outside his College, the river, and the airfield. Yet the war had already done for him what it did for tens of thousands of us who were older. He had become concerned.

Sitting in a room almost next to his old rooms, with his papers by me, I read Denise's account. Denise called him Dick.

Before his speech he and Eric [Linklater] and Rache and I met at the Dorchester. Eric said to Dick, 'What will you have?'
'Whiskey.'
'Have something else,' said Eric, only just omitting the 'dear boy'.
'Whiskey,' replied Dick, unperturbed, and proceeded to continue his order several times, hugely enjoying the growing concern on our faces.

And I imagine them all listening at Grosvenor House, with Mary and his parents, and the guests, some men, some women, in uniform, and the rationed food.

It reads as rather an ambling rough-cut speech, that begs many questions, but has a bearing on his fate, and throws light on him. He speaks of himself not as an artist 'in the strict sense of the word', but as one of those 'who would dearly love to be creative artists, but are not; those of us who are novelists, art critics, columnists, and who write, not because we have something in us which must come out, something to give, but because we have the facility – it is the thing we do best, and it makes of us a success, gives us power, and a certain position . . .' He confesses to being 'a passionate believer in free trade, private enterprise, and laissez-faire'. It comes with an odd ring from that time. No place for Marxism? But he was growing interested. Round about then, he decided to do battle with Victor

177

Gollancz, doyen of the Left Book Club, and, taking his customary and necessary short-cut, wrote to his old English master at Shrewsbury, Mr McEachran, for 'half a dozen of the best and most convincing arguments for liberalism, individualism, and so forth', as he might have ordered half a dozen eggs. 'They should be good enough to make Mr Gollancz unmask his batteries, for I want to see what his case looks like in action.' Unhappily this confrontation never took place.

To his audience at Foyle's he took up roughly the position of the anarchist with a small 'a'; 'I have always abhorred the State, or any form of control from above . . . I should like to live to see the day when a Government realised that its only proper function is to vote itself out of existence.' He recognised that such a day was a long way off, and that 'after this war some form of planned society is absolutely inevitable'. Diffidently he mentioned his book, and that 'emotional' peroration. He and his kind had believed before all in self-realisation and in personal relationships. What about that 'Humanity' he had invoked at the end, to whose cause he claimed to have been converted? What did he mean? he asks, interrogating himself at least as much as the audience, and comes to his main theme, 'Which of us is a Fascist?'

If we believe that man is basically good, we must accept mankind as a whole, 'or else call ourselves Fascists. Do we then accept the Australian aborigine? No, we do not.' And 'from excluding him, it is not such a very big step before we exclude the sweating masses at Marble Arch tube station – those masses who prevent us getting our seat in the train, and clutter up the restaurants when we are home on leave . . . unable to avoid them, we should like to throw them out. Every thinking man has something of the Fascist in him.'

He supposes that, having lost the war, we have a collaborationist Government here, 'just as they have in France'; or have not even lost the war, but simply have a Fascist Government under another name. 'What will our position be . . . will we go Nazi?' And to illustrate the theme he comes to the world that he knows best.

Many artists, journalists, and authors, together with those of us who profess and call ourselves intellectuals, are now in the

Services – men who before the war were a success, had a position. Let us take from them an imaginary example. Let us assume that one of us before the war was a successful art-critic, with a column read and admired daily in some newspaper. Now he is in the Air Force; nobody reads his column; nobody knows his name. He has become a cog. He does not like it. He despises the dull, factual men around him, their lack of imagination, perception, awareness, sensibility. 'What have I to do with thee, Oh sweating masses?' Let us say that he is sitting in the Mess, feeling bored with the Station Medical Officer, who can do nothing but tell garrulous and slightly drunken stories, but who before the war had a large and flourishing practice . . . or is irritated by that very dull pilot sitting beside him, with a glass of beer in one hand and the *Daily Mirror* in the other; that pilot who is limited in his expression of emotion to the words 'Wizard' and 'dim', and who reacts in just the same way to the most cultivated of women and to a barmaid, for to him they are both simply Women. But that boy realises himself in the sky; that is where his life lies. Our friend would say he had no sensibility, but how wrong he would be! . . . in the air the pilot acquires awareness, acquires sensibility, from the combination of deep humility and immense power that, alone with the wind and the stars, every pilot must feel. Neither that doctor nor that pilot will go Fascist. [One wonders, but here it need only be in passing, if he had not yet learned what doctors did to inmates of concentration camps; or had never heard of the early and brilliant record as a pilot of one who was by now Field-Marshal Hermann Goering, or of that flying circus of D'Annunzio, another founder of Fascism. He goes on:]

What of our friend? It seems to me that in his frustration he is an intellectual snob. If his life cannot be apart from those he despises, if he cannot ignore them, then he will seek to dominate them. And is not this man representative of all of us, of anyhow the subconscious in all of us, whose art is not great enough to be a thing in itself, but merely a means to power? For Fascism is not a national creed: it is a state of mind – and all those who love power more than people will go Fascist, if Fascism is a majority movement. We must each of us ask ourselves . . . are there no conceivable circumstances in which I might turn Fascist? If we can face up to that question, the battle's already half-won; then if we can, having seen the danger and looked into our hearts, honestly say 'It's all right, I shall not fail', we shall have a spiritual armour that, come what may, will see us through to the end.

The speech evidently met with great applause, perhaps rather muted from any novelists, art critics, or columnists who happened to be among the audience. The theme is concern for people versus desire for power or success, and there are echoes in the letters. Remember, for example, his letter to Kennington: 'the answer is simple – does one write for power, or because one has something to give?'; the pilots he had sometimes despised when drunk; in his reply to Mary's letter of 'dismissal', his own awareness of power – 'frozen, hard, and powerful!'; and one comprehends that he is thinking of a danger to himself. It is an old, even trite theme, but one he refreshes by coming to it straight from the experience of the war. He is remembering the Carburys and Berrys he wrote of in his book, 'the tough practical men who had come up the hard way, to whom Britain must look . . .'.

And it strikes me, lying these forty-five years later with the carbon copy of his speech beside me on the lawns of Trinity, or by the waterfall at Llanfrothen, that just as the lawns are the same, as the waterfall is the same, so is the memory the same, for myself and many others, of all those of all ranks, in whom self-reliance, imagination, and many other qualities flowered momentarily only to be struck down and wasted, and of the cohesion and the common purpose that has long since vanished.

He had been speaking to a circle of friends; of cultured friends. How many there, I wonder, knew or guessed that, within a month, he would be leaving them for those others who, by their standards, 'might be lacking in any form of feeling, but who in their own way were fully orientated . . . who realised themselves in the sky'. And would he find what he was looking for?

*　*　*

180

Richard dined with Mary the evening after his speech, was with her the following evening, Friday 23 October, and again on Sunday. Something must have happened on the Friday, which transcended the past weeks of separation and conflict, and set a seal on the letters earlier in the month. He wrote to her on Saturday, suddenly answering all her queries in a kind of parody of his hard, impersonal self, as if she had posted him a questionnaire, with the point in an off-hand postscript:

Saturday [24 October]

Darling

I don't know about ROCK-BOTTOM TRUTH, but here are your answers.

Q. Do I ever have ups and downs?
A. Yes.
Q. Am I always so sure, calm, & serene about everything as I seem?
A. Yes.
Q. Have I achieved such power of detachment, that I never feel sadness at this separation?
A. No.
Q. Did I feel a quickening of the heart when I saw you at Yvonne's?
A. Yes.
Q. Were your jet black nails the only thing I noticed?
A. No.
Q. If you were much in my thoughts over the week-end, what did I think?
A. Where is she? What is she doing? What is she wearing? What is she thinking? What do I care?
All of which answers are superfluous after Friday night.
Richard

And of that same Friday, looking back over the whole week-end, she had this to say in her own romantic manner, but with a radiance her letters to him had not possessed for months:

181

27.

10.

42. (Tuesday)

My darling – Was it my imagination, but was Sunday a very charming evening? I remember it with a smile and am happy. You asked me a question about the previous Friday night, and I said, 'Yes,' in rather your way – just yes. Shall I answer it in my way? My way, when I am not sitting opposite your mocking smile? When I am writing for companionship – the only companionship I really need?

I always find it difficult to put into words – even to myself – that strange magnetism that exists between us. Something disturbing and exciting, yet with the gift of utter peace. That Friday night I will remember always as a fragment of perfection. So strange that it should come then – so suddenly & unexpectedly in those incongruous surroundings – a vision of spirit and body such as I have never before experienced. Nothing can take that moment from our lives; nothing for me has ever touched it. No starlit sky above the Mediterranean shore, with the scent of magnolia in the warm night air of the South could have added to that perfection – There was nothing existing apart from you and me – Alone, together, and as one.

Whenever that inevitable antagonism rises up between us, when you are at your most unbearable Bassington, and I most maddening, so that you long to beat me, I shall remember and hug the memory to my secret heart. *This* is my answer.

My darling, I take your head between my hands and kiss your lips.

They were together again on 27 October, and again on Sunday the 30th. Five weeks before she had written to him that 'the very memory of the few occasions I saw real happiness in your face strikes me each time in wonderment, as though a miracle had happened'. Evidently it had happened that Sunday, for in her diary she put against the 30th, 'Dine Richard. Miracle.'

'Miracle' is, during his lifetime, the last word about their relationship in Mary's handwriting that has survived.

They spent many evenings together during November. The friends, like Job's comforters, had withdrawn, their counsels and their supplications fruitless. In terms of a Greek tragedy the hero has now opened all the sealed envelopes, read his fate, and is steeled to face it; all that remains will be the ultimate rendezvous, and the concluding comments of the chorus. But not quite so in this story of real life, where the place of the Fates is to be taken by the faceless ones of the Medical Board. With them it will rest whether to pass him fit or not. If yes, then he can go forth like someone doomed according to the ancient style; if not, then all his stern accumulation of resolve will have been, theatrically, anticlimax.

He was with Rosie Kerr on the morning of his interview. He had not told McIndoe, as he should have done, that he was going. Rosie recorded him as not at all confident he would get through, and terribly worried for his mother, to whom he knew it would be a desperate blow. He was soon back. They had passed him. The encounter had been quite short. Few questions had been asked him. It had been left to him to declare whether or not he was equal to operational flying, and he had said that he was. 'Was he jubilant?' Rosie was asked. 'No,' she replied. 'Not jubilant. Not at all jubilant.'

Jubilation seems to have been left for later. 'One day,' wrote Sir Sholto Douglas in his memoirs, 'he appeared in my office [at Bentley Priory], triumphantly waving a favourable medical report, and he called on me to live up to my promise. I felt in honour bound to keep that promise even though I believed that, for all that the doctors might say, he was not fit for operational flying. But I did tell him that I considered that it would be impossible for him to go back to single-seater fighters, and that instead he should go to an Operational Training Unit with a view to becoming a night-fighter pilot, in which the flying was not as rough-and-tumble as it was in the day-fighters. My proposal was accepted gratefully enough, although I sensed that Hillary was a little disappointed and he went off to a night

Operational Training Unit, with plans at the back of his mind about possibly joining Max Aitken's squadron . . .'

Here there might still be a moment for a chorus. One can imagine them, moving on to the stage and dividing into two opposing chants, one side intoning the arguments for passing him, as put by his biographer:

The Royal Air Force is an enlightened Service . . . and had, I think rightly, conceived the view that young men desperately injured who craved to go back to fight again should, if it were at all possible, be allowed to do so; that it was better to lose a plane and the man, though this would not necessarily be the outcome, than have a nervous frustrated psychological case, not injured enough to be discharged, carrying on a ground job, and infecting with his disillusionment and despair all the others;

and the other side reiterating Rosie's (and other people's) astonishment:

Incomprehensible. He was not fit. They had only to say, once and for all, that they could not afford to lose more planes, let alone two lives, his and his radio-observer's, and reject him. After a few weeks he would have accepted it, and found something else. Incomprehensible.

Rosie spoke with feeling, not only for Richard. Later in the war she became engaged to a brilliant fighter-pilot in the Free French Air Force, Commandant Jacques-Henri Schloesing. He had been awarded the George Cross and had shot down eighteen planes. In February 1942 he was shot down himself, and received severe burns. The French Resistance nursed him back to health and enabled him to escape. He was treated at East Grinstead, but after D-Day resolved to return. He was killed on the day of the liberation of Paris. Two French generals had come to see Rosie's mother, to ask her to ask Rosie to dissuade him. Rosie declined. It was not for her, she had felt, but the authorities. Mary had felt, and acted or refrained from action, in the same way about Richard, although 'I find myself *with* Linklater'. How much it cost her to hold back, her farewell to him reveals; how much it meant to him, he wrote to her soon after he had been passed.

> Rutland Court
> 19.11.42

Mary darling,

I can't find it in my heart to write much at the moment, but I want you to know that I am grateful to you. I know my instinct is right about this thing and you have never questioned my decision. Bless you for that.

I say very little, but though you upbraid me for it I think you know well enough that you are the one person who means anything to me.

Just keep faith and I shall be all right & when I come through, which I know I shall – it will be gain – not loss.

I love you with all my heart.

> Richard

The same night, alone in his club, he wrote to Edwyna Hillary:

Mother darling,

I just want to say thank you for always having faith, for not questioning my decision, for never betraying that you feel unhappy and above all, for your unfailing sense of humour.

We do not often speak together about it and for this and many other things I am so deeply grateful. I know what you think about my going back, and if I were outside looking on I would agree with you. Yet I am glad the decision has been left to me. One can go on arguing the thing out rationally ad nauseam. I can write, I am more useful on the ground, I only want to go back so that people may say, 'Well done!', and to get a medal, I am frightened of going back, I only want to make a name, and so forth.

Finally one must listen to one's instinct, and the time will come when I shall know that my instinct was right and my reason wrong. You must try not to worry about me and to

185

have the same faith I have that I shall be all right, for I know it.

It may be that —— has the inside information to which he pretends and that I am to be given something else to do. It may be a thousand things will happen. I do not know. But that it will be all right, I do know. So please try not to be unhappy and lonesome . . . I should not be at peace if I did not go back. Afterwards it will bear fruit and I shall write.

There are few things to which one can cling in this comic war. To see straight and know where one is heading is perhaps the most important of all.

God bless you always,
Richard

He wrote a letter for the Commanding Officer of the night-fighter station on the Border to which he had been posted, requesting that, if he was killed, the telegram announcing his death should be sent to Mary four hours before his mother was told. He believed that Mary would be better able to 'take it'.

He made his will, unwitnessed. Apart from his bequest to Mary of Eric Kennington's portrait, and other clauses,

To Mary Booker I also leave £20 that she may give a dinner for me to which she will invite Michael & Barbara Astor, Denise Maxwell-Woosnam, Eric Linklater, & Rache Lovat Dickson.

To Tony Tollemache, I leave my gold watch.

To Merle Oberon (Lady Korda), I leave my gold aeroplane clip.

To my mother I leave my everlasting love and gratitude . . .

I want no one to go into mourning for me.

As to whether I am buried or cremated – it is immaterial to me, but as the flames have had one try I suggest they might get their man in the end.

I want no one to feel sorry for me. In an age where no one can. make a decision that is not dictated from above, it was left to me to make the most important decision of all. I am eternally grateful to the stupidity of those who left me that decision. In my life I had a few friends. I learnt a little wisdom and a little patience. What more could a man ask for?

This phrase about 'the stupidity of those who left me that decision' cannot mean those who vainly attempted to dissuade him. I take it to refer to the bureaucracy, who had only to tell him, once and for all, that it was out of the question for him to go back, but allowed themselves to be persuaded that he could. It is omitted in Lovat Dickson's biography, and by those who followed him without reading the original manuscript.

Richard did all this on the night of 19 November. On the 23rd he had dinner alone with Mary in her new flat. Her furniture had been moved in that day. It was her first night in that place they had hoped for so ardently since the spring, where 'what he needed was to be able to come in and sit by the hour and talk', where 'we will read all through our meals and afterwards too'. Next day his father Michael Hillary saw him into the train at Kings Cross, said goodbye, and suddenly reappeared with a packet of cigarettes; and Richard went off to the aerodrome.

Sir Sholto Douglas, who was about to take over command in the Middle East, heard of Richard's death on his way overseas. In his memoirs he concluded his account of him:

There have been many times when, in thinking about what happened, I have reproached myself for having allowed Richard Hillary to win me over. I should never have made him that promise. Perhaps in doing what he did he found something of whatever it was that he was looking for. But there was an additional feature about his death that has always troubled me. There has never been a full explanation of the reason for the crash in which this talented young man died. That was sad enough; but in it the young navigator who was training with Hillary was also killed. That adds to my own feelings of regret about having allowed Hillary, through a rash promise on my part, to have his own way.

One does not always encounter such generous admissions of an error of judgment in great commanders.

Here the play, if this were a play, might be expected to end. The truth was otherwise. Only the interchange of letters ends, since all Mary's written to Richard at the aerodrome were destroyed. His to her continue. The story continues. He had another decision to make, and the faceless ones yet another entry.

Chapter Ten
November - December 1942

Mary wrote to Richard at the aerodrome almost every day, and kept his replies. All her letters were burnt by the RAF. What they contained we can only guess from his replies. 'We had that extraordinary affinity of mind and spirit', she wrote to his mother, 'that he talked and wrote to me as if to his other self. Over and over again I would ask him a question, and I would receive the answer in the letter crossing mine . . . It helped that aloneness that was so terrible up there.'

Rosie also wrote; her letters too were burnt, and doubtless others from other friends. What documents went into the flames may be guessed from the following masterly letter, written by Richard's father, a warm-hearted, upright and straightspoken man, from whom Richard had much of his independence. Dated two months after Richard's death, it is addressed to the RAF officer who came to London to inform his parents how he had been killed.

> 26 Rutland Court
> Knightsbridge S.W.7
> 8th March 1943

Dear Group-Captain L.,

I want to thank you most sincerely on behalf of my wife and myself for your very great kindness and thoughtfulness in coming personally to explain to us the circumstances of our son's death. I bitterly resent those circumstances. One braces oneself to meet the hazards of action against the enemy, but finds it very difficult to accept the senseless waste of a valuable life in training. However, our minds are now at rest, and we can disregard any rumours that reach us. The truth, however gruesome, is preferable to the uncertainty in which we have been living.

The position in regard to the letters and papers which were burnt is not so satisfactory, and I am writing to say some of the things I had to leave unsaid in the short time available on Saturday.

I do not question the motives of your Effects Officer, but the wisdom and prudence of his actions are open to grave doubt. His mistaken zeal in his attempts to save pain has dealt us perhaps the blow next hardest to our son's death, for, apart from the indignity of his and others' inquisitorial examination of our son's letters and papers, we have been irrevocably prevented from knowing our son's last thoughts and state of mind in the last days of his life. To anyone not entirely devoid of the finer feelings and perceptions, the destruction of his correspondence because of some quite unimportant letters from women suggests the sort of callous act that springs from a form of moral righteousness that does incalculable harm.

Being the man you are, I quite understand your readiness to support your Effects Officer's actions; but it seems to me that, in exercising moral censorship of my son's affairs, he gratuitously usurped a private right that no amount of blessing by you can extenuate or justify, especially when the censorship was exercised with a rigidity of mind which apparently did not admit of any discretion, and a criterion was applied that was surely more suitable for a Girls' Sunday School than a fighting service. I could understand indiscreet letters not being sent to a young wife; but my son was not married, and the fact that he had a father was either overlooked, or his father was not considered competent to decide the moral issues involved. I maintain it was for me, and not your Effects Officer, to decide upon the disposal of my son's letters and papers; and I should have thought the obvious course would have been to seal these up and send them to me by Squadron-Leader Gregory, when he accompanied the body.

Having expressed these views, I should not wish to pursue

the matter further. My son is dead, and nothing else matters. And I loathe publicity. But you will appreciate that other people are concerned, whose interests are of a different kind; and they have already made it abundantly clear that they are profoundly dissatisfied with the position. It is common knowledge that my son was engaged in the preparation for the background of another book, and several people had seen what he had already written, and were aware of what he was writing. The letters to him from some of these people were, at his request, written in narrative form with a view to incorporation in a publication at a later date. Most of these people are closely associated with literature and the press and, with all respect to your Effects Officer, flatly refuse to believe his statement that Richard had written nothing at Charter Hall. On the contrary, they know that he wrote a daily journal; and part of that journal, written up to the 4th January, is in the possession of one of his friends. They know too that some of the matter he had written was derogatory to the administration of the R.A.F. Station at Charter Hall, and would at once conclude that the material was destroyed with a view to the suppression of damaging criticism.

Almost daily I am told of letters that were written to my son and were not returned; and only this morning I received a letter from the Chief Intelligence Officer at Hornchurch, stating that he wrote to Richard on 6th November. I enclose a copy of this letter. It was not returned and was presumably one of those destroyed.

Ever since Richard's death the press have been trying to obtain information as to what he had left of written material, and two at least of the leading London papers have made offers to buy this material for publication. So far they have been told that the effects have not been delivered. Now they have to be told that there are no literary effects, and I shall have to ask my son's publishers, who dealt with these matters for my son, both to close off these enquiries, and in addition not to expect any material for the Memoir which they have already commissioned two popular authors, Eric Linklater and Arthur Koestler, to write.

It is all very disturbing. Like my son, the letters have been uselessly and unnecessarily destroyed, and nothing can bring them back. It is only another instance of the mischief and harm that can be done by well-intentioned stupidity and moral righteousness, and a lack of courage to face criticism.

I am sorry to have had to write at such length, but I wanted you to know the position. All I ask personally is that I may be allowed to forget the whole painful episode as quickly as possible, and for that reason I shall not expect a reply to this letter.

Yours sincerely,

Michael Hillary

Eric Kennington had just visited Mrs Hillary about his picture 'The Heart of England,' which he offered her as a tribute to Richard, and wrote to Mary, whom she put in charge of distribution of reprints:

March 8

. . . She was suffering from a foul blow received the day before. No doubt it will strike you too. They burnt his letters and Mss. For myself I feel a savage resentment against that destruction. I know so well the stage and players where the tragedy was carried out, having lived on numerous stations, and have seen the pain (though not so severe) that such callousness causes.

And on 7 April Mrs Cazalet Keir, Member of Parliament for East Islington, asked the Secretary of State for Air, Sir Archibald Sinclair,

whether it is the usual practice of the Ministry to destroy after their death, letters and personal papers belonging to officers and other ranks killed on service?

Sir Archibald Sinclair: No, sir. The normal practice is to hold the private books and papers of deceased personnel in safe custody until they can be handed over to the person entitled to receive them.

192

Mrs Cazalet Keir: Is it a fact that under the regulations no station commander has the right to destroy any private letters or papers?
Sir Archibald Sinclair: Yes, sir. That is so.

Thirty-seven years later Gordon Watkins, a senior producer at BBC Television, considered making a documentary programme about Mary's and Richard's letters. He managed to trace the officer to whom Richard's father had written, by then a retired Air Commodore, who also turned out to have taken command of the aerodrome about three weeks before Richard was killed. Watkins asked about the destruction of Richard's papers. In November 1980 this officer replied with a long and helpful letter, in the course of which he said: '. . . a word about the duty of Courts of Adjustment and therefore of an Effects Officer. Apart from the duties implied by the title it is an unwritten law in the three Services and strictly adhered to, that the Effects Officer should destroy any letters, papers, correspondence etc., which might cause pain to next of kin, relations, etc.' Some letters had been found among Richard's belongings which 'had obviously been written to him by a married girl . . . They could have caused shock or pain to the parents (or to some parents) – who could tell? Not least, the girl concerned could have been put in a very tricky position.' The Effects Officer therefore destroyed them.

As for notes for or a manuscript of a book, 'the Effects Officer had searched everywhere and there was no trace and I believed him'. The Effects Officer turned out to be the same man to whom Richard refers with some affection in a letter on New Year's Day as being in charge of R/T speech training and also running a music circle at the aerodrome. Years later, during the sixties, the Air Commodore happened to meet him. 'He had returned to the Guildhall School of Music after the war and had just retired . . . I said we were both now out of the service and could talk quite freely. I told him I'd often wondered what had happened to that Ms. Once again he swore he had never found it and knew nothing about it. And once again I believed him with complete confidence.'

* * *

The name of the aerodrome to which Richard had been posted was Charter Hall. It may stand for the deadest of all dead ends, the graveyard of all illusions, desolate, run-down, swept by freezing winds, abstract as a setting for a play by Samuel Beckett. 'The forgotten man's last stop,' Richard called it in a letter to America, relishing, if only as an artist, its *Umheimlichkeit*. Lawrence's Uxbridge was by comparison mere melodrama. Warmth came from Mary's letters, the first of which was already waiting for him; and an immediate ray of hope from the off-chance that he might get leave for Michael Astor's wedding in London on 28 November.

Richard to Mary:

25th November	Officers Mess
	R.A.F. Station
	Charter Hall
	near Duns. Berwickshire
	a million miles from anywhere

My darling,

Your letter greeted me on my arrival very late in the evening. I crept away with it to my wooden hut two miles away from the Mess and read it. Then I cried myself to sleep . . . until I remembered old ——, and then I had to laugh . . .

I am stealing odd moments between marching – yes, marching – to and from lectures to write this, so it will be very incoherent. I will do better tonight when I get back to my hut.

At the moment I am filled with an overmastering depression.

Later.

We have just had the list of fatal casualties in the last few weeks read out to us as a warning – very encouraging.

I now have a suspicion that I am sitting in a room reserved for instructors – they are of no senior rank, but they look at me oddly.

This is indeed a queer place for journey's end and yet in a way it is good. It is so utterly bare and without human contact that one must at last be self-sufficient. That is the best way to go.

194

But I wish you were here. I shall write to-night, all night if I cannot sleep. Now it's impossible.

I love you
R.

Charter Hall
25th November

My most darling Mary,

I feel like the Hollywood gangster hero, who voluntarily walking back into gaol hears the prison gates clang to behind him for the last time.

First the journey. I left Kings Cross at 10 am and arrived foodless at Berwick about 6 pm – strangely touched by a last gesture of my father, who after bidding me goodbye came back with a packet of cigarettes. I avoided thought all the way up by reading Hesketh Pearson's Life of G.B.S.

At Berwick night had fallen and the platform was cold, but the train to Reston arrived after ten minutes. In the compartment were a couple of youngsters, fresh from training school and eager to get on the course. It was largely to get back into communion with these, that I made up my mind to return in the first place – but I felt outside, or rather not so much outside, but as though I was back again two years, and though somewhat the same they were less fine than those I knew then.

. . . At Reston we changed again and I went to a compartment by myself, and watching the sparks fly by I felt very low and in need of you. Finally at Greenlaw we all decanted, & after half an hour a van trundled us the five miles into the camp. It is perhaps the camp more than anything which is likely to break me.

The sleeping huts are dispersed over a distance of a couple of miles – [in my room] there is no fire, coal being scarce. The walls are horribly damp. All this I could bear if it were not that in the Mess – such as it is – there is no chance of ever being alone, and yet I am alone all the time. This is the end of the world; —— [a senior officer] a cad and a bully, and the ground staff deadbeats who can get in nowhere else.

The whole atmosphere is the one I dread most – emptiness – Do you remember the line in my book about Sunday lunch at Shrewsbury – the bars on the windows, the boys crouched dispiritedly over plates of cold trifle. This is the same.

They have told me that as I am a Flight Lieutenant I need not march to lectures with the others. Kindly meant, but it puts me still further from them. Not that I'm aloof. I think they like me well enough, considering me rather a droll fellow who may save them some 'bullshit'. (They consist of six officers and ten sergeant pilots.)

The telephone in the Mess – the only one I can get at – is in full view of everyone . . . The baths, which have no plugs, are in a separate building, though I don't see why this should worry me, as I shall never have the rapid organising power necessary to fit one in.

The worst moment was an armament lecture – an exact repetition of the one we had at Kinloss [in *The Last Enemy*]. I kept on expecting to look up and see Noel [Agazarian] beside me, instead of which there was a pinched little boy who picked his nose.

All day my eyes have pricked with tears, and now at last in the privacy of my room I have been weeping like a child for an hour. Why? Is it fear? I have not yet seen an aeroplane, and I know not yet whether the night will terrify me or not. Is it just the atmosphere? Very largely, I know. But perhaps this is what they mean in the Air Force by 'lack of moral fibre'. I have often wondered. Maybe this is what happens when a man's nerve goes. And yet I am not *consciously* frightened of anything, merely unutterably wretched and missing you most frightfully.

This is an awfully egotistical letter, and not much of a showing on my first day. But I suddenly know that I should have listened to advice and not come back.

Phyllis Bottome said that it was only Nazis who forced themselves to do things and that that way was unnatural for me. I should like to believe her now, but perhaps that is a mere bleat of fear. Certainly my London period must have sapped my will, but I did not think I would break as quickly as this. And

196

yet it is so largely the surroundings and the sense of being trapped . . .

Funny, your instinct about Kennington . . .

The encounter between Eric Kennington and Richard has something of allegory about it. A stranger comes across a lost traveller, and sets him on his way. In such stories the stranger sometimes gives the traveller a gold token, or a talisman, as Kennington had given Richard Lawrence's *The Mint*. Now it is as though, having taken the road indicated to him, he had found the token not to be of gold, the talisman false, or false for him. The discovery came suddenly, by accident: 'I have been looking through the scant library here and, coming across T. E. Lawrence's letters, I took the book out and, believe it or not, opened at this page – [David] Garnett speaking about Lawrence wanting to go back to the R.A.F. "Since the period at Uxbridge had been a time of great suffering, when he was continually on the verge of breakdown, one wonders whether his will had not become greater than his intelligence."'

The passage continues, though Richard does not quote these lines: 'Such a predominance of will was Lawrence's chief danger. It shows itself frequently in his treatment of his body, on which all his life he was apt to impose quite unfair strains, often of a stupid character. For example, he neglected a broken arm in 1926 and so made a less than satisfactory recovery, just as he had gone back to work in his class with a broken leg in 1904.'

Richard ended the quotation as it goes on: 'The courage of a boy too proud to make a fuss is something we admire; in an educated man it is ridiculous and a sign of abnormality', and continued his letter:

And yet am I to go crawling to them on my knees, snivelling to be let out? They already regard me askance – 'Done no twin-engined stuff? Only six hours at night? Are you sure you want to go into night fighters? Don't forget it isn't only your life, but your air gunner's' – a damnably cruel, but true point.

Perhaps they're right – perhaps it is the night which is subconsciously too much. I *know* I'm not frightened of flying by

197

day. Perhaps it is merely the fear of being so much alone – a bitter pill, when I always thought I liked it so much, but the total lack of human contact is awful – they are machines, not men. At Fighter Command they were people. One could talk to them and like them.

I spoke to Dirty Watkins at Headquarters Fighter Command. How surprised he'd have been if he knew how I hated to let him go. He is prepared to fly me to Northolt on Saturday [for the wedding] if I can get half-way – a miracle if I can get permission or a plane, but I will try.

He mentions here that he has received a *'charming'* message from K., and adds,

I sometimes wonder, had she not called me a coward – oh well, one can't go on rationalising for ever.

Please excuse pencil, but I can find no pen and must go ten miles to buy one.

Rache and Koestler are both in on some scheme – both very secretive about it, for getting me out to do something 'soon'. What the devil do they mean? If I get through this three months, and am then dragged out, I think I shall break up altogether. If they know something, why don't they tell me? . . .

Forgive this long and (yes, I believe it's true) self-pitying epistle, but I feel much happier for having written it, and for having you to send it to. Don't be ashamed of me if you can help it, my darling.

I shall think of you in your new surroundings and hope to dream of you.

I love you so very much that at moments I think my heart will break. You are everything that is not here – warmth, humanity, humour, and intelligence.

I thought I might write an amusing book here. Perhaps I yet shall, if I can ever be alone, but what escapism it will be.

Good night. God bless you. You are very near to me and the tears are over.

                              Richard

The miracle happened. He got leave and a plane, and flew south the day before the wedding: a war-time one in Mayfair, a flock of Astors, most of 'Society' that was not overseas in strength, the bride in 'a gown of heavy ivory satin with a bouquet of white lilies, gardenias, and stephanotis', a reception in Grosvenor Street, Miss Rosemary Kerr with her new face among the guests, and Mr Archibald McIndoe from East Grinstead. According to Rosie, he met Richard, who told him that he had lost his nerve. McIndoe was horrified at Richard's mental condition, and wrote to the Medical Officer at Charter Hall. Both meeting and letter are facts attested by McIndoe's biographer, who had the use of his papers; but according to him they belong about a fortnight later, and I shall place them there.

Richard had dinner with Mary that evening, and returned to Charter Hall next day.

In his protest to the Group-Captain, Michael Hillary had referred to a 'daily journal' Richard was known to have been keeping, 'and part of that journal, written up to 4th January, is in the possession of one of his friends'. This seems to be the 'notes' mentioned at the beginning of the letter of 30 November, cited hereafter. Expecting to be killed, and that the authorities would destroy them, Richard sent them in the form of letters to Mary, perhaps with similar letters to others. Of those that follow, one or two are still mainly about his own depression and the icy weather, but from 1 December, when he had at last flown, the tone alters and becomes less wretched. Aeroplanes, the aerodrome, and the personnel take over. It matters less now that the fire in his room has gone out. Mary's flat is too spacious for her, and she has taken a lodger, one of those distinguished Americans who used to write admiring books about Britain, but Richard is no longer jealous. He has grown more tolerant of K.; and of the official he had once thought wished to 'write him off', he says only: 'Poor ——. He is a pathetic figure really . . . One should feel sorry for him, not hate him.' After she has written to him of some plan for him, perhaps meaning employment with Miles Aircraft, he warns her, 'Here I am beginning to settle in.' And he has begun to write, 'which I could not do in London'.

How sad it is that nothing of hers is left. Her diary shows her seeing her old friends. She asks Richard's mother round. But we have no record of what she felt as she opened his quickly pencilled letters and read of the ill-serviced aircraft, the savage weather, the gales across the runway, his shattering headaches, and the weakness of his hands. We know only that after he had left she went back and wept; and but for her last letter would only be able to guess at what she went through, the effort of will it cost to go on giving him heart and keep somehow the note of lightness. She had become one of millions of women.

His two passions, for flying and for writing, had begun to merge again, as they had in *The Last Enemy*. One seems almost sure to lead to death; the other belongs to the future she believes in for him. And so she sends him word of something she has read, for example, a book by Gerald Heard on mysticism, or ideas for him to comment on, and all the time encouragement to go on with those notes which one day are to become his second book, in letters that to him seem 'wonderful', all of them destined for the Charter Hall incinerator.

> Officers Mess
> Charter Hall
> near Duns, Berwickshire
> Tel. No. Coldstream 134–135
> Sunday 29th November

My darling,

Such a very wonderful letter. I will make the promise that IF I get the chance to *really* do something, then I will take my friends' advice [to give up operational flying].

It was like some extraordinary dream to see you again so soon, and to have you again in my arms. Never have I felt so close to you, nor felt the need of you more . . .

Please excuse scrawl, but I am just off to bed – as my fire has not been lit – a proper letter tomorrow.

I shall dream of you.

> R.

P.S. You spoil me outrageously.

200

Charter Hall
30th Nov. 1942

I will take your advice, darling, in that I will make notes – not of a book, but in diary form, and I will write them to you. But to-day I cannot start properly. I am too weary and again very low. For I have a splitting headache; my teeth are chattering and I fear I am in for a chill. And yet I *must* fight this, for if I go to bed now I shall have to drop a course and I shall still not have flown. I expect to start tomorrow. Any more of the nerviness of this waiting will be calamitous.

After a morning of lectures, and a wonderful letter from you, written before the wedding, I set off for 'A' Squadron, already unable to move my eyes without feeling as though I had been hit by a hammer . . .

The wind was very bitter on my hands and face, & I arrived chilled to the marrow. (This wind has a peculiar quality – it bores into your very soul.) All afternoon I sat there, and having brought no book I could only brood. Then at 5.30 I climbed out of my flying kit and walked the 35 mins back to sick quarters, where with much mystery and hand-waving the Station M.O. produced two aspirin and vanished off somewhere to play bridge.

My eyeballs are aching, so I must turn in, for I must not pack up tomorrow.

First, however, thank you for buying such a lovely present in my name. I hope you are being truthful about the price.

Second, I love you dearly.

Third, to-night has been a near thing, but it has not ended in tears.

R.

Charter Hall
3.12.42

Much better to-day, for I have finally flown; with no particular distinction and only dual, nevertheless I have flown. My greatest difficulty is taxi-ing these heavy brutes. I find that I have not the strength in my right thumb to work the brakes, so I am to have an extension fitted to the brake lever.

My headache is still with me, but better. If only I could lay my hands on a car, life would be quite tolerable. The evenings here, with the snow-dusted mountains pale under an orange sky, are very lovely.

Were it not that one's chattering teeth force one to walk on, it would be time well spent just to sit on the aerodrome and look across the great stillness. For it is still; the roar of machines taking off and landing only seeming to emphasise it.

It's curious psychologically that I have only to step into an aeroplane, that monstrous thing of iron and steel just waiting for the chance to get me down, and all fear goes. I am at peace again.

Not that this course is going to be easy. It is so utterly different from day fighting – no question of 'There they are, let's have a go', but very cold, calculating, and scientific. One must acquire a quite different temperament and learn that one's greatest enemy is one Isaac Newton.

A letter from you to-day with the criticism of Gerald Heard. As you say, hardly the answer to my problem.

Tomorrow the C.O. has ordained a station parade in the morning, to make quite sure of wasting time and to give himself the pleasure of telling some of us (me without doubt) to get our hair cut.

In their correspondence they had often used the word 'faith', and the exhortation 'have faith'. Mary had evidently used the word again in one of her destroyed letters, for he goes on:

You ask me to have faith, darling. Yes, but faith in what? 'That things will be all right,' you say. Depends what you mean by 'all right'. If you mean faith that some miracle will happen, and I shall be ordered to some job which I can not only do well, but enjoy, then I say no. It is bad to have that faith, and undermining. If you mean faith that I have done the right thing in coming back, then yes. But if you mean faith that I shall survive, then again no. If this thing plays to its logical conclusion, there is no reason why I should survive. After a few hours flying, my instinct will tell me that I shall survive, while my reason will tell me that I shall not – and this time reason will be right.

It may be of course that I shall come through, but it does not do to think so. I came back not expecting to come through – it was a very part of my decision to come back, and suddenly to see a pink spectacled light through all that darkness would be merely hedging the bet.

How self-consciously priggish that sounds! However, I mean it. I am so unhappy that you went back after I had gone and wept. As you wrote it, I had the picture vividly clear, and I was not there to comfort you.

No more to-night as I must sleep – with your picture by my side.

R.

In the letters that follow, the tone is altering almost entirely. Excuses, moans, apologies, jealousies, seem to be of the past. He is becoming extrovert, turning as one turns a coat from fighting himself to fighting the aeroplanes, the elements, and beginning to wear the sky; and liking other people; and practising a style.

Charter Hall
3.12.42

My darling,

The morning started badly; bitterly cold, a long walk over to flights, and an indifferent dual performance on a Blenheim. Then this afternoon something clicked. My instructor climbed out and in an over-casual voice said, 'O.K., off you go. Just time for a couple of circuits and bumps,' and I was on my own.

Round I go, twice without mishap, and am exhilarated as after my first solo three years ago. I saunter into the mess, my battledress carelessly undone, and a voice calls out, 'So you made it.' Pilots cluster round: they have been watching. 'I saw

203

you take off.' 'Very nice landing.' – 'The old ace back on the job again.' So they are human after all. I feel a new-old warmth begin to course through me; the potion is already at work.

I pick up a newspaper – Beveridge Report? Oh, the fellow is thinking about after the war: we'll probably all be dead anyway. Let's find out what Jane's doing in the Daily Mirror. We turn the page: we comment on her legs, and I look more closely at the faces around me, and what I see pleases me. I am happy.

We wander into dinner and afterwards we crowd round the fire, order beers, more beers, and talk shop. Time passes. Am I bored? A little, but only a very little, for to-morrow I shall be up again. This morning I was thinking seriously of asking for a transfer to a day O.T.U. – Spitfires again – easy to handle, people I know. Now I'm off on a new adventure.

That was to-day darling – that and your letter. So you're turning into a miracle worker now, along with everything else. I refuse resolutely to believe it: there must be something you cannot do. And be warned – here I am beginning to settle in – here, funnily enough – if I only had time I could write, whereas in London I could not . . .

Charter Hall
7.12.42

Only a line to-night, as my poltroon of a batman has left the window open and my fire has gone out.

A sixty mile an hour gale has been blowing all day with a cloud base of 600 ft, so flying has indeed been a battle with the elements. Taxi-ing round the perimeter track develops into a fierce tussle between pilot and machine. One wrestles with the wheel as though forty thousand gremlins were blowing on the rudder and tail-fin. In doing so I took most of the skin off one hand, and as a result I'm in a lowering temper.

And yet the whole thing grows on me, and in a curious way I am beginning to enjoy myself.

It appears likely that during the next two months we shall be snow-bound, and any chance of finishing the course on time has already gone overboard.

Letter from you to-day. Happy you like those I send and bless you for having Mamma along.

R.

Next day he wrote to Mrs Lee, one of his hostesses in America.

Dear Jeanette,

I have at last managed to get back to flying, and after three months in this wilderness I shall be a fully fledged night fighter and go to a squadron. Reason and my friends told me it was madness to return, but in London I felt out of touch and though I am half-way through a new book I listened to my instinct and not my reason, with the result that here I am. My hands caused me some trouble at first with these heavy machines, but now I'm settling in and enjoying myself.

The general situation is better, especially for us in the R.A.F. What a difference from this time two years ago!

This is the forgotten man's last stop. We expect to be snowed up shortly, which will put an end to flying. Then I tremble to think what will happen, for flying is the only thing that keeps one sane. Write and tell me your news, Jeanette dear. I'm very cut off here.

The same day he wrote a similar letter to Mary Warburg in New York, with some differences and additions:

. . . I'm pretty scared and my hands give me quite a lot of bother, but anyhow I am back.

In London I was well into a new book and had written the script for a picture to be filmed next month [he never saw it] and yet I felt more and more out of touch with reality – and here I am, learning to get pleasure from ordinary people and ordinary things again.

It's a little hard learning to go to school again after three years – it makes one very nostalgic for all those, now dead, who

205

trained with me, yet I'm beginning to enjoy myself and the old glow is returning . . .

Apart from the intense cold and driving winds, it is difficult to keep clean as some maniac seems to delight in stealing the bath plugs!

The news generally is encouraging at last, especially for us in the R.A.F. What a difference from two years ago. Now finally it looks as if it's our turn.

And then, revealingly but also surprisingly,

My love life, now suspended, has been for the last year one of quiet domesticity, slippers by the fire, etc. – a great and pleasant change, though a sign of advancing years, I fear . . .

The next letter to Mary, dated 10 December, has been printed in Lovat Dickson's biography. It describes laconically how one of the trainees on Richard's course loses direction, crashes, and is killed. It ends with dining-in night in the Mess, when, to Richard's astonishment and delight 'a dear old buffer, permanent unsuccessful Liberal candidate for the County, came to give us the Liberal view of the way, and HE TALKED LAND VALUES AND HENRY GEORGE. Between us we kept them all there till half-past twelve, and he left *Progress and Poverty* and *Protection and Free Trade* for the library. Both are out to-day. There's hope for this place yet! That's all for to-night. I love you, darling, and when I say [about the cockpit] "quite alone in that confined space," I don't mean it. I always fly with you beside me . . .'

Charter Hall
14.12.42

My darling,

The most agonising headache, so I'm off to bed. I'll write to-morrow . . .

There is no letter from to-morrow in the collection, and none until after his Christmas leave.

CHAPTER TEN: NOVEMBER – DECEMBER 1942

It is in this gap, according to the dating in Mosley's biography of McIndoe, that we should place Richard's interview with him. After Richard was dead, McIndoe wrote:

> I have always been certain he knew what his end would be. Three weeks before his time he came to see me, and said that, unless he could be shifted from night-flying, he could not last out much longer. But he stipulated that the course on which he was flying should not be interrupted, lest someone should say he was afraid to continue. The idea was, that he should be returned to East Grinstead for another operation. Disturbed by his news and impressed by the passive way in which he gave it, I wrote immediately to the Station Medical Officer. Richard was suffering from the common complaint where his body could not tolerate what his mind could contemplate. His nervous system had not brought his physical responses under control.

The text of the letter, dated 17 December, which McIndoe wrote to the Station Medical Officer, is as follows:

> Re Flight Lieutenant Hillary. This officer, as you know, has had a long series of plastic operations for the repair of severe burns of the face and hands. I saw him the other day and was impressed by the fact that his left eye did not appear to be standing up to the strain of night flying as might be expected, a fact of which Hillary is aware, but which I think he is loth to admit.
>
> As you know, he is a very able young writer, and I feel very strongly that flying under these conditions can only end one way. This would be a great pity. He unfortunately was boarded by the Central Medical Establishment before I knew he was going, and I am afraid he brought great pressure to bear to get back to operative work. I have in fact more to do to his face, and particularly his left lower eyelid, which will necessitate his attendance at East Grinstead in the future, and I would therefore be glad if you would arrange his return to me at an early date.
>
> In the meantime I do feel that if you could with discretion restrain him from further flying, it might save him from a very

207

serious accident. After I have dealt with his eye, I can reopen the matter with the C.M.E., and a more satisfactory disposal could be made for him.

Would you be so good as to treat this letter as private and confidential to yourself? The feelings of these young men are very apt to be hurt in relation to this vexed question of operative work following an injury. I feel however there is a strong case for intervention.

The Station Medical Officer was on leave, and McIndoe's letter remained among his mail unopened.

9   Alexander Korda and Merle Oberon leaving Buckingham Palace
    after receiving his Knighthood, September 22, 1942

10   Eric Kennington portrait of Richard

Monday,

Darling
Not writing today as am off to bed. flew last night till late am. Lovely machine — everything working, she just purred. I'm quite sure aeroplanes are human. the one before was determined to get me
I'm hoping Probably to get down toward end of month.
Love you
R.

11   Richard's last letter to Mary

8. 1. 43.

Richard, I bow before this blackness of despair; this loneliness of night. The first of an eternity of nights. I feel your spirit stretching forth to me from out the stars; through all of this world's tears I see your face trying with infinite compassion & understanding to comfort me. But you must let me cry. These tears held back with all the courage that lay between us these last months can no longer be held back.

You once wrote, "I had a sudden vision of what life would be without you. It was like a shadow passing across the sun." That same shadow has passed across my sun. You who were my light are gone from me into light itself. Help me to share that light with you in spirit as we shared everything together here in life. I must achieve this; I must not be so desolate. You will help me I know. I must find a new & selfless happiness in the knowledge that your search for those circles of peace is now ended; that your

12   Mary's last letter to Richard

Chapter Eleven
December 1942 - January 1943

Richard came to London for Christmas leave and stayed with his parents. He had dinner the first evening with Mary. Next evening he went to have a drink with Denise. Her brother was with her, and he stayed to supper, and talked for a long time like one who has become a spectator of life. He was not depressed, but dispassionate and fatalistic, and several times repeated that he had found the key to life. Denise was wearing khaki. About midnight he asked her to change into her loveliest clothes, which after some protest she did. He stayed silent for a while, thanked her, and went.

On Christmas Eve Mary had dinner with him and Arthur Koestler. She spent Christmas Day with her mother and her family, and had dinner with Brigadier Charles Haydon and his wife, one or two other friends, and Richard. Next day Richard returned to Charter Hall.

Twenty-three years later Michael Hillary was asked to write something about him for the twenty-fifth anniversary of the Battle of Britain; to help him, Mary described what Richard had been like during that Christmas leave.

The main point, which I remember very vividly, was the change in his attitude from that of his previous leave for Michael Astor's wedding.

At that time he knew that various people of authority were pulling strings to get him grounded, and this somehow seemed to prevent him from making the effort to integrate himself with the life of the community up there. It had been a shock to him when he first arrived, to find none of the same spirit of comradeship with his fellow men that had existed with all his

209

friends in the past. They naturally treated him as someone special, someone whom they regarded with respect as being one of the original Battle of Britain 'heroes'. This threw him back, and gave him a feeling of being alone in a place where human warmth and friendship were essential to combat the bleak isolation of it all.

As time went on, a change took place.

1. Richard gained confidence in overcoming the disabilities, which at first he had thought he would never overcome.
2. He found a bond of friendship, first with Fison, his Radio Observer, and then with his fellow pilots, who showed genuine pleasure and friendly interest in his achievements against such heavy odds.

A Sergeant-Pilot called Handel Miller, who according to a letter from his mother to Richard's mother, shared a room with Richard, went home at Christmas 'and could talk of nothing but your boy, so great was his admiration for him'. His fiancée bought him *The Last Enemy* for Christmas, and he took it back to Charter Hall for Richard to autograph.

'All this', Mary continued to Michael Hillary,

added up to the change in him when he came down the last time. It seemed to me that he had accepted the fact that he would have to go through with it. Facing this decision had aged him in maturity. He was much quieter. He didn't want to meet people, excepting those he was most fond of – Denise, Tony – He gave me the impression that he wanted them to be clear regarding his devotion and the value of all they had given him of themselves, so that there should be no hurt or misunderstanding. He spoke to me of the importance of this on several occasions, always adding, 'But I need never *explain* anything to you.'

If he didn't see much of you and Edwyna it was because it was too sad, and he thought you would see through his façade – for there is no doubt about it, that he was convinced that he wouldn't come through. I did all I could not to let him know I guessed this, and we talked of the future. That he would fight physically for life is undeniable. He talked of its fulness, and how he felt more fitted than ever to try to make a fresh start, with the new confidence and strength he felt within himself; beneath it all I felt he had lost hope that he would ever be given the chance.

He wanted our letters, edited by him, to be published, and talked of ideas for other things he hoped to write about, but he knew I knew, and underlying it all our hearts were heavy.

He talked a good deal about you and Edwyna – saying that he didn't want you to find a telegram on the mat. I didn't know then that he had made arrangements with his C.O. that I should have the telegram 4 hours ahead, so that I should perhaps be of some help in breaking the news if the worst should happen. Whatever happens, what is written must be so worded that there is no hint of that suicide which is so utterly false. He was gay and always full of hope for the future and had everything to live for. But he was calm and ready for anything that came which would put an end to it all . . .

As soon as he was back at the aerodrome, Richard wrote to Mary:

> Charter Hall
> 27th December
>
> Darling,
> Coming up in the train I pondered over how you spoiled me. It's really terrible and I must not accept it as a matter of course.
> I was so happy over Christmas; thank you for it.
> To-night somehow I cannot write, so I'm not going to try. Tomorrow however I shall produce a screed. I shall also take to *answering* your letters as my New Year's resolution.
> Thank you for such a wonderful Christmas present also.
> A small boy's letter, but to-night I feel spent.
> I love you,
> R.

Charter Hall
30th December

There has been no moment at all in which to write or think in the last few days, for we are flying night and day. And yet somehow I must get all this down, these three months, even if it's only notes and impressions so that it may not be wasted. As long as you don't mind it scrappy, disjointed, and rambling, I will send it all to you, and then maybe some day I shall have peace and time to put it together.

He describes the Boxing Night dance, and a formal parade of the whole station with a speech about Christmas being over, 'shoulders to the wheel, etc', and then:

There will be no ground crews to service my aircraft, but those four of us who are on night flying detail must do a night flying test, so we get our aircraft and fly it round the aerodrome once each – the others starting it up.

I go first, in a Blenheim. I have never flown one before, always having been put in 5's (Bisleys) in A Squadron to save my hands. The Bisleys have a switch to shut the gills – the Blenheims a wheel somewhere behind the pilot that needs about 50 turns.

The Bisleys have a simple lever up and down to raise and lower the undercarriage. The Blenheims have a catch out from the handle, which must be pushed in with the thumb, before the undercarriage can be pulled up. No one has ever shown me the cockpit, but I think I can manage, and take off. I find I cannot reach the catch with my thumb. Ground Control calls up. 'Hullo One Zero Two your undercarriage is still down.' It is indeed and I cannot be bothered to answer. I have let go of the stick and am wrestling with the lever with both hands. It will not budge. I curse and sweat blood, but it will not come up, so I land again, very dispirited.

My Squadron Commander comes up. 'Can't cope, old boy. Too bad.' Genially: 'We'll have to throw you off this course. No

212

Bisleys in this squadron.' Finally he arranges for someone to go up and pull it up for me, until I get on to Beaufighters, which I shall find simpler.

In the afternoon I go with my Radio Observer for an hour on the Link trainer. This is really the only flying I enjoy here, because it is warm.

At 4.30 we go down again. Night flying begins at 5. A 50 mile an hour wind is blowing from the North, and some light snow is falling.

Then begins the worst part – the getting ready. No blithe leaping in and taking off as in a Spitfire.

There follows a comic-exasperated account (St-Exupéry wrote one similar in *Flight to Arras*) of the bulging upholstery and accessories essential to transform a peaceful earth-bound creature into one of those 'Knights of the Air', modern version of the medieval, to whom combat pilots so much disliked being compared: Irving suit and boots, Mae West, maps, torch, gloves (difficult for Richard), helmet, R/T connexion, miles of oxygen tubing, parachute. Their armour on, the flight is scrubbed.

My R.O. and I look at each other. Then we sit down slowly and beg a cigarette. Our own are buried away beneath layers of what almost amounts to our skin.

But finally we may go . . . I scramble along the hatch – which is locked. I call out to an airman who must crawl up inside and undo it. Inevitably he says, 'Fuck,' before disappearing from view, but he gets it open and I wallow in – my R.O. following, for on this trip he is to sit beside me and work the u/c.

I settle into my bucket seat and together we dig around for the straps . . . they will not meet . . . Oh well, by now I really don't care. If we do a crash landing, we do a crash landing. If I go through the windscreen, I go through the windscreen. I switch on the petrol. 'Petrol on.' I plug in my R/T and by slewing sideways in the seat and feeling behind me find the oxygen plug. My R.O. tells me he cannot find his. I switch on the torch. There is none . . .

'Contact starboard!' I strain my eyes through the shoddy unclean perspex, but I can see neither the fitter nor his torch, only the night, starry but very dark, and, light against that darkness, furtive clouds hustled before the wind. I shout again . . . This time I see the fitter, but not out in front. He has scrambled up on to the wings and clutching on to the cockpit hood he puts his head in out of the wind.

'Scrubbed again, sir,' he says hoarsely. 'Switch her off' . . . Six pilots and their R.O.'s climb aboard [transport] and we rattle round to the night-flying canteen and get some hot sausages and tea. W. (my R.O.) settles down beside me, and asks me if I'm going to hear the gramophone concert in the R/T hut the following night.

'They're playing Beethoven's 5th,' he adds.

Next comes a page or two of four-lettered badinage, Australian pilots mocking the Pommies, and vice versa, and

Suddenly I felt quite exhausted. I wasn't trying to be funny or even to get a rise out of George [an Australian], as W. loves to do, but I was quite suddenly unutterably weary of it . . . [and yet] I think what an ideal crew George and his R.O. make . . . I also ponder Koestler's theory that *l'espoir de la fraternité* is always a wild goose chase unless one is tight or physically exhausted in a crowd – as after long marches. To-night I am almost convinced he is right, but he must not be – for it was for that reason I returned . . .

Snowing heavily. Bitterly cold.
I love you,
R.

Charter Hall
1st January 1943
Friday

Darling,

Another year is past – a year in which I have written little and done nothing that can be measured in objective terms, but for

214

me a great year. I had you and I grew up. 1942 was ours, and with all the horrors that occurred all over the world nothing can make me anything but grateful to it for what it granted to me. I thought we must founder, but we did not, only grew ever more strong. I only hope that 1943 will allow me to put into action the personality which now, (thanks largely to you) is me, be it good or bad.

The evening before last I thought that the great snow had begun. As night fell down it came – driven across this bleak wilderness by a vicious wind.

Here follows an account of the New Year's dance and the gramophone recital, in the R/T hut.

It was my first visit. Outside the beating of the snow, unutterably dreary across the camp against the huts: inside, another world – a breath of lost civilisation. My first impression was of breaking in on a private family party. About thirty people, mostly airmen and WAAF's – curiously enough no pilots – and all with a knowledge and appreciation of music to which I doubt if I shall ever be able to pretend. (My 1st visit – their 17th.)

Flying Officer How, the R/T speech officer, who gives the programme, is an old gentleman of upright carriage, protruding ears and an academic manner – ex-choirmaster–music teacher and voice trainer. Each work is carefully explained – we are told what to listen for – the undertones 'like this' – he plays a couple of bars, 'and now this' – two more. He reads from a marked passage in some book, and the snow and the aerodrome are forgotten.

Programme.

        Wilhelm Tell .... Rossini
        Meistersinger .... Wagner
        5th Symphony .... Beethoven
        Karelia .... Sibelius

His explanations are above my head, but I listen as eager to learn and accept his authority, as I am unwilling and disinclined when he tries to standardise my R/T patter and voice control by day. Now he is at home – the master. Before he was uncertain – trying to teach me my job.

Mary had written him something about beauty and about orientation, and he replies:

I reject appreciation of the beautiful if you mean it in the purely aesthetic sense, for whether beauty – aesthetic beauty – is of any but selfish value is a moot point. But if you mean it in the sense of Plato's 'Beauty is the splendour of Truth' then I agree.

What in terms of action has the well orientated man got that anyone else has not? Creative imagination and all that follows from it, eg production of an intellectual theory which reorganises understanding and opens new vistas before the mind's eye; the production of an original and significant work of art; the production of a personal relationship which drives both individuals to greater integrity; the production of vitalising social changes.

But more of this to-morrow – I must to bed as I am flying to-morrow day and night.

My love and prayers that together we may achieve something great in 1943.

R.

On 3 January Richard wrote to his mother:

There are moments, far too many, when you make my heart turn over, and I am filled with such unutterable tenderness for you and all you have done for me, that in my happiness I feel quite sad . . . in the last two years I have made many mistakes, but I have gained a little wisdom and living up here seems to point to it rather than lessen it. For I try to live now on the principle, 'I live this day as my last.' Here it is not difficult. I can summarise my tiny drops of wisdom quite easily. The first is:

I have not the right to make any man small in his own image; and the second is:

216

Time is very short, and there are a great many people in the world. Therefore of these people I shall try to know only half a dozen. But them I shall love and never deceive.

The same day he sent Mary a long letter, reproduced here in full for several reasons. It is the last long descriptive letter he wrote her. Next, the book by Group Captain Bill Simpson, *One of our Pilots is Safe*, had just come out. Simpson was one of the worst burnt and injured of the fighter-pilots. He had had the terrible experience of being left almost alone in France at the time of the collapse, and then being shifted across the shattered refugee-thronged country for many months and imprisoned by the Vichy Government, before he was finally repatriated by way of Portugal. Rosie Kerr was among those who looked after him when at last he arrived at East Grinstead. The book is noble and well-written, possessing an extraordinary calm, and Richard's tribute to it has the generosity it deserves. Richard's letter is also interesting and important for its account of a night-training flight; for the style he was now developing for the book that was not to be, which makes clear that his return to flying had carried forward the creative surge he had felt at Kennington's; and for his relationship with his Radio-Observer, Sergeant-Pilot Kenneth Wilfrid Young Fison. Fison was thirty-seven, fourteen years older than Richard, married and with two young children. He had been educated at Marlborough and Clare College, Cambridge, where he got an honours degree in modern languages and a hockey Blue. After going down, he qualified as a chartered accountant. During the Blitz on London he had been head warden at an ARP post in Bermondsey; but in December 1941, when his firm moved out into the country, he left it and joined the RAF Volunteer Reserve. He was now in the final stages of his training.

Charter Hall
3rd January 1942 (Sunday)

Simpson's book I see is going very well, but I do not grudge its success. About all the others which have been well received I have felt a petty exasperation – due largely to having written

217

nothing further myself. And yet I know that they are people who happened to be watching an accident with a camera in their hands and thus got a good picture, while I am a professional cameraman and will always – on the rare occasions when I use my camera – get a good picture. They will never do it again. Is this arrogance on my part? Certainly the exasperation is because I am beginning to fear that either through force of circumstances or lack of concentration I am rapidly becoming an amateur myself.

S. on the other hand has suffered so much, and has emerged with so little bitterness that I am genuinely glad of his success. I do not mean by this that I think that anyone who has an inclination to write, and passes through a time of great physical and mental suffering, will write necessarily better than before. That happened to me; but to apply it as a general rule seems to me as a sceptic as logically unsound as the man who has a deep emotional experience in which he feels a great love of humanity and feels himself a part of the universe, and deduces from his own personal experience that *therefore* there must be an all loving God. I accept the experience, but I reject its inference.

Or to take it further. Most really religious (say rather spiritual) people have suffered terribly during the process of their own self-mastery; but to infer from that that suffering is a necessary and beneficial thing imposed on mankind by an all seeing Deity seems to me nonsense. As well say 'God made the wind to fill the sails of ships.'

But I am rambling.

Yesterday I got as far as the cockpit of a Beaufighter before flying was cancelled owing to weather – the nearest I have got yet. As soon as I can fly a Beau I am to go over to the 3rd leg of this course and do all the rest of my training on Beaus, for although it is a much more powerful aircraft the cockpit lay-out is much easier for my hands.

In the evening the weather cleared and I was on first detail night flying. My Squadron Commander had arranged for me to fly a Bisley from A Squadron, as frankly I'm scared stiff of the old Blenheims at night – you can't even see your instruments –

and also as I was to do a height test the cold would have been too much for me – quite apart from fighting with the under-carriage.

It was bitterly cold but clear and starry. W. and I clambered into all our equipment and were driven over to A Squadron to pick up No 238. We only had to try two other A/C before getting the right one in the dark, so we were in not too bad a temper. As there was nothing for him to do on a height test W. sat up in front with me. We plugged in our oxygen and turned it on full, squeezing the tube to see if it was coming through.

Mine seemed O.K. – his also. We taxied out – always a nightmare to me as I cannot reach the brake – and last night 40 mph cross wind. The serviceability rate of these A/C is so low that I always marvel whenever we leave the ground at all. Of course at any other unit we wouldn't – they would put every aeroplane unserviceable at once – this had been proved by aircraft from here – diverted to another aerodrome, being refused permission to take off again.

But anything goes here and off we went. As soon as we were off the ground I knew something was wrong. The old monster started plunging away to starboard. We flashed a torch through the filthy perspex to see if the gills had not shut, but they seemed O.K. so I continued. (I wonder if W. knows just how terrified I am at night? I hope not.) Then we started to climb. At 10,000 feet the pitch control of the port engine jammed. At 19,000 I was waffling about at 100 mph with the outside temperature 50° below. Then my R.T. packed up. (I could receive from the ground, but not transmit.)

I told W. to get a homing. I listened to him calling up. His voice very drowsy. Oh God he's going to pass out. Down I pushed the nose, down until I thought my ears would crack – all the time hearing ground control giving us homing vectors and W. repeating them, slowly, happily and quite wrong.

I should of course have kept a mental note of the courses we were flying, but having so much else to do I had left it to W. What if the R.T. packs up altogether? A moment later it did so. A feeling oddly of resignation – not panic. Then I saw it, the flare path, way below us. We were all right. I came down slowly, feeling very sick (my own supply of oxygen cannot have been too good) and started to flash my navigation lights at 1,000 ft. Nothing happened. Why the Hell can't they answer? I glanced again at my instruments. 11,000 ft! What a fool – mustn't get drowsy. That might have led to disaster – a quick circuit at what I took to be 1,000 ft; turn on nicely over the East funnel of lights at 800 ft – wheels down, flaps down, throttle back, down to 100 ft. Why no chance light? & then the stall. Too late I realise what has happened. We are not at 100 ft but at 10,000 ft & all the time the plane is spinning and spinning.

Well that's what might have been. Another lesson learned.

I lose more height and when I really am at 800 ft start flashing my navigation lights. A green lamp flashes back. I can land. I turn to W. and put up my thumb. He grins back, quite unaware that he was nearly out. (He has great confidence in me! If he did but know.)

Round the circuit and down with my wheels – a flood of light comes on where the ground crew have not put strips over the undercarriage positive indicator lights. I am quite blinded, but W. gets down on his knees and holds his hand over the glare. We are coming in – Hell of a cross wind – we're drifting badly. I straighten up over the runway, throttle back, we're still going like a crab. Then the wheels touch and we are down. As I turn off the runway I can feel the sweat running down inside my Irving suit and my hands are trembling. Climbing out I put my foot gingerly to the ground. Oh how welcome it is. Solid earth beneath my feet.

In the air twice I had promised myself that if I got down I should go to the Wing Commander and say that I'd had enough. Already the mere thought of it amused me. What was for supper? That occupied the first place in my mind.

We staggered back to the crew room, weighed down by our parachutes, fears forgotten, chattering and laughing.

We were met by the Officer i/C Night flying, the M.O. and an ambulance.

What happened?

Are you all right?

'Yes,' I said, 'My R.T. packed up and Fison was answering for me. He doesn't know the patter – that's all. Actually his supply was a little short, I think.'

'Oh, that's what happened. We thought you'd had it.'

Grinning with relief they sent off the ambulance and offered us a cigarette. I took one from the M.O. wondering what he'd think if he knew how nearly I had made use of that ambulance, said that I was ill, sick at altitude, anything. Nobody could blame me. There was still time. W. helped me out of my kit, I relit my cigarette and we walked over to night supper.

Then no transport – somebody had boobed again and so the long weary, cold walk up to the mess. Time midnight.

Outside I bade W. goodnight (how much rather that he were allowed in our mess than some of the dregs) and walked in for a moment before going to bed.

A party was going on. I could hear a piano playing, and a huge barrel of beer frothed past, carried by four drunken clowns. I collected some letters from my locker and turned to go out to my room, but one of them saw me – my Flight Commander.

'What ho, Hil! How did it go?'

I told him. He answered quite soberly.

'Christ old boy. Shaky do eh? I wouldn't fly one of these Blenheims at night for any price – tried once – shook me to the tits – Can't even see the instruments and fuck all outside. Oh it's a grand life we lead here old boy. To-morrow you'll have all that and your engine'll cut too just for full measure, and if you prang they'll say it was your fault. Come on in. Someone's birthday – good excuse for getting pissed – only thing to do here.'

He took my arm, but pleading tiredness I slipped away – put my calling time of 7.15 on my door, climbed into my night-pullovers and socks and then into bed.

Well darling, that was yesterday – illegible, unrevised, and very hurried, but I hope you understand it.

All hope of getting on with the book has vanished for the moment. Flying, or rather waiting to fly night and day; at the moment I'm writing this with my feet too hot in front of the writing room fire and the back of my neck freezing from the inevitable draught. Night flying has been put to 60 minutes as a snow storm is expected. I am on second detail – normally nine o'clock, but to-night I imagine we shall not get off before midnight – down about 3 am – God willing.

Your letters to me keep me sane my darling – and both 'masks' now look down on me in bed. The second will not fit the frames alas. What a pity about the cottage. If you do see anything you might let me know and we can have fun imagining how it might be if we could only have managed it.

Max [Aitken] I hear will be leaving the Squadron very shortly, but who will take his place I know not.

Write soon.

You will fly beside me.

R.

Max Aitken did in fact leave to join Sir Sholto Douglas in the Middle East in early 1943 and take up an important air command, covering the defences of Cairo and Alexandria and the whole North African coast from Tripoli to the Nile. It was this appointment Richard must have heard of, making him feel more than ever left behind.

Charter Hall
Monday, 4.1.43

Darling

Not writing to-day as am off to bed. Flew last night till 4 am. Lovely machine – everything working, she just purred. I'm quite sure aeroplanes are human. The one before was determined to get me.

I'm hoping desperately to get down towards the end of the month.

Love you
R.

Three days later, 7 January, the Station Medical Officer sent his answer to McIndoe's letter of 17 December (of which the Station Commander knew nothing), asking that Richard should be grounded:

I am sorry to have delayed replying, but have been away from the unit. Until I had returned I haven't had the opportunity of checking up the points you raised.

I find Flight Lieutenant Hillary difficult to deal with, as any indication that his condition was not progressing as it should would result in him immediately withholding his personal feelings.

Without indicating that I had had a personal letter from you, I asked how things were going. I suggested that his left eye looked a little irritated, but he insisted that it was better than it was before he came to this unit, a matter, of course, on which I have no information.

I may have imagined it, but I think there was a certain caution exercised to prevent me from finding out Hillary's real view.

I agree with you that intervention is suitable in such a case, but I am also sure that Hillary's self-respect is an enormous obstacle. He is due to go to London about the 19th of this month and promised to call on you while in London. I did not tell him you had specifically desired it, but I said it was only fair to the surgeon who had devoted so much time and trouble to effect a cure to let him check up from time to time to see how things are going. I will remind him when I see him making preparations to go off and hope this will meet with your approval.

The same day, in his address to the 78th Congress in Washington, President Roosevelt described the Allies' turning of the tide towards victory during 1942: the Russian encircling of huge German armies on the Stalingrad front; the British advances along the Mediterranean coast of Africa; the Anglo-American landings to meet them in North

West Africa; the growing threat to Mussolini's Italy; the naval triumph at Guadalcanal in the Pacific; the vast reinforcing of the air forces.

That night a Polish pilot training at Charter Hall noticed Richard in the briefing-room as looking 'tired, strained, and very red about the eye'.

Sergeant-Pilot Miller had supper with Richard and went up. He was detailed to go up again, but because of severe icing returned to base. Meanwhile Richard and Fison had gone up. As Miller was starting to change, he heard a whine and a terrible crash. It was just after half past one on the morning of 8 January. Eric Linklater used the official account to describe what happened.

The weather was not exceptionally severe, though the cold cloudy sky was unfriendly, and occasional sleet was falling. Richard, who had made a normal flight before midnight, took off for the second time, and was told by radio telephone to circle a flashing beacon. This was ordinary drill, in which the pilot, turning gently to port, would keep the beacon off his port wing and make a series of circles round the aerodrome.

After a little while the telephone asked him, 'Are you happy?' and Richard answered, 'Moderately. I am continuing to orbit.' The question was part of the routine of training, but the answer, with its honest admission of discomfort, is in Richard's own voice.

When he was spoken to again, a minute or two later, there was no reply, and an officer on the ground, watching his navigation lights, saw that he was losing height.

Some two or three miles from the aerodrome his aircraft hit the ground with great force, and both Richard and his navigator (Fison) were instantaneously killed.

At the official inquiry into the accident, it was found that the flight had been properly authorised, the weather suitable for such an exercise, but the pilot had lost control of his craft while circling the beacon in cloud. An official finding, however, is not necessarily an explanation and what actually happened during those last minutes will never be told.

224

Mary received the telegram announcing Richard's death the same morning, and went to tell his mother, who was working with the Red Cross at St James's Palace. When Edwyna saw her enter, and before she had spoken, she came towards her and said, 'Is it Richard?' Mary took her home, and stayed with her and Richard's father during that day. That evening Rosie Kerr, on twenty-four-hour leave from East Grinstead, was having dinner at a London restaurant. A young man was going round the tables, asking people, 'Have you heard? Richard Hillary's been killed.' Rosie heard him and collapsed.

Mary went home from the Hillarys to her own flat, and that night wrote Richard this goodbye, the last letter from the brown paper envelope:

8.1.43

Richard, I bow before this blackness of despair, this loneliness of night. The first of an eternity of nights. I feel your spirit stretching forth to me, from out the stars, through all of this world's tears I see your face trying with infinite compassion of understanding to comfort me. But you must let me cry. These tears held back with all the courage that lay between us these last months can no longer be held back.

You once wrote, 'I had a sudden vision of what life would be without you. It was like a shadow passing across the sun.' That same shadow has passed across my sun. You who were my light have gone from me into light itself. Help me to share that light with you in spirit as we shared everything together here in life. I must achieve this. I must not be desolate. You will help me, I know. I must find a new selfless happiness in the knowledge that your search for those circles of peace is now ended, that your desires are fulfilled beyond the dreams of our imagination. I must not grieve that it had to be thus without me. I must overcome these black waves of the never any more. I cannot believe it. The realisation comes only in sudden spasms as daggers in the heart. I see no life without the joy your presence gave me – the sound of your voice, the touch of your hands, your laughter, and the tenderness of your complete understanding of me. I am alone as I was before you came. Alone yet not alone, for your spirit is all about me in these rooms which held our happiness. So near I hold my breath and yet so far beyond my human longing as to break my heart. I seem to see you smile with an infinity of wisdom and I strain to think only of you who have stepped gloriously out of all this sadness into eternity. You have left me rich in the memory of completeness and fulfilment of love and with much to do in honour of that memory.

My darling I will do my best and if I fail in the small things of this earth it will be because I no longer belong down here, but always 'fly beside you'.

Epilogue

[i]

The story of Mary and Richard recalls another, which also closes in a tragedy brought on by the non-delivery of a letter. If Friar John had managed to deliver Friar Laurence's letter to Romeo, Romeo would have known that Juliet's death was a feigned death and fetched her away to settle down in exile, have children, and neither of them would ever have been heard of again. If the Station Medical Officer at Charter Hall had not been on leave when McIndoe's letter arrived; or had authorised a deputy to open it; or had acted on it immediately after his return and grounded Richard, Richard might still be alive today, and we might be hearing a great deal of him.

In the play we are interested in the two lovers, in the two bungling friars not at all. We accept the accident of the letter as a theatrical device, and do not inquire how it might have been prevented. In the story of Mary and Richard, we do inquire. We become curious about this doctor, who 'with much mystery and hand-waving produced two aspirin and vanished off somewhere to play bridge', as we are already curious about those other officials with power over life and death, the faceless ones on the Central Medical Establishment, of whom we know nothing at all. How many of them were there? Two? Five? Ten? Did they sit at a desk, or on a dais in a semi-circle? Did they perhaps wear masks? Remembering the numerous successive impediments to Richard's hopes, well may we wonder if we are farther back than Shakespeare's tricks and accidents, in that most ancient theatre dominated by gods and Fates and predestined victims.

But all this is fantasy. There were, in our own time, this real life and real death that caused a real heart-break, and there remains a real question: not merely why did 'they' pass him fit, but how and why did he compel them? He, Hillary, is the question. Why did he insist on going back?

Thus we come to those sensational theories and supposed facts about him, which I mentioned in Chapter One as so large a part of the published material any student would have had available hitherto; namely, that he may have committed suicide, and/or that he had had an unhappy love affair.

[ii]

In the April 1943 issue of *Horizon* three months after Richard's death, Arthur Koestler published an article 'The Birth of a Myth', which was later re-published in his book of essays *The Yogi and the Commissar*. Mary had met him with Richard. He called on her two days after the death, and again while she was copying the letters, and she introduced him to Richard's parents. Once the copies were done, she gave them to Rache Lovat Dickson, with permission for Koestler to see them on condition that he used them only as background. In his essay, however, he quoted directly from about a fifth, and always selectively in order to fit a thesis. The thesis purports to describe the crystallisation of a myth as it begins to gather around the life of someone lately dead. The myth, we are told, destroys the man. What was Richard's myth?

Koestler instances Richard, from the passage I quoted in Chapter Two from *The Last Enemy*, as 'not displeased' to have the Press style himself and his Oxford friends 'the Lost Generation . . . without any Holy Grail in which to lose ourselves . . .'; and, says Koestler, 'if one is exceptionally sensitive and exceptionally brave, and if one caught the bug of the great nostalgia of one's time – in search of a redeeming emotion; of a credo, neither sentimental, vulgar, nor archaic, whose words one could say without embarrassment or shame . . . then indeed a man's longing for the Holy Grail may become so strong that he flies like a moth into the flame; and having burnt his wings, crawls back into it again.' He concludes: 'There the man ends and the myth begins . . . the myth of a crusade without a cross, and of desperate crusaders in search of a cross. What creed they will adopt, Christ's or Barabbas's, remains to be seen.'

It is a clinical thesis, dotted here and there with epigrams, and interesting about the formation of myths; but it seems to me to use Richard as a guinea-pig and to be irrelevant to him.

Richard appropriated the label 'Lost Generation' (attributed to Gertrude Stein as a description of the expatriate American writers of the twenties) for an attitude at Oxford just before the war. By the time his book had been published, he had recognised the war to be a crusade, and was so little 'lost' that, in the short time granted him, he had begun seriously to consider what kind of Britain might arise once the war was over. His creed was forming, out of many strands. He still believed in Henry George, and in laissez-faire, but knew that post-war society would have to be in some degree and for some time regulated. He was eager to take on Victor Gollancz and 'draw his fire', in order to learn more about Socialism than the clichés. He was returning to active service in order to be among 'ordinary people', and discover, or re-discover, what sort of creed they might have. Koestler, a European politically minded from necessity and from the outset, was years older than Richard, and had been through the mill of militancy and disillusion. His 'God' in the title of another influential book to which he contributed, had been Soviet Russia and had 'failed'. Why Richard, at twenty-three, in the middle of war, and thronged with personal problems, should be in a hurry to find a 'God' himself, or have already formed any permanent creed; why Richard, or anybody else, should have to choose between Christ and Barabbas, Koestler does not elucidate. Indeed, in the last essay in *The Yogi and the Commissar*, he advocates something of both: 'Neither the saint nor the revolutionary can save us; only the synthesis of the two.'

Richard was neither. The myth Koestler invented for him was far too complicated to take hold, and has not. But the phrase about the moth that 'crawls back into the flames' was cruel and vivid, causing great grief to Richard's parents and to Mary, and caught on sufficiently to be taken to mean deliberate self-destruction. Thus it was Koestler who, wittingly or unwittingly, suggested suicide, leading Merle Oberon's biographers, only five years ago, in a well-publicised paperback, to declare that 'according to Koestler Hillary committed suicide. He was no longer able to endure his uselessness in time of war.' Such was the impression 'The Birth of a Myth' had given them, and others since.

In 1944 John Middleton Murry published an essay 'Richard Hillary' in his magazine *Adelphi*. It was re-published in *Looking Before and After*, one of the first productions of the pacifist Sheppard Press, which Murry helped to found. Murry was more explicit than Koestler, on even less evidence; one might say, on almost no evidence at all. Although he had read *The Last Enemy*, he had never met or corresponded with Richard; nor consulted anyone close to him; nor read any of his letters, relying entirely on Koestler's snippets; nor studied any other relevant documents. He too had a thesis, similar to Koestler's, but with vaguely religious undertones; and because he too was an old hand at criticism, and wrote well, it might convince someone who knew nothing else about the subject.

After paying his tribute to Richard as a 'writer born', and to the 'plane of sheer veracity on which the greater part [of *The Last Enemy*] was written', he tells us regretfully that Richard was a liar. In those sentences which conclude the book 'he faked the record'. We have been misled; he did not go up into the air again 'in order to help to stamp certain ideals for ever on the future of civilisation. Neither did he write his book to commemorate men who believed that that was why they fought and died . . . That the record is faked admits of no doubt whatever.' In support Murry quotes, first, 'the internal evidence of the writing', which appears to mean no more than that those closing sentences are rather rhetorical, and, second, 'the evidence of Richard's subsequent letters', of which Murry had read only a small number in Koestler's extracts. He informs us that, even after that vision of the dying woman in the ruins of London, Richard did not genuinely believe that the war had become a crusade. It does not matter how often Richard says that it had, Murry knows better. He could not resist the temptation to dramatise Richard as a 'tragic hero', of that kind already mentioned here, in whom the gods employ some fatal weakness to drive him stage by stage to his annihilation. Perhaps one should not say 'the gods', since Murry is more modern, more specific: 'in the total story of Hillary', he tells us, 'the veil is lifted for moments, and we glimpse the purposes of God.' Richard's 'weakness' had been to write what the public wished to hear, but he himself did not believe, thereby landing himself with a phoney literary role which he had to play out to the end in life. 'It was no crusade on which he was flying. He was seeking Death.'

Murry ignores, as did Koestler – or perhaps neither knew, since neither thinks it worth a mention – that Richard had a radio-observer who was killed with him. The charge therefore which Koestler hints at, and Murry asserts, is one not merely of suicide, but of murder.

Richard could have believed, Murry next instructs us, if the Battle of Britain had been the end. But it was not, 'and *The Last Enemy* was written in growing awareness that it would not be . . . The glory of the fighter-pilot grinds slowly and inexorably down to the shame of Bomber Command', inflicting 'with calculated purpose upon the simple families throughout the length and breadth of Germany the same obscenity' of blasting the Germans to death as they had attempted to inflict on Britain. This 'terrible event would dissolve the very foundation of Richard's half-won faith'. We are not told how, or when, or in which documents or letters, the 'half-won faith' was dissolved, nor on which page of *The Last Enemy* we are to look for this 'growing awareness', for the reason presumably that the evidence is not there; nor had Murry read Richard's letters to Mrs Lee and Mrs Warburg of 8 December – 'It's our turn now' – in which he shows anything but repugnance against the bombing, so far as it had gone in 1942. (What he might have thought of the 'round-the-clock' offensive we cannot say, since it was not decided upon until 1943, after he had been killed.)

All this is merely something Murry 'feels', and is attempting to argue without reference to fact, but with a good deal of attention to drama and high-sounding phrases. The necessity imposed on Richard becomes 'cosmic', his urge to suicide symptomatic and symbolic. 'He could not live. He could not have lived . . . In Hillary the deep urge of contemporary society towards death is made visible. He is the dazzling white of the foam on the great wave of death which Lawrence [D.H. this time] prophesied . . . "We are fighting for survival", said Churchill in 1940. Hillary is the essence of what survives – the impossibility of life. What Hillary foreknew as an individual, Britain will discover as a nation.'

Murry wrote only eighteen months after Richard's death, without regard to his parents or to Mary, or to Fison's family. He called Koestler's essay 'penetrating', and to a great extent apes it. Penetration was not difficult for either of them, since both were working on a dummy. Koestler says nothing of Mary's influence on Richard, except to describe her in passing, in a later work, as 'an attractive mistress'. Murry does not mention her at all; his dummy might have been pouring its heart out to a statue.

In 1950 Lovat Dickson, Richard's publisher, issued his biography *Richard Hillary*. He was a kind and able man, devoted to Richard's memory, and gave a useful account of his early life, the production of *The Last Enemy*, his friends' dismay and powerlessness before his decision to return, and many affectionately portrayed characteristics. The biography is a corrective to Murry's and Koestler's essays, but suffers from a poverty of analysis as theirs from an excess; from incompleteness of information; and from under-use of what he had. It is hero-worship. He will have no weakness in his subject, and appears to know nothing of his last interview with McIndoe, nor of McIndoe's request that he should be grounded.

Mary permitted Lovat Dickson to quote direct from Richard's letters, but those he chose were mainly written from the aerodrome, describing the grimness of life there and the ordeal of night-flying. He knew nothing of Mary's letters. Thus very little space is given to the love-affair, a most unfortunate defect, since it helped to give rise to, or did not prevent, the ancillary theory that this had been unhappy. So far as I have been able to ascertain, this theory comes first from a Frenchman, Admiral André Jubelin, Grand Cross of the Légion d'Honneur, and Croix de Guerre, who in 1953 wrote a preface for a translation into French of *The Last Enemy*. Forty-two pages long, it is immensely interesting and appreciative, and a striking honour to Richard's memory from this illustrious and intrepid Provençal officer. It exemplifies the respect in which Richard and his book have been held abroad.

Admiral Jubelin ('old Ju' to the RAF) gave a new meaning to the word 'amphibian', used most commonly for someone or something adept in the two elements, land and sea; with him they became sea and air. In 1940, at the time of the fall of France, he was in Indo-China, then still part of a French Empire. Officially he was a sailor, trapped at Saigon and under suspicion from the French authorities. His heart was set on getting somewhere where he could continue the fight. Although he held a pilot's licence, he pretended to wish to learn to fly, and managed to escape seven hundred miles across the Gulf of Siam, piloting a ropey old trainer-plane which his two companions refuelled by climbing on to the wings; an adventure as audacious and as poetically told as anything in St-Exupéry. He arrived in Scotland at the beginning of 1941, joined General de Gaulle, was put in command of an ancient French cruiser, and transferred himself to the RAF.

One of his own books, *Marin de Métier – Pilote de Fortune (The Flying Sailor)*, pays one of the warmest tributes that any Frenchman can ever have paid to the British, though only to a few of them; to those young men of Richard's kind with whom, aged thirty-four, the Admiral flew by day in the famous 118 Squadron, and afterwards by night in the equally famous Squadron 1, throughout most of 1942. He left the RAF to return to the Free French Navy, in 1945 commanded the aircraft-carrier *Arromanches* at the liberation of Saigon, and in 1963 became Commander-in-Chief in the Mediterranean. In the same year, by then aged fifty-five, he still listed as his hobbies in the French *Who's Who*: boxing, pelota, squash, and flying. The only enemy he ever ran away from seems to have been a rhinoceros he met while stationed in Africa.

Admiral Jubelin has no hesitation in calling *The Last Enemy* a masterpiece. He sets Richard as a literary meteor (though in no other sense) alongside that French prodigy, Raymond Radiguet, who was born in 1903, wrote *Le Diable au Corps* when he was seventeen, and *Le Bal*, and died when he was twenty. He speculates in his preface that, since Richard is his own book's romantic hero, he might well become to English literature what Benjamin Constant's *Adolphe* and Stendhal's Julien Sorel are to French. He has not the slightest doubt that Richard felt he had a mission to his dead comrades. How extraordinary, he writes, that out of that diminutive band of fighter-pilots, there should have arisen one young man, able to immortalise not only them but 'a gigantic battle on which past all question hung the future of the world'.

In only one respect is he at fault, and then only through lack of information, compensated by a chivalrous imagination. He confesses in his preface to a complex dilemma, as difficult to avoid as to write about. He tells us that all Richard's biographies are inadequate about his love life. (There is only one, Lovat Dickson's, and the Admiral is right.) 'They are all', he says, 'in English, and English modesty [*pudeur*] expects them to stay within the bounds of discretion. All the same, without probing too far into something which might give pain, I think there is a point which needs to be made more clearly.'

And so, he asks, what was the true reason, first, that Richard went off to America, and, second, that he went back to active service? He finds his answers, which he admits to be entirely hypothetical, in disappointed love. The first disappointment was partly with Denise, 'whose religious scruples were too deep, and whose mourning too absolute, to offer Richard the slightest hope of satisfaction'; and partly with his own disfigurement. So off Richard went to the United States in despair. On his return a new love [Mary, although the Admiral does not name her] had come to take the place of the old. 'But we get the impression [*nous devinons*], reading between the lines of certain intimate letters published in England [Koestler's and Lovat Dickson's snippets], that Richard got nothing out of it but *une plénitude morale*. For the woman to whom he was writing insists too often on the necessity of considering love as *l'union de deux âmes*.'

It is often difficult, even impossible, to translate French categorisations of love into English. But I take these two phrases to mean that all Mary required of, indeed insisted on, in her relationship with Richard, was that they should be 'soul-mates'; that she was a kind of war-time, twentieth-century, rather prudish Princesse de Clèves. And so, in the Admiral's elegantly composed fantasy, Richard remains 'still unsatisfied . . . still a man of vigour, but inspiring a kind of repulsion. Had love been enough to conquer it? It does not seem fanciful to suppose that, alongside the idealistic impulses which undoubtedly sent him back to active flying, there were equally a succession of cruel disappointments in regard to love [*une suite de déceptions sentimentales cruelles*].' How well it sounds, and plausible! But what a pity that, through no fault of his, the Admiral read so few of Richard's letters to Mary, and none of hers to him.

In 1957 Colin Hodgkinson, another terribly injured fighter-pilot

234

who had made his way back to active service, and a friend of Richard's from East Grinstead days, published an autobiography *Best Foot Forward*. He described a chance meeting with Richard towards the end of 1942. As they took leave of one another, Richard said: 'I don't think I'll see you again . . . I don't think I'm going to last it out,' on which Hodgkinson commented, 'I know, personally, that he had had a frustrating love affair. Perhaps, quite simply, he wanted to die.' Perhaps Hodgkinson did not realise what a journalist in need of a sensation would make of this aside. Ostensibly reviewing the book in the *Sunday Express*, Robert Pitman seized on it and built it up into a half-page article with a picture of Richard and a banner headline *Did This Hero Crash His Plane On Purpose?* 'It fits in', he claimed, 'with all the facts save one . . . that Richard was not alone', and then proceeded to reveal that neither Hodgkinson nor any other of Richard's fellow pilots would have anything to do with the theory of suicide, and withdrew what he had himself advanced. One wonders why he published it at all.

Since Max Aitken, who had shown readiness to take Richard into his Squadron and been a good friend of his, was Lord Beaverbrook's son and a power on Express Newspapers, Mary wrote to him in protest against Pitman's article, with a letter for publication. He was away, the editor asked her to shorten it, and nothing came of it then. But in 1960 Leonard Mosley wrote a full-page article in the *Sunday Express*, which made some amends. He called the theory of suicide 'an insult' and also 'a misreading of Richard's character and preposterous. He was, and he knew it, a symbol of the fighter-pilot of the Battle of Britain, and had he chosen to die he would have died in character, as his comrades had died.' And in 1981 Geoffrey Page, who had known Richard well, who often argued with him and wrote of him with respect towards the author and affection for the friend, put in his *Tale of a Guinea-Pig*: 'It has been said by irresponsible persons that Richard deliberately crashed his aircraft as an act of suicide; but knowing him I refuse to believe that his nature would allow him to take his observer to a violent death.'

In the sentence immediately following, Wing-Commander Page wrote: 'I am quite sure I know what caused him to crash.' In 1987 I asked the Wing-Commander what he had meant by this sentence, and he not only replied in detail, but was kind enough to allow me to quote his reply, which I give in his own words.

Soon after rejoining a fighter squadron, he was based at Martlesham Heath near Ipswich.

This particular time of the year, November, was grey and desolate beyond belief. During one morning I was on the duty roster to carry out a boring routine task of providing air cover to one of the dozens of small shipping convoys, plying up and down the East coast. A sergeant pilot in another Spitfire would accompany me.

We took off on time into the grey murk, and I immediately contacted ground control to obtain a compass bearing to intercept the convoy. Settling down on course at an altitude of five hundred feet, we flashed over the damp fields and hedges towards the North Sea. After a few moments the distinctive coastline showed, and beyond it – nothing. Grey sea and grey sky merged to form a canvas on which no horizon or ships appeared. Then the germ of fear began to grow and grow. Was I climbing or diving, in a turn or flying straight? The perfectly reliable instrument panel in front of me showed that no outstanding change of altitude had taken place in the aircraft's flight.

I could feel the perspiration trickling down my neck from under my oxygen mask.

More and more wildly I began a desperate rhythm, firstly checking my instruments, then looking out at the bleak seascape and then back to the instruments. I trusted neither my vision beyond the aeroplane nor the reliable facts the rows of little dials were telling.

I was bewildered and terrified.

Knowing that my life expectancy was limited to mere seconds if I didn't take a grip on myself, I forced my mind and eyes to remain glued on those faithful instruments until the period of stark panic had passed. Without question, if I had relied on my senses, I would have crashed into the sea a few feet below.

Richard, on a pitch dark night, I am utterly convinced, went through the same traumatic experience, leading to his death and that of his observer.

If I had dived into the sea, my companion in the other Spitfire in close formation with me, would undoubtedly have perished as well.

Would an investigation into my death suggest I had committed suicide, taking an innocent partner with me?

I think not.

This professional document, coming from a highly experienced fighter-pilot, who like Richard had been shot down in the Battle of Britain, who knew him well, and like him had undergone innumerable skin-grafts at East Grinstead, seems to me to have great importance for anyone attempting a study of Richard's life and death, and to carry greater weight than the accusations and insinuations which have hitherto been published.

Nonetheless these suggestions remain in print. (Both biographers of McIndoe repeated the story of a disappointment in love, but gave no authority for it.) They are still an important part of the record about Richard, and it may be imagined what distress they caused to those who loved him; meagre ingredients out of which to concoct an unhappiness, a shallow pool from which to dredge a suicide, and, on the part of one or two of the recorders, a rather shoddy exercise. The personal, as distinct from the professional answer, if answer there need be – and sometimes to defend a person who has been slandered seems almost as insulting as the slander itself – is surely to be found in passage after passage in the preceding chapters. In regard to the love affair, even if Mary's final letter were to be removed entirely from the correspondence, we have Richard's own words: 'it is you and you alone who mean anything to me; and that anything is more than the whole world'; 'For me a great year. I had you and I grew up,' and all the rest. As to suicide, he himself wrote, 'Somehow I must get all this down . . . and then maybe I shall have peace and time to put it all together,' and 'I only hope that 1943 will allow me to put into practice the personality which (thanks largely to you) is me . . .' – hopes which Mary's letter to his father, and her unpublished letter to the *Sunday Express*, confirm: 'He loved life and lived it with absorbed interest and delight. He did NOT want to die . . .'

There remains with me, nearing the end of this story, as there came to me at the beginning, the thought of the radio-observer Sergeant Wilfrid Fison, who was killed with Richard. He was chosen, the Station Medical Officer wrote after their death, as 'a very special observer, an old Cambridge Blue, of a temperament just calculated to suit Hillary, and the prospects were that they would make a good pair'. Thirty-seven, Fison's age, was old to start training for night flying. He had never been in combat, and had joined the RAFVR only a year before. His reactions would have been slower than Richard's, as his experience too was much less. It seems, from Richard's references to him, that they got on well together, and that Fison had confidence in Richard; Fison's son, who was only eight when his father was killed, has told me that his letters home to his wife suggest nothing to the contrary. It may be said that he was taking a risk, and Richard a responsibility, which war demands of innumerable people: the one of trusting himself to someone whose secret fears he does not, and perhaps must not, know, and the other, with knowledge of what war is really like, of concealing them. After Fison's death a friend wrote of him in *The Times* that 'his greatest happiness lay in the work he did for others. His enthusiasm and good fellowship were unbounded, and in all he did he showed the breadth of vision and sympathetic understanding which only comes to those few who can learn from both life and reading.' He must also have been a most courageous man.

[iii]

What was it that drove Richard back to active combat?

Lawrence, trying to tell Robert Graves why he had joined up, wrote, 'I honestly could not tell you . . .', and having listed a few reasons, already given here, went on: '. . . all these are reasons, but unless they are cumulative, they are miserably inadequate.'

Richard's too were cumulative; not a single romantic need for a 'redeeming emotion', but, more prosaically, a number of influences and circumstances which can be listed.

There was, first, the first question of all injured pilots, 'When can I fly again?'; the magnetic imperative of the air, that liberation, lure, spell, ecstasy, of which the chronically earth-bound had best say no more – even though the greatest poem about it, Yeats's 'An Irish Airman Foresees His Death', was written by someone who metaphorically may have 'hid his face amid a crowd of stars', but physically never came closer than a VIP flight could take him.

There was that perpetual haunting of Richard by his dead pilot friends, that shock that 'I, who had given least' should have become the sole survivor, that sense of a debt he had meant to be quit of through his book, only to find that the book increased the debt.

There was the feeling, 'I was stopped too soon'; that as a pilot he had failed; a bitterness which gnawed at him the more as surviving friends, like Max Aitken, went on to ever more challenging and exacting jobs, leaving him behind on that 'forgotten man's last stop'.

There was his writer's block, the block of someone most at ease with action, adventure, danger, and the rebuff of all his eager initiatives which might have breached it; beginning with his project in America, rejected on political grounds; going on to his request to report on the RAF in the Middle East, and then to train American pilots, both refused on medical grounds; and finally his transfer to Combined Operations, deferred week after week, to be turned down on bureaucratic grounds. This particular frustration made him imagine enemies where there may have been merely incomprehension, and sometimes caused him to resent those who were doing their best to help him, whether it was Mary, or, as Sir Sholto Douglas wrote, the staff at Fighter Command. A 'born writer' is liable to be a freak, and Richard was a freak: a freak to his parents, a freak very often to his fellow-pilots, a freak to McIndoe. 'He was not on Archie's beam,' said Rosie Kerr. He was different from the other patients, the tough, the cheery, the Australians and New Zealanders with whom McIndoe, himself from New Zealand, was naturally at ease. Among the most touching things in the whole story are McIndoe's understanding and concern for him, his tolerance of the occasional rows which Richard caused, and his effort to save him from the end.

There was the war, the crusade against Evil, still continuing, still far from won.

There was disgust with the futility of 'my high-flying London life', and the role of wounded hero-author he could so breezily assume, suddenly off-loaded in the peace on Kennington's farm; the excitement of reading *The Mint*; the yearning back to simpler company. Unwittingly, Kennington and the ghost of Lawrence of Arabia must be reckoned signallers on his way to death.

There was the fear, which Richard and Geoffrey Page mutually confessed in hospital, of what would be said if they did not go back. Even at Charter Hall, after his nerve had gone and he had seen McIndoe, this fear stayed with him, stipulating that his course should not be interrupted, 'lest someone should say he was afraid to continue'. Some people lose this kind of fear as they grow up. Because combat in the air could age, or seem to age, a pilot by many years in a few hours, one forgets too easily that Richard was only twenty-three, and 'what people would think' could still affect him as it might a schoolboy. He cared about the alteration in his looks, and the massacre of his hands. He cared profoundly for a certain image of himself – and then, and in front of others, to have been called a coward! This, no matter that it came from an unhappy and thwarted woman, he never forgot. He called her 'evil', a word he only used once elsewhere, linking her spite with the world-force he sensed behind the mother and child's death in the wreck of London. He remembered the insult on the aerodrome. Some who knew him well believed that it was this, more than anything, that drove him to go back.

Any one of these provocations and incitements would be enough to agitate any highly sensitive young man, let alone the combination of them all. Add to them fear of the night sky he had not yet thrown himself against, and of another failure, and further maiming, and the responsibility for the other airman who would be flying with him, none of which he mentions until he has gone back and is faced with them, all of which he must have hour after hour imagined in solitude; and the need for Mary is explained, for somewhere 'to come in and talk for hours on end'. The inward torment is explained which, lacking her, lost him his hold on happiness after they came back from Wales. The withdrawal into himself is explained, the obstinacy, the truculence, and the concentration of energy into a single-minded will which silenced his friends and enabled him to stalk his way past the bureaucracy. What all those pressures come to in the end were a few

words. Like Lawrence's, 'I want to join up, that's all,' or St-Exupéry's
'*Je dois participer. Je ne peux pas rester témoin*,' so Richard's
reiterated, 'I must trust my instinct,' and to his mother 'I should not
be at peace if I did not go back.'

That power of detachment, that relish of an ironical situation, and
that tireless curiosity, could have made the prospect of death less
awful. One recalls those questionings of McIndoe. Before the war
Richard had written a short story about a vain man jilted on a sea
voyage, who decides to commit suicide by throwing himself overboard. Poised on the rail, he changes his mind, because it seems
ridiculous. But as he draws back, he slips, falls in, swims around a
bit, then drowns. He drowns laughing. Not long afterwards Richard
himself was in the drink, a blazing torch quenched by the North Sea.
He described it in that first chapter he forced on Lovat Dickson.

He had fallen out of his Spitfire at 10,000 feet, unconscious, then
regained consciousness, and pulled the rip-cord of his parachute.
The water was quite warm and his life-jacket was keeping him afloat.
He noticed his hands. 'Down to the wrist, the skin was dead white
and hung in shreds: I felt faintly sick from the smell of burnt flesh.
By closing one eye I could see my lips, jutting out like motor tyres.
The side of my parachute harness was cutting into me particularly
painfully, so that I guessed my right hip was burnt.' He tried to undo
it, but the pain in his hands was too great. He lay back and reviewed
his situation. He was a long way from land and unlikely to have been
seen. 'After about half an hour my teeth started chattering, and to
quiet them I kept up a regular tuneless chant, varying it from time
to time with calls for help. There can be few more futile pastimes
than yelling for help, alone in the North Sea, with a solitary seagull
for company, yet it gave me a certain melancholy satisfaction, for I
had once written a short story in which the hero had done just this.
It was rejected.'

He noticed with surprise that the sun had gone in, though his face
was still burning. 'I looked down at my hands, and not seeing them,
realized I had gone blind. So I was going to die.' He considered
death. 'Within a few hours or a few minutes I was to learn the great
answer. I decided it should be in a few minutes. I had no qualms
about hastening my end and reaching up, I managed to unscrew the

241

valve of my Mae West.' His head went under, but came up again, and he could not keep it under. 'I was so enmeshed in my parachute that I could not move. For the next ten minutes I tore my hands to ribbons on the spring-release catch. It was stuck fast. I lay back exhausted, and then I started to laugh. By this time I was probably not entirely normal and I doubt if my laughter was wholly sane, but there was something irresistibly comical in my grand gesture of suicide being so simply thwarted.'

He surveyed his life. 'It is often said that a dying man re-lives his whole life in one rapid kaleidoscope. I merely thought gloomily of the Squadron returning, of my mother at home, and of the few people who would miss me. Outside my family, I could count them on the fingers of one hand. What did gratify me enormously was to find that I indulged in no frantic abasements or prayers to the Almighty. It is an old jibe of God-fearing people that the irreligious always change their tune when about to die: I was pleased to think that I was proving them wrong'; and pleased later, no doubt, that he was rescued and survived to say so. He was always pleased to be able to prove that a well-established belief was wrong, disconcerted when he could be proved wrong himself; as, for example, in deciding that he had no intention yet of falling in love, and promptly doing so.

He does not go easily into myth or legend. He was an individualist, and individualists do not make good legends. Legends accrue out of men and women who have done, or are thought to have done, things which appeal to commonly felt personal, national, or ethnic aspirations. It might have been different if Richard had got through his course, and then been killed in battle, but nobody aspires to being killed on training. Had he not met Mary, his courage and his pose of cynicism might have been welded into some minor legend agreeable to the present age, and his death neatly morticed into it, as the gestures of a young hero knocking his pipe out on the grate of an unpleasant world. But he did meet her. He wrote and received these letters, and cynicism does not fit. What does begin to fit is something like the opposite.

His life has something truly remarkable, and much more than superficially attractive, which causes one to forget his petulant and childish moods, enables one to understand why Mary thought him a 'grand person', and singles him out beyond his writer's gift, his compelling personality, and the charm. He was extremely honest with himself, and one should therefore pay all the more heed to the accusation he makes against himself, over and over again, of selfishness or synonyms for being selfish. To be intensely aware of one's own selfishness, and to combat it, are traits unusual in one so young until, perhaps, one recalls the heights of show-off and conceit from which he was seeking to descend; the golden boy, insisting on diving backwards from the highest springboard; the stroke of the twice-champion crew; his mother's 'cad'; the adored of young girls; the silver-spoon, ball-at-his-feet Adonis.

For there the traits are, unmistakable, emerging into print in *The Last Enemy*, which is the legend of a conversion, and passing on into his letters from the moment he falls in love. The clues are continuous, like a well-laid paper-chase. He rejects the wish to go back to America, recognising it as a selfish wish to get material for another book. One writes, he told Kennington and his audience at Foyle's, not for success or power, but for what one has to give. He knows what humility is, as well as supreme self-confidence, because he has felt it in the air. To Mary, as we have seen already, he feels remorse for being casual, for being thoughtless, for being egocentric, for being Blimpish, and then fury for being 'spoilt'. With no loss of joy in life, no lessening of ambition to know and experience all he could, he was trying to correct that all-but-fatal endowment of facility, and in the end took on what was most difficult. Linklater wrote: 'Irony had its final triumph when to Mary, who knew him so well, he the arrogant left the memory of his humility.' 'It is not humility,' wrote St-Exupéry, 'it is self-forgetfulness – the right to sit at table with my comrades and be silent.' However it is put, perhaps 'The last enemy that shall be destroyed' is selfishness.

What would have become of him? Such promise, so many possibilities – the practical joined to or warring against the imaginative, the seeker after adventure with the artist. Writing from the aerodrome on his last New Year's Day he had listed among the achievements of that 'orientated man' he aspired to become, 'the production of vitalising social change'. Charles Haydon thought that this was a field where he might have partly found fulfilment.

Michael Astor, who became chairman of the Richard Hillary Trust, wrote to me: 'Richard used to talk about a book he wanted to write one day about politics; by which he meant (as he stated) the need for society to reduce the role of politics and politicians to a minimum. The true voice of the romantic, the artist, of all who find ourselves agnostics without a party we can believe in (much). Here, I imagine, he was trying to find his own position rather than prescribe anything in particular for society as a whole.'

'Creative imagination' Richard listed too, of course. Had he survived the war in combat, he might have brought off that majestic story of the RAF which Lawrence had yearned to write ('I had meant to go on to a squadron and write the real R.A.F. and make it a book – a BOOK, I mean. It is the biggest subject I have ever seen, and I thought I could get it, because I felt it so keenly . . .'). Koestler reckoned (in 1943) that 'With the "bourgeois" novel getting more and more exhausted and insipid as the era which produced it draws to a close, a new type of writer seems to take over from the cultured middle-class humanist: airmen, revolutionaries, adventurers, men who live the dangerous life; with a new operative technique of observation, a curious alfresco introspection and an even more curious trend of contemplation, even mysticism, born in the dead centre of the hurricane. St-Exupéry, Silone, Traven, Hemingway, Scholochow, Istrati, may be the forerunners; and Hillary might have become one of them.'

Well, perhaps (though I know nothing of Istrati). To my mind, because of Mary, Richard might have reached out further and wider, to describe 'that personal relationship driving both individuals to greater integrity', which he also listed. He had a desperate need to prove himself, as a pilot, as a writer, and with Mary. It became his strange fortune to love and to be loved by a woman almost entirely opposite, to whom, so far as is humanly possible, concern for others appeared to come quite naturally. In her letters to him she sees straight into and through his egocentricity, and does not judge or reprimand, but appropriates it, makes fun of it, plays with it, lightly, delicately, deliciously, entertained or pretending to be entertained by its 'enormity'. And he responds. She gave him confidence and the total security of her love, and at the same time she changed him. She changed him, Rosie said, out of recognition, and would have changed him more. The poses were falling away. The 'tiny king of self-realisation' was beginning to realise himself through her. One day, his purpose in the air fulfilled, what he was learning from her must have shown in an enlargement of his writing; might have enabled him, one day, to write a love-story, and in life gain something of her own inner happiness and peace.

But he lived only long enough to write one book, for which he has not yet been remembered as other one-book writers are remembered: Alain-Fournier, Choderlos de Laclos, the Prince of Lampedusa, Emily Brontë. His second book lay in embryo in the conflicts of the one and a half years left to him, in the papers burnt by Charter Hall, and his letters.

Mary did not forget that promise she made him in her goodbye letter. Year after year, until their death, she gave strength to his parents and helped to found and further the Trust established to give grants to young writers in his memory. She would be glad that I have tried to vindicate and commemorate him. In that hope, for him if not for herself, I am convinced she left those letters for me to find; and it may be that, because of the story they wrote together, Charter Hall will turn out not to have been his 'last stop'. It is a story, on both sides, of love, nobility, and courage against cruel odds. There were many such during the war, and are many still, lived out daily, in all countries, in all walks of life; but few see the light, because few who live them have the words. Perhaps it is one of those stories which must await some later and freer re-creation of their joys and their frustrations, allowing their passion to overflow the bounds of documents and interpretation of documents into a play, a poem, or a novel.

She remembered also their other mutual promise, that personal happiness should not be an end in itself, but used 'even if only its little drop . . . for the betterment of mankind'. After the war she came out to Eastern Europe, there to witness an enforced revolution, more ruthless and more thorough, although more subtly disguised, than any which had preceded it, and in all its manifestations utterly alien to the world of ease and friendships into which she had been born. For three years critical in modern history she left all that behind; and on the edge of that smouldering political volcano she listened, as at home. She listened to the Soviet journalists who were for a time our friends, to whom she appeared as an almost fabulous figure from a long-discarded epoch, an untormented Anna Karenina. She listened to the young peasants from the People's Colleges with whom we travelled through the villages, and to their visions of a society to be transformed.

It was an all-too-brief time, during which people still cherished the illusion that East and West might meet and understand each other, an interregnum which did not last. The iron curtain descended, the cold war froze round us, our telephone was tapped, our house watched, overnight people from all walks, of all political ranges, disappeared, some never to be seen again. It was then, with personal loyalty and compassion raised almost to offences against the State, that her humanity shone at its most serene, and seemed never more essential. Through her, three or four people were enabled legally to start a new life in the West, who would otherwise have been destroyed or dead. It gave others heart simply to know that she was there. When we returned to Britain, this was the role that she resumed.

Richard wanted her to write a book. She never did. Her book, her poem, were in her life. How generous-hearted it had been, how diverse those it had enchanted, enriched, and helped, was seen in the many dear friends who joined her daughters, her grand-daughters, and her family, at the Masses said for her in Wales and London: Michael Hillary, Rosie Kerr, and others from this book; Diana Cooper, the tribute of one beautiful woman to another, alongside the old Hungarian Bolshevik Edith Bone, sent by her Stalinist comrades for seven years in solitary confinement for speaking her mind, set free in the rising of 1956, to whom Mary in Budapest had been 'the kindest person I have ever known'; young David Jones from Gwynedd, who as a child, fearful of some harm befalling his parents, made Mary promise to be his foster-mother; and others young, to whom she had become a legend. And remains so. There are still those who, faced with some difficult decision, recall her tenderness, her gaiety, and her faith, and still ask

246

themselves what she would have thought or done. Her spirit dances on, 'continuing to orbit', as if in a ballet of the perpetuity of love; and I have laid her own letters like flowers at her feet.

Bibliography

1 Manuscript sources

The letters of Richard Hillary, for the most part unpublished, together with other papers, photographs, press cuttings, etc. relating to him, are held by the Richard Hillary Trust, Trinity College, Oxford.

The letters, diaries and other papers of Mary Booker, all unpublished, are in the possession of the author.

2 Published sources

Richard Hillary, *The Last Enemy*, 1943. (*Falling Through Space*, U.S. edition, 1943; *Le Dernier Ennemi*, French edition, 1953.)

R. Lovat Dickson, *Richard Hillary. A biography*, 1950.

Arthur Koestler, 'The Birth of a Myth', *Horizon*, April 1943. Reprinted in *The Yogi and the Commissar*, 1945.

Eric Linklater, in *The Art of Adventure*, 1947.

J. Middleton Murry, 'Richard Hillary', *Adelphi*, July 1944. Reprinted in *Looking Before and After*, 1948.

Geoffrey Page, *The Tale of a Guinea-Pig*, 1981.

Lord Douglas of Kirtleside, with Robert Wright, *Years of Command*, vol. 2, 1966.

Colin Hodgkinson, *Best Foot Forward*, 1957.

Charles Higham and Roy Moseley, *Princess Merle: The Romantic Life of Merle Oberon*, 1983.

Leonard Mosley, *Faces from the Fire: A Life of Sir Archibald McIndoe*, 1961.

BIBLIOGRAPHY

Hugh McLeave, *McIndoe, Plastic Surgeon*, 1961.
William Simpson, *One of our Pilots is Safe*, 1943.
Antoine de St-Exupery, *Pilote de Guerre (Flight to Arras)*, 1943.
Christine Mill, *Norman Collie, A Life in Two Worlds*, 1987.